Presented to:

_____

From:

_____

Date:

_____

Jesus Listens®

Daily Devotional Prayers
of Peace, Joy, and Hope

Sarah Young

Thomas Nelson
Since 1798

I dedicate this book to Jesus—Immanuel—who is with us continually, listening to all our prayers. The Bible assures us that Jesus is able to save forever those who come to God through Him, because He always lives to intercede for us with our Father-God (Hebrews 7:25). And when we pray, the Spirit Himself intercedes for us with groans that words cannot express (Romans 8:26). How great and glorious is our triune God!

ACKNOWLEDGMENTS

I am thankful to work with such a gifted, dedicated team. Laura Minchew and Michael Aulisio shepherd my publishing so creatively and effectively. Kris Bearss, my faithful editor, knows my work wonderfully well and edits my writing with just the right touch. Finally, I want to thank Joey Paul, my first publisher, who came up with the idea for *Jesus Listens*, and Jennifer Gott, who worked to pull everything together. I'm blessed to have the help of all these talented friends!

INTRODUCTION

I love Jesus' beautiful invitation to us: *"Come to Me, all who are weary and burdened, and I will give you rest"* (Matthew 11:28 NASB). My hope is that this book, *Jesus Listens*, will encourage you to approach Him confidently and joyfully—finding peaceful rest in His Presence. It's such a blessing to know that Jesus listens to every one of our prayers! He loves us perfectly and is constantly caring for us, whether we're aware of His Presence with us or not.

All of my devotional books, including this one, are designed to help you grow closer to Jesus. This quest is my deepest longing— for you and for me. As you may know, I wrote my previous books from the perspective of Jesus speaking to you, the reader. But *Jesus Listens* is written from the vantage point of you praying to God. I hope you will not only read these prayers but make them your own—using them to guide you as you express your heartfelt longings to the Lord.

You will find prayers of peace, joy, and hope throughout this book. As I was writing, I drew on themes from *Jesus Calling: Enjoying Peace in His Presence*, *Jesus Always: Embracing Joy in His Presence*, and *Jesus Today: Experience Hope Through His Presence*. Other topics are also emphasized in the prayers—especially Jesus' boundless, unfailing Love for all who belong to Him.

Jesus Listens contains prayers for every day of the year. They are *devotional prayers*: designed to lead you into deeper, richer, more continual communion with God. These daily prayers are meant to be a starting point for your other prayers—helping you to enjoy your time with Jesus and bring all your concerns to Him.

I admit that praying doesn't come naturally to us; in fact, it is frequently viewed as a chore. Prayer certainly does require effort, but we need to remember that communicating with the Creator and Sustainer of this vast universe is an amazing privilege! Jesus' sacrificial death for our sins opened the way for us to commune freely and fully with our Father-God. The moment Jesus died, *the curtain of the temple was torn in two from top to bottom* (Matthew 27:51). So our unrestricted access to God in prayer is a glorious, blood-bought privilege!

I'm thankful that God uses our prayers not only to change circumstances but to change *us*. We bring our prayer requests to Him, trusting that He hears and He cares. As we devote time to communicating with Jesus and enjoying His Presence, we gradually become more like Him.

I consider it a wonderful privilege and responsibility to pray for readers of my books. So I commit quite a bit of time to this pursuit each morning. I've found that no matter how I feel when I first get out of bed, I feel better and stronger after spending this precious time with Jesus. And you readers can start your day feeling encouraged because you know that I'm praying for you!

One of my favorite verses about prayer is Psalm 62:8. In this psalm King David urges us to *trust in God at all times and pour out our hearts to Him*. Jesus knows everything in our hearts, and He longs for us to trust Him enough to open up and be real with Him in our prayers. Since He understands us completely and loves us eternally, we can safely unburden ourselves to Him. He is indeed *our refuge*.

The prophet Jeremiah assures us that God listens to our prayers:

"You will call to Me and come and pray to Me, and I will listen to you. You will seek Me and find Me when you search for Me with all your heart" (Jeremiah 29:12–13 HCSB).

While Jesus lived on this earth, He listened wonderfully well to the people around Him. I'm grateful that He continues to listen—to us! Moreover, we have the miraculous help of the Holy Spirit. As we're praying, *the Spirit Himself intercedes for us with groans that words cannot express. And He who searches our hearts knows the mind of the Spirit, because the Spirit intercedes for the saints in accordance with God's will* (Romans 8:26–27). Our prayers may be inadequate and fragmented, but the Holy Spirit transforms them and makes them consistent with God's will.

I'm convinced that prayer is extremely important in all areas of our lives. Alfred Lord Tennyson famously wrote: "More things are wrought by prayer than this world dreams of." The influence of our prayers goes far beyond what we can see and comprehend.

Scripture repeatedly instructs us to pray, and Jesus taught His disciples to pray what we call the Lord's Prayer:

> Our Father in heaven,
> Hallowed be Your name.
> Your kingdom come.
> Your will be done
> On earth as *it is* in heaven.
> Give us this day our daily bread.
> And forgive us our debts,
> As we forgive our debtors.

And do not lead us into temptation,
But deliver us from the evil one.
For Yours is the kingdom and the power and the
    glory forever. Amen.

                    Matthew 6:9–13 NKJV

I realize that unanswered prayers can be discouraging. While we're waiting for answers, we need to trust that God hears our prayers and responds to them in ways that make perfect sense—from His infinite, all-knowing perspective. God tells us in His Word that *His ways are higher than our ways, as the heavens are higher than the earth* (Isaiah 55:9). Although we would love to understand more, it's often impossible for us finite creatures to fathom God's ways.

The Bible encourages us to persevere in our prayers. I've been praying for the salvation of some people for decades, and I plan to continue. I love the parable of the unjust judge versus the persistent widow. This parable teaches that *we should always pray and not give up.* Even though the judge didn't care about people or justice, the persistence of the widow eventually wore him down and he granted her request (Luke 18:1–8). How much more will God, who is loving and just, answer our prayers in His perfect way and timing!

We live in stressful times, and many of us struggle with anxiety. The apostle Paul's teaching in his letter to the Philippians is very practical and timely: "*Do not be anxious about anything, but in everything, by prayer and petition, with thanksgiving, present your requests to God. And the peace of God, which transcends all understanding, will guard your hearts and your minds in Christ Jesus*" (Philippians 4:6–7).

Instead of focusing on our problems when we're feeling anxious, we can bring everything to Jesus—our struggles and confusion, our prayers and petitions, our thanksgiving and praise. After pouring out our hearts to Him, we can ask Him to fill us with His wondrous peace. To receive this glorious gift, we need to relax in Jesus' Presence and *trust Him wholeheartedly*—instead of *relying on our own understanding* (Proverbs 3:5 NET).

Sometimes when I'm feeling stressed, I sit quietly and breathe slowly while praying, "Jesus, help me relax in Your peace." If I continue praying this way for a few moments, I invariably relax and feel calmer.

The prayers in *Jesus Listens* emphasize trusting Jesus and living in dependence on Him. The Bible is full of the tender directive to trust in the Lord, a crucial condition for living close to Him. The trust-emphasis in my book reflects this biblical teaching and also my personal struggle to trust God at all times—even when the world is full of uncertainties and things are not going as I'd hoped. At such times, I find it helpful and encouraging to whisper, "I trust You, Jesus; You are my Hope."

As I've spent time with Jesus and studied His Word over the years, I've come to grasp the importance of having a thankful attitude. So the theme of thankfulness appears frequently throughout this book. First Thessalonians 5:17–18 instructs us to *pray continually* and *give thanks in all circumstances*. There is power in thankful prayers! They keep our focus on Jesus' priceless promises and His perpetual Presence with us.

Recently, I wrote a personal story called "The Power of Thankful Prayers." I'll share part of the story here. When our two children, Stephanie and Eric, were young teenagers, they were scheduled to travel alone from Nashville, Tennessee, to Melbourne, Australia, where we were living and working as missionaries. This was a very long journey, requiring multiple changes in major airports. I was feeling anxious about their making this trip by themselves, and I was praying about it almost constantly. However, as I prayed, I was actually worrying more than I was trusting God. Eventually I realized that this kind of praying was displeasing to God—and it certainly wasn't relieving my anxiety. So one morning I brought my concerns to Jesus and asked Him to show me a better way to pray. He taught me to change my prayer focus from voicing my concerns over and over to thanking Him for how He *was* answering my prayers. This change in my focus really did help me calm down. Yet little did I know the amazing adventures that were awaiting all of us! I don't have space in this introduction to tell you the full story, but my many thankful prayers were answered in ways that seemed miraculous! The rest of this story is recorded in *Jesus Calling: 365 Devotions with Real-Life Stories.*

Thankfulness and praise go together extremely well. I've found that prayers of praise deeply refresh me—and they increase my awareness of Jesus' Presence. Again and again throughout Scripture, we find the vital command to praise the Lord. We can joyfully obey this command because God is altogether worthy of our worship—and praising Him blesses us immensely. Our words of worship help us remember how great and glorious God is! Praising Him strengthens our confidence that the One to whom we pray is in control, even when our world feels terribly out of control.

Many years ago I went to Covenant Theological Seminary in St. Louis to get a master's degree in counseling and biblical studies.

I especially enjoyed a course on the Bible's wisdom literature, and the professor was indeed very wise. From the vast array of wisdom he imparted, one simple teaching has stayed with me all these years. He shared with us his personal practice of praying, "Help me, Holy Spirit" throughout the day—before answering the phone or doorbell, when engaged in an important conversation, when attempting to do something difficult, and so on. I followed my teacher's advice until this brief prayer became a part of me. Now I find myself praying it effortlessly, and it reminds me that I am not alone. The third Person of the Trinity is always available to help me!

The devotional prayers in this book are full of God's promises. To benefit from these precious promises, it's essential for you to know Jesus as your Savior. Because He is God, Jesus' death on the cross was sufficient to pay the penalty for all the sins of those who come to Him. If you have never acknowledged your sinfulness and asked Jesus to be your Savior, I urge you to do so. *Whoever believes in Him will not perish but have eternal life* (John 3:16). I will be backing you up with my prayers. Every day I pray that God will use my books to bring into His forever-family many readers who are not yet believers.

Finally, dear reader, I encourage you to delve into the prayers in *Jesus Listens*. You don't need to begin on January 1. Simply start with the prayer for today—and keep going, day by day. Remember that I will be praying for you. Most importantly, remember that Jesus is with you, listening to all your prayers.

Bountiful blessings!

Sarah Young

January

"I know what I have planned for you," says the Lord. "I have plans to prosper you, not to harm you. I have plans to give you a future filled with hope." —JEREMIAH 29:11 NET

My living God,

As I begin a fresh year, I rejoice that You are continually working newness into my life. Because *You are doing a new thing*, I must *not dwell on the past*. I refuse to let last year's disappointments and failures define me or dampen my expectations. This is the day for a fresh start! I know there are no limits to Your creativity, so I anticipate some lovely surprises in this year that stretches out before me.

Lord, I receive *today* as a precious gift from You. I realize that the present moment is where You meet with me. *This is the day that You have made.* I know You have carefully prepared it for me—with tender attention to every detail. So I have good reason to *rejoice and be glad in this day*!

As I journey along *the path of Life*, I'll search for signs of Your loving Presence. I delight in finding the little blessings You sprinkle alongside my pathway—sometimes in surprising places. As I discover them, I'll thank You for each one. This keeps me close to You and helps me find Joy in my journey.

In Your blessed Name, Jesus, amen.

"Forget the former things; do not dwell on the past. See, I am doing a new thing! Now it springs up; do you not perceive it? I am making a way in the desert and streams in the wasteland." —ISAIAH 43:18–19

This is the day that the LORD has made; let us rejoice and be glad in it. —PSALM 118:24 ESV

You will show me the path of life; in Your presence is fullness of joy; at Your right hand are pleasures forevermore. —PSALM 16:11 NKJV

Beloved Jesus,

I want to be all Yours! I invite You to wean me from other dependencies. You have shown me that my security rests in You alone—not in other people, not in my circumstances.

Trying to depend only on You sometimes feels like walking on a tightrope. Yet I don't need to be afraid of falling because Your *everlasting arms* are a safety net underneath me.

Please help me to keep looking ahead to You, Jesus. I know that You're always before me, beckoning me on—one step at a time. As I spend quiet time with You, I can almost hear You whispering, "Follow Me, beloved."

Lord, *I am convinced that neither death nor life, neither angels nor demons, neither the present nor the future nor any powers, neither height nor depth, nor anything else in all creation, will be able to separate me from Your loving Presence!*

In Your precious Name, amen.

The eternal God is your refuge, and underneath are the everlasting arms; He will thrust out the enemy from before you, and will say, "Destroy!" —DEUTERONOMY 33:27 NKJV

In his heart a man plans his course, but the LORD determines his steps. —PROVERBS 16:9

For I am convinced that neither death nor life, neither angels nor demons, neither the present nor the future, nor any powers, neither height nor depth, nor anything else in all creation, will be able to separate us from the love of God that is in Christ Jesus our Lord. —ROMANS 8:38–39

Compassionate Lord,

You tell me in Your Word: *"I have loved you with an everlasting Love. I have drawn you with loving-kindness."* This means that You knew me and loved me before time began! Yet for years I swam around in a sea of meaninglessness—searching for Love, hoping for Hope. All that time, You were pursuing me, ready to embrace me in Your compassionate arms.

When the time was right, You revealed Yourself to me. You lifted me out of that sea of despair and set me down on a firm foundation. Sometimes I felt naked—exposed to the revealing Light of Your Presence. So You wrapped an ermine robe around me, *a robe of righteousness.* You sang me a Love song whose beginning and end are veiled in eternity. You infused meaning into my mind and harmony into my heart. I want to join You in singing Your song. Please use my voice in whatever way You will, as *You call people out of darkness into Your marvelous Light.*

In Your brilliant Name, Jesus, amen.

The LORD appeared to us in the past, saying: "I have loved you with an everlasting love; I have drawn you with loving-kindness." —JEREMIAH 31:3

I delight greatly in the LORD; my soul rejoices in my God. For he has clothed me with garments of salvation and arrayed me in a robe of righteousness, as a bridegroom adorns his head like a priest, and as a bride adorns herself with her jewels. —ISAIAH 61:10

But you are a chosen generation, a royal priesthood, a holy nation, His own special people, that you may proclaim the praises of Him who called you out of darkness into His marvelous light. —1 PETER 2:9 NKJV

All-knowing God,

I delight in the truth that *I am fully known*! You know absolutely everything about me, yet You love me with perfect, *unfailing Love*. I've spent many years searching for greater self-understanding and self-acceptance. Underlying this search is the desire to find someone who truly understands me and accepts me as I am. I've discovered that *You* are the Someone who can satisfy my deep-seated longing. In my relationship with You, I become more completely who I really am.

Help me to be increasingly real with You—dropping all pretenses and opening up fully to You. *Search me, O God, and know my heart; try me and know my anxious thoughts.* In the Light of Your holy gaze, I can see many things I need to change. But I know You are with me in my efforts, so I won't despair. Instead, I'll rest in Your Presence, receiving Your Love that flows freely into me through my openness to You. As I take time to soak in this powerful Love, it fills up my empty spaces and overflows into joyous worship. I rejoice that I am perfectly known and forever loved!

In Your loving Name, Jesus, amen.

For now we see indistinctly, as in a mirror, but then face to face. Now I know in part, but then I will know fully, as I am fully known. —1 CORINTHIANS 13:12 HCSB

The LORD delights in those who fear him, who put their hope in his unfailing love. —PSALM 147:11

Search me, O God, and know my heart; try me and know my anxious thoughts; and see if there be any hurtful way in me, and lead me in the everlasting way. —PSALM 139:23–24 NASB 1995

Sovereign God,

Help me to make friends with the problems in my life. Many things seem wrong to me, but I need to remember that You're in control of everything. Your Word assures me that *all things work together and are fitting into a plan for good for those who love You and are called according to Your purpose.* I can access this magnificent promise through trusting You.

Every problem can teach me something—transforming me little by little into the person You designed me to be. Yet the same problem can become a stumbling block if I react with distrust or defiance. I realize I'll have to choose many times each day whether or not I will trust You.

I've discovered that the best way to make friends with my troubles is to thank You for them. This counterintuitive act opens my mind to the possibility of blessings emerging from my difficulties. Moreover, when I bring You my prayers *with thanksgiving*, my anxiety diminishes and *Your Peace that transcends all understanding guards my heart and my mind.*

In Your wonderful Name, Jesus, amen.

Consider it pure joy, my brothers, whenever you face trials of many kinds. —JAMES 1:2

All things work together and are [fitting into a plan] for good to and for those who love God and are called according to [His] . . . purpose. —ROMANS 8:28 AMPC

Do not be anxious about anything, but in everything, by prayer and petition, with thanksgiving, present your requests to God. And the peace of God, which transcends all understanding, will guard your hearts and your minds in Christ Jesus. —PHILIPPIANS 4:6–7

My Lord,

Help me to thank You *for everything*—including my problems. As soon as my mind gets snagged on a difficulty, I need to bring the matter to You *with thanksgiving*. Then I can ask You to show me *Your* way to handle the situation. The very act of thanking You frees my mind from its negative focus. As I turn my attention to You, my difficulty fades in significance and loses its power to trip me up. You guide me to deal with the problem in the most effective way—either facing it head-on or putting it aside for later consideration.

Most of the situations that entangle my mind are not today's concerns: I've borrowed them from tomorrow, next week, next month, or even next year. When this is the case, please lift the problem from my thoughts and deposit it in the future—veiling it from my eyes. Then draw my attention back to Your Presence in the present, where I can enjoy *Your Peace*.

In Your perfect Name, Jesus, amen.

And give thanks for everything to God the Father in the name of our Lord Jesus Christ. —Ephesians 5:20 nlt

Do not be anxious about anything, but in everything, by prayer and petition, with thanksgiving, present your requests to God. —Philippians 4:6

Show me Your ways, O Lord; teach me Your paths. Lead me in Your truth and teach me, for You are the God of my salvation; on You I wait all the day. —Psalm 25:4–5 nkjv

"Peace I leave with you; my peace I give you. I do not give to you as the world gives. Do not let your hearts be troubled and do not be afraid." —John 14:27

Holy Lord,

I love to *worship You in the beauty of holiness.* The beauty of Your creation reflects some of who You are, and it delights me! You are working Your ways in me: the divine Artist creating loveliness in my inner being. You've been clearing out the debris and clutter within me, making room for Your Spirit to take full possession. Help me to collaborate with You in this effort—being willing to let go of anything You choose to take away. You know exactly what I need, and You have promised to provide all of that—abundantly!

I don't want my sense of security to rest in my possessions or in things going my way. You are training me to depend on You alone, finding fulfillment in Your loving Presence. This involves being satisfied with much or with little of the world's goods, accepting *either* as Your will for me. Instead of grasping and controlling, I'm learning to release and receive. To cultivate this receptive stance, I need to trust You more—*in any and every situation.*

In Your beautiful Name, Jesus, amen.

Give unto the LORD *the glory due to His name; worship the* LORD *in the beauty of holiness.* —PSALM 29:2 NKJV

One thing I ask of the LORD, *this is what I seek: that I may dwell in the house of the* LORD *all the days of my life, to gaze upon the beauty of the* LORD *and to seek him in his temple.* —PSALM 27:4

And my God will supply all your needs according to His riches in glory in Christ Jesus. —PHILIPPIANS 4:19 NASB 1995

I know what it is to be in need, and I know what it is to have plenty. I have learned the secret of being content in any and every situation, whether well fed or hungry, whether living in plenty or in want. —PHILIPPIANS 4:12

God, my Refuge,

Help me *not to dwell on the past*. I can learn from the past, but I don't want it to be my focus. I know I cannot undo things that have already occurred, no matter how hard I try. So I come to You and *pour out my heart*—remembering that *You are my refuge*, worthy of my trust *at all times*.

One way I can build up my confidence in You is to tell You frequently: "I trust You, Lord." Speaking these affirmations of trust brightens my day immensely—blowing away dark clouds of worry.

You are always *doing a new thing!* So I'll be on the lookout for all that You're accomplishing in my life. Please open the eyes of my mind and heart so I can see the many opportunities You've placed along my path. And protect me from falling into such a routine way of living that I see only the same old things—missing the newness.

I'm learning that You can make a way where there appears to be no way. *With You all things are possible!*

In Your amazing Name, Jesus, amen.

"Forget the former things; do not dwell on the past. See, I am doing a new thing! Now it springs up; do you not perceive it? I am making a way in the desert and streams in the wasteland." —ISAIAH 43:18–19

Trust in him at all times, O people; pour out your hearts to him, for God is our refuge. —PSALM 62:8

And looking at them Jesus said to them, "With people this is impossible, but with God all things are possible." —MATTHEW 19:26 NASB 1995

Mighty God,

You are the God who makes me strong. So I come to You just as I am—with all my sins and weaknesses. I confess my many sins and ask You to *remove them from me as far as the east is from the west.* I rest in Your Presence, with my shortcomings in full view.

I am like a *jar of clay* filled with weaknesses, but I know that *Your Power is made perfect in weakness.* So I thank You for my insufficiency—it helps me depend on You to infuse strength into me. How I rejoice in Your infinite sufficiency!

You are also the One *who makes my pathway safe*—protecting me not only from dangers but from worry and excessive planning. Instead of gazing into the unknown future, I want to be mindful of You as I journey through this day. I'll endeavor to stay in close communication with You, relying on Your guiding Presence to keep me on course. Though You are always beside me, You also go before me—clearing away obstacles on the path up ahead. I trust that You're making the conditions on my pathway the very best for accomplishing Your ways in my life.

> In Your strong Name, Jesus, amen.

He is the God who makes me strong, who makes my pathway safe. —PSALM 18:32 GNT

As far as the east is from the west, so far has he removed our transgressions from us. —PSALM 103:12

But we have this treasure in jars of clay to show that this all-surpassing power is from God and not from us. —2 CORINTHIANS 4:7

But he said to me, "My grace is sufficient for you, for my power is made perfect in weakness." Therefore I will boast all the more gladly about my weaknesses, so that Christ's power may rest on me. —2 CORINTHIANS 12:9

Dear Jesus,

Please help me learn to appreciate difficult days—being stimulated by the challenges I encounter rather than becoming distressed. As I journey through rough terrain with You, I gain confidence from knowing that *together* we can handle anything. This knowledge is based on three blessings: Your Presence continually with me, the Bible's precious promises, and my past experiences of coping successfully by depending on You.

When I look back on my life, I can see how much You have helped me through difficult days in the past. Yet I easily fall into the trap of thinking, "Yes, but that was then, and this is now." Instead, I need to remember that though my circumstances change immensely, *You remain the same* throughout time and eternity. Moreover, *in You I live and move and have my being*. As I live close to You—aware of Your loving Presence—I can go confidently through my toughest times.

In Your worthy Name, amen.

"Do not fear, for I am with you; do not be afraid, for I am your God. I will strengthen you; I will help you; I will hold on to you with My righteous right hand." —ISAIAH 41:10 HCSB

"But you remain the same, and your years will never end." —PSALM 102:27

I can do all things through Christ who strengthens me. —PHILIPPIANS 4:13 NKJV

"God did this so that men would seek him and perhaps reach out for him and find him, though he is not far from each one of us. 'For in him we live and move and have our being.' As some of your own poets have said, 'We are his offspring.'" —ACTS 17:27–28

Ever-near Jesus,

You've been calling me to a life of constant communion with You. Part of the training involves living above my circumstances, even when I'm up to my neck in clutter and confusion. I yearn for a simplified lifestyle—with fewer interruptions to my communication with You. But You have been challenging me to relinquish the fantasy of an uncluttered world. I need to accept each day just as it comes to me—and *search for You* in the midst of it all.

I'm thankful that I can talk with You about every aspect of my day, including my feelings. Help me remember that my ultimate goal is *not* to control or fix everything around me; it's to keep communing with You. You've been showing me that a successful day is one in which I have stayed in touch with You—even if many things remain undone at the end of the day.

I must not let my to-do list become an idol directing my life. Instead, I can ask Your Spirit to guide me moment by moment. He will keep me close to You.

In Your guiding Name, amen.

Devote yourselves to prayer, being watchful and thankful. —COLOSSIANS 4:2

"You will seek Me and find Me when you search for Me with all your heart." —JEREMIAH 29:13 NASB 1995

In all your ways acknowledge him, and he will make your paths straight. —PROVERBS 3:6

Since we live by the Spirit, let us keep in step with the Spirit. —GALATIANS 5:25

Jesus, my loving Companion,

I am on an adventurous trail with You. This is not an easy time, but it is nonetheless good—full of blessings as well as struggles. Help me to be open to all that You're teaching me as I journey with You through challenging terrain. And enable me to let go of familiar comforts so I can say a wholehearted "Yes!" to this adventure.

I know You will give me everything I need to cope with the challenges I face. So I don't want to waste energy imagining myself in future situations—trying to walk through those "not yet" times in my mind. I realize this is a form of unbelief—doubting Your ability to provide what I need *when* I need it.

I want to make wise choices as I journey with You. I need to *pray continually* about these decisions, trusting in Your perfect wisdom. You know *everything*—including what lies ahead on my path. My busy mind tends to make various plans about the way I should go, but *You* are the One who *directs my steps and makes them sure.*

In Your infinitely wise Name, amen.

And my God will supply all your needs according to His riches in glory in Christ Jesus. —PHILIPPIANS 4:19 NASB 1995

"The secret things belong to the LORD our God, but those things which are revealed belong to us and to our children forever, that we may do all the words of this law." —DEUTERONOMY 29:29 NKJV

Pray continually. —1 THESSALONIANS 5:17

A man's mind plans his way, but the Lord directs his steps and makes them sure. —PROVERBS 16:9 AMPC

My risen Savior,

I'm so thankful that *You have given me new birth into a living hope through Your resurrection from the dead*! Moreover, *I am a new creation; the old has gone, the new has come!*

My adoption into Your royal family occurred the moment I first trusted You as my Savior-God. At that instant, my spiritual status changed from death to life—eternal Life. I have *an inheritance that can never perish, spoil or fade—kept in heaven for me.* My heart overflows with gratefulness for Your provision of this glorious inheritance!

You've shown me that even though I'm *a new creation*, my conversion was only the beginning of the work Your Spirit is doing in me. I need *to be made new in the attitude of my mind and to put on the new self*—becoming increasingly righteous and holy. This strenuous, marvelous, lifelong endeavor is preparing me to spend an eternity with You in Glory! Please help me to receive this assignment with courage and gratitude—staying alert and looking for all the wonderful things You are doing in my life.

In Your magnificent Name, Jesus, amen.

God . . . has given us . . . an inheritance that can never perish, spoil or fade —kept in heaven for you. —1 PETER 1:3–4

If anyone is in Christ, he is a new creation; the old has gone, the new has come! —2 CORINTHIANS 5:17

You were taught . . . to put off your old self . . . ; to be made new in the attitude of your minds; and to put on the new self, created to be like God in true righteousness and holiness. —EPHESIANS 4:22–24

Just as Christ was raised from the dead . . . , even so we also should walk in newness of life. —ROMANS 6:4 NKJV

Trustworthy Lord,

Help me to *trust You and not be afraid.* Many things seem out of control, and my routines are not running smoothly. I feel much more secure when the circumstances of my life are more predictable. Please *lead me to the rock that is higher than I.* Lord, *I long to take refuge in the shelter of Your wings*—where I am absolutely secure.

When I'm shaken out of my comfortable routines, I need to grip Your hand tightly and look for opportunities to grow. I can accept the challenge of something new—refusing to waste energy bemoaning the loss of my comfort.

Protect me from adding to my difficulties by anticipating problems that could possibly arise in the future. I recognize this tendency for what it is: grasping for control. Instead of *worrying about tomorrow,* I want to relax in Your Presence and trust You to help me deal with problems as they come. Rather than dreading my difficulties, I invite You to use them to *transform me from one degree of Glory to another—* making me fit for Your kingdom.

In Your sheltering Name, Jesus, amen.

"I will trust and not be afraid. The LORD, *the* LORD, *is my strength and my song; he has become my salvation." —*ISAIAH 12:2

*From the ends of the earth I call to you . . . lead me to the rock that is higher than I. For you have been my refuge, a strong tower against the foe. —*PSALM 61:2–3

*"Don't worry about tomorrow, for tomorrow will bring its own worries. Today's trouble is enough for today." —*MATTHEW 6:34 NLT

*We all, with unveiled face, beholding the glory of the Lord, are being transformed into the same image from one degree of glory to another. For this comes from the Lord who is the Spirit. —*2 CORINTHIANS 3:18 ESV

Gracious God,

As I journey with You today, please help me to thank You all through the day. This practice makes it more feasible for me to *pray without ceasing*, as the apostle Paul taught. I long to be able to pray continually, and thanking You in every situation facilitates this pursuit. My thankful prayers provide a solid foundation on which I can build all my other prayers. Moreover, it's so much easier for me to communicate freely with You when I have a grateful attitude.

If I keep my mind occupied with thanking You, I'm less likely to fall into hurtful patterns of worrying or complaining. I've seen that when I practice thankfulness consistently, negative thought patterns gradually grow weaker and weaker.

A grateful heart opens up the way for me to *draw near to You*. And Your glorious Presence fills me with *Joy and Peace*.

> In Your joyous Name, Jesus, amen.

Rejoice always, pray without ceasing, give thanks in all circumstances; for this is the will of God in Christ Jesus for you. —1 THESSALONIANS 5:16–18 ESV

Draw near to God and He will draw near to you. Cleanse your hands, you sinners; and purify your hearts, you double-minded. —JAMES 4:8 NKJV

May the God of hope fill you with all joy and peace as you trust in him, so that you may overflow with hope by the power of the Holy Spirit. —ROMANS 15:13

Sovereign God,

Please help me to live joyfully in the midst of my struggles. I yearn for a freer, more independent way of life than I'm currently experiencing.

I pray fervently and then wait expectantly for the changes I desire. When You don't answer my prayers as I'd hoped, I sometimes get discouraged. It's easy for me to feel as if I'm doing something wrong—as if I'm missing out on what's best for me. But when I think that way, I'm overlooking a most important truth: You are Sovereign. I need to remember that You're always in control and You are taking care of me.

Teach me to accept my dependent way of living as a gift from You. Moreover, help me receive this gift joyfully—with a glad and thankful heart. I've found that nothing lifts me out of the doldrums faster than thanking and praising You. And nothing enables me to enjoy Your Presence more delightfully! As I seek Your Face, I'm blessed to hear Your loving words of instruction: *Enter My gates with thanksgiving and My courts with praise.*

In Your dependable Name, Jesus, amen.

See, the Sovereign LORD comes with power, and his arm rules for him. See, his reward is with him, and his recompense accompanies him. —ISAIAH 40:10

Cast all your anxiety on him because he cares for you. —1 PETER 5:7

But indeed, O man, who are you to reply against God? Will the thing formed say to him who formed it, "Why have you made me like this?" —ROMANS 9:20 NKJV

Enter his gates with thanksgiving and his courts with praise; give thanks to him and praise his name. For the LORD is good and his love endures forever; his faithfulness continues through all generations. —PSALM 100:4–5

Exalted Lord Jesus,

You are my Strength and my Song! Yet I confess that I'm feeling wobbly this morning—looking at difficulties looming ahead and measuring them against my limited strength. But these challenges are not tasks for today, or even for tomorrow. I need to leave them in the future and come home to the present, where I can enjoy Your Presence. Since You are my Strength, I know You can empower me to handle each difficulty as it comes. And because You are my Song, You're able to give me Joy as I work alongside You.

Please draw my mind back to the present moment—again and again. The amazing ability to anticipate future events is a blessing from You, but it becomes a curse whenever I misuse it. If I use my mind to *worry about tomorrow*, I cloak myself in dark unbelief. Instead of this sinful wallowing in worry, I want to trust You more and more.

I've found that the Light of Your Presence envelops me in Peace when I fill my thoughts with the hope of heaven. You are *my Salvation*, Lord, so I have good reason to *trust and not be afraid*.

In Your heavenly Name, amen.

*"Surely God is my salvation; I will trust and not be afraid. The Lord, the Lord, is my strength and my song." —*Isaiah 12:2

*We take captive every thought to make it obedient to Christ. —*2 Corinthians 10:5

*"Therefore do not worry about tomorrow, for tomorrow will worry about itself." —*Matthew 6:34

*Blessed be the God and Father of our Lord Jesus Christ! According to his great mercy, he has caused us to be born again to a living hope through the resurrection of Jesus Christ from the dead, to an inheritance that is imperishable, undefiled, and unfading, kept in heaven for you. —*1 Peter 1:3–4 esv

My great God,

I love hearing You speak through Your Word: *"I am making every-thing new!"* This is the opposite of what is happening in my world of death and decay. I realize that every day I live means one less day remaining in my lifespan on earth. But because I belong to You, Jesus, this thought doesn't trouble me. At the end of each day, I'm mindful of being one step closer to heaven.

The world is in such a desperately fallen condition that Your prom-ise to *make everything new* is my only hope. Help me not to get dis-couraged when my efforts to improve matters are unsuccessful. I must keep in mind that all my efforts are tainted by the brokenness around me and within me. I won't stop trying to do my best—in dependence on You—but I know that this world needs much more than a tune-up or repairs. It needs to be made completely new! And this is absolutely guaranteed to happen at the end of time, for *Your words are trust-worthy and true.*

I have good reason to rejoice because You have promised to renew all things—including me—making everything gloriously perfect!

In Your triumphant Name, Jesus, amen.

He who was seated on the throne said, "I am making everything new!" Then he said, "Write this down, for these words are trustworthy and true." —REVELATION 21:5

For to me, to live is Christ, and to die is gain. —PHILIPPIANS 1:21 NKJV

We know that the whole creation has been groaning as in the pains of childbirth right up to the present time. Not only so, but we ourselves, who have the firstfruits of the Spirit, groan inwardly as we wait eagerly for our adoption as sons, the redemption of our bodies. —ROMANS 8:22–23

Peaceful Savior,

May Your Peace protect my mind and heart. Help me to *rejoice in You always*, remembering that *You are near*. As I spend time with You, *presenting my requests to You with thanksgiving*, You bless me with *Peace that transcends all understanding*. This is how You *guard my heart and my mind*. It's a collaborative, You-and-I-together effort. I'm grateful that I never face anything alone!

Because I belong to You, aloneness is just an illusion—but it's a dangerous one that can lead to depression or self-pity. The devil and his underlings work hard to cloud my awareness of Your Presence. So it's crucial for me to recognize and resist their attacks. I can fight back with Your powerful Word, which is *living and active*—reading it, pondering it, memorizing it, speaking it out loud.

Even when I'm feeling alone, I can talk freely with You, trusting that *You are with me always*. I've discovered that the longer I talk with You, the more aware of Your nearness I become. And this awareness of Your Presence with me fills my heart and mind with Your Peace.

In Your beloved Name, Jesus, amen.

Rejoice in the Lord always. I will say it again: Rejoice! Let your gentleness be evident to all. The Lord is near. Do not be anxious about anything, but in everything, by prayer and petition, with thanksgiving, present your requests to God. And the peace of God, which transcends all understanding, will guard your hearts and your minds in Christ Jesus. —PHILIPPIANS 4:4–7

For the word of God is living and active and sharper than any two-edged sword, and piercing as far as the division of soul and spirit, of both joints and marrow, and able to judge the thoughts and intentions of the heart. —HEBREWS 4:12 NASB 1995

"And teaching them to obey everything I have commanded you. And surely I am with you always, to the very end of the age." —MATTHEW 28:20

Jesus, my Guide,

Help me to go gently through this day, keeping my eyes on You. I ask You to open up the way before me as I take steps of trust along *the path of Life*—with You as my Guide.

Sometimes the way before me appears to be blocked. I've discovered that if I focus too much on the obstacle or on searching for a way around it, I'm likely to go off course. So I need to stay focused on You, the Shepherd who is leading me along my life-journey. If I keep my eyes on You, the obstacle will be behind me before I know it—and I may not even understand how I passed through it.

This is an important secret of success in Your kingdom. Though I remain aware of the visible world around me, I want to be primarily aware of *You*. When the road before me looks rocky, I know I can trust You to get me through that rough patch. No matter what is happening, Your Presence with me enables me to face each day with confidence.

In Your encouraging Name, amen.

You will show me the path of life; in Your presence is fullness of joy; at Your right hand are pleasures forevermore. —PSALM 16:11 NKJV

"I am the good shepherd; I know my sheep and my sheep know me —just as the Father knows me and I know the Father —and I lay down my life for the sheep." —JOHN 10:14–15

The path of the righteous is level; O upright One, you make the way of the righteous smooth. —ISAIAH 26:7

For the LORD will be your confidence, and will keep your foot from being caught. —PROVERBS 3:26 NKJV

Gentle Jesus,

As I look at this day that's stretching out before me, I see a twisted, complicated path—with branches going off in all directions. I start wondering how I can possibly find my way through that maze. But then I remember: *You are always with me, holding me by my right hand.* I recall Your promise to *guide me with Your counsel,* and I begin to relax. When I look again at my pathway, I notice that a peaceful fog has settled over it—obscuring my view. I can see only a few steps in front of me, so I turn my attention more fully to You and start to enjoy Your Presence.

You've been showing me that the fog is a protection You provide for me—calling me back into the present moment. Though You inhabit all of space and time, You communicate with me *here* and *now.* Please train me to keep my focus on You and on the path just ahead of me. Then the fog will no longer be necessary as I walk through each day with You.

In Your comforting Name, amen.

Yet I am always with you; you hold me by my right hand. You guide me with your counsel, and afterward you will take me into glory. —PSALM 73:23–24

Show me your ways, O LORD, teach me your paths; guide me in your truth and teach me, for you are God my Savior, and my hope is in you all day long. —PSALM 25:4–5

Now we see but a poor reflection as in a mirror; then we shall see face to face. Now I know in part; then I shall know fully, even as I am fully known. —1 CORINTHIANS 13:12

For we walk by faith, not by sight. —2 CORINTHIANS 5:7 NKJV

Sovereign God,

I want to live in Your Presence more consistently—open to You and Your will for me. But when something interferes with my plans or desires, I tend to resent the interference. Instead of pushing down those resentful feelings, I need to increase my awareness of them—letting them come all the way up to the surface. As I bring my negative feelings into the Light of Your Presence, You're able to set me free from them.

The ultimate solution to my rebellious tendencies is submission to Your authority over me. Intellectually, I rejoice in Your sovereignty. Without it, the world would be a terrifying place. Yet when Your sovereign will encroaches on my little domain of control, I often react with telltale resentment.

Your Word teaches that the best response to losses or thwarted hopes is praise: *The Lord gives and the Lord takes away. Blessed be the name of the Lord.* Help me remember that all good things are gifts from You. Please train me to respond to my blessings with gratitude rather than feeling entitled to them. And prepare me to let go of anything You take from me—without letting go of Your hand!

In Your praiseworthy Name, Jesus, amen.

And see if there be any hurtful way in me, and lead me in the everlasting way. —PSALM 139:24 NASB 1995

Humble yourselves, therefore, under God's mighty hand, that he may lift you up in due time. —1 PETER 5:6

And he said: "Naked I came from my mother's womb, and naked shall I return there. The LORD gave, and the LORD has taken away; blessed be the name of the LORD." —JOB 1:21 NKJV

My living Savior,

Your Word shows me that it's possible for Your followers to be joyful and afraid at the same time. When an angel told the women who came to Your tomb that You had risen from the dead, they were *afraid yet filled with Joy.* So I don't have to let fear keep me from experiencing the Joy of Your Presence. This pleasure is not a luxury reserved for times when my problems—and the crises in the world—seem under control. Your loving Presence is mine to enjoy today, tomorrow, and forever!

Lord, help me not to give in to joyless living by letting worries about the present or the future weigh me down. Instead, I need to remember that *neither the present nor the future, nor any powers, neither height nor depth, nor anything else in all creation, will be able to separate me from Your Love.*

I'm thankful that I can talk freely with You about my fears, expressing my thoughts and feelings candidly. As I relax in Your Presence and entrust all my concerns to You, please bless me with Your Joy—*which no one can take away from me.*

In Your delightful Name, Jesus, amen.

So the women hurried away from the tomb, afraid yet filled with joy, and ran to tell his disciples. —MATTHEW 28:8

For I am convinced that neither death nor life, neither angels nor demons, neither the present nor the future, nor any powers, neither height nor depth, nor anything else in all creation, will be able to separate us from the love of God that is in Christ Jesus our Lord. —ROMANS 8:38–39

"Therefore you too have grief now; but I will see you again, and your heart will rejoice, and no one will take your joy away from you." —JOHN 16:22 NASB 1995

My Savior-King,

Thank You for Your precious *robe of righteousness* that covers me from head to toe. The price You paid for this glorious garment was astronomical—Your own sacred blood. I realize I could *never* have purchased this royal robe, no matter how hard I worked. So I'm extremely grateful that Your righteousness is a free gift! If I forget this amazing truth, I feel ill at ease in my regal robe. Sometimes I even squirm under the velvety fabric as if it were made of scratchy sackcloth.

Lord, I long to trust You enough to remember my privileged position in Your kingdom—and to relax in the luxuriant folds of my magnificent robe. I need to keep my eyes on *You* as I practice walking in this *garment of salvation.*

When my behavior is unfitting for a child of the King, it's tempting to try to throw off my royal robe. Help me instead to throw off the unrighteous behavior! Then I'll be able to feel at ease in this garment of grace, enjoying the gift You fashioned for me before the creation of the world.

In Your regal Name, Jesus, amen.

I will rejoice greatly in the LORD, my soul will exult in my God; for He has clothed me with garments of salvation, He has wrapped me with a robe of righteousness, as a bridegroom decks himself with a garland, and as a bride adorns herself with her jewels. —ISAIAH 61:10 NASB 1995

God made him who had no sin to be sin for us, so that in him we might become the righteousness of God. —2 CORINTHIANS 5:21

You were taught, with regard to your former way of life, to put off your old self, which is being corrupted by its deceitful desires; to be made new in the attitude of your minds; and to put on the new self, created to be like God in true righteousness and holiness. —EPHESIANS 4:22–24

Glorious Jesus,

I want to follow You wherever You lead. Help me to chase after You wholeheartedly, with glad anticipation quickening my pace. Though I don't know what lies ahead, *You* know—and that is enough! I believe that some of Your richest blessings are just around the bend: out of sight, but nonetheless very real. To receive these precious gifts, I need to *walk by faith, not by sight.* I know this doesn't mean closing my eyes to what is all around me. It means subordinating the visible world to You, the invisible Shepherd of my soul.

Sometimes You lead me up a high mountain with only Your hand to support me. The higher I climb, the more spectacular the view becomes—and the more keenly I sense my separation from the world with all its problems. This frees me to experience more fully the joyous reality of Your brilliant Presence. How I delight in spending these Glory-moments with You!

Eventually, You lead me down the mountain, back into community with other people. May the Light of Your Presence continue to shine on me and make me a blessing to others.

In Your majestic Name, amen.

For we walk by faith, not by sight. —2 CORINTHIANS 5:7 NKJV

Splendor and majesty are before him; strength and glory are in his sanctuary. —PSALM 96:6

When Jesus spoke again to the people, he said, "I am the light of the world. Whoever follows me will never walk in darkness, but will have the light of life." —JOHN 8:12

For with You is the fountain of life; in Your light we see light. —PSALM 36:9 NKJV

O Lord,

You keep my lamp burning; You turn my darkness into Light. Sometimes, when I am *weary and burdened*, I feel as if my lamp is about to go out. It's flickering and sputtering—on the verge of running out of fuel. Whenever this happens, I need to cry out to You and draw near to You. As I rest in Your Presence, You remind me that *You* are the One who provides fuel for my lamp. You are *my Strength*!

You are also my Light. As I keep turning toward You, the Glory of Your Presence shines on me. Your radiant beauty brightens my life and changes my perspective. When I turn away from Your brightness and look toward the darkness of the world, it's easy for me to get discouraged. Yet even though there's so much trouble in this broken world, I can always rejoice in You, Lord. *You are the Light that shines on in the darkness.* So I don't need to be afraid, no matter how bleak things may look.

Rather than focusing on trouble, I want to trust You wholeheartedly. Help me to wait expectantly for You to transform my darkness into Light.

In Your bright, blessed Name, Jesus, amen.

> *You, O Lord, keep my lamp burning; my God turns my darkness into light. With your help I can advance against a troop; with my God I can scale a wall.* —Psalm 18:28–29

> *"Come to me, all you who are weary and burdened, and I will give you rest."* —Matthew 11:28

> *I love you, O Lord, my strength.* —Psalm 18:1

> *The Light shines in the darkness, and the darkness did not comprehend it.* —John 1:5 nasb 1995

Generous God,

You are a God of both intricate detail and overflowing abundance. When I entrust the details of my life to You, I'm often surprised by how thoroughly You answer my petitions. The biblical instruction to *pray continually* helps me feel free to bring You all my requests. And I've found that the more I pray—with a hopeful, watchful attitude—the more answers I receive. Best of all, my faith is strengthened as I see how precisely You respond to my specific prayers.

I rejoice that You are infinite in all Your ways! Because *abundance* is at the very heart of who You are, I don't need to fear that You will run out of resources. I can come to You in joyful expectation of receiving all I need—and sometimes much more!

I'm so grateful for the bountiful blessings You shower on me! Even the hardships in my life can be viewed as Your blessings—they train me in perseverance, transforming me and preparing me for heaven. So I come to You with open hands and heart, ready to receive all that You have for me.

In Your great Name, Jesus, amen.

Pray continually. —1 Thessalonians 5:17

How priceless is your unfailing love! Both high and low among men find refuge in the shadow of your wings. They feast on the abundance of your house; you give them drink from your river of delights. —Psalm 36:7–8

"I will abundantly bless her provisions; I will satisfy her poor with bread." —Psalm 132:15 esv

Compassionate Jesus,

Help me remember how safe and secure I am in You. The Bible assures me that Your Presence with me is a fact—totally independent of my feelings. Because Your death on the cross covers all my sins, I know I am on my way to heaven. *Nothing* can prevent me from reaching that glorious destination! There I will see You *face to Face*, and my Joy will be off the charts!

I'm thankful that even in *this* world I am never separated from You. For now, though, I must be content with seeing You through eyes of faith. I delight in Your promise to walk with me till the end of time and onward into eternity.

Though Your continual Presence is guaranteed, simply knowing this truth doesn't automatically change my emotions. When I forget to focus on You, I'm vulnerable to fear, anxiety, loneliness, and other unwanted feelings. Yet I've found that *awareness* of Your Presence with me can dispel those painful feelings and replace them with Your Peace. Please train me in the discipline of walking attentively with You through each day.

In Your calming Name, amen.

*"I give them eternal life, and they will never perish —ever! No one will snatch them out of My hand. My Father, who has given them to Me, is greater than all. No one is able to snatch them out of the Father's hand." —*JOHN 10:28–29 HCSB

*Now we know that if the earthly tent we live in is destroyed, we have a building from God, an eternal house in heaven, not built by human hands. —*2 CORINTHIANS 5:1

*For now we see in a mirror dimly, but then face to face. Now I know in part; then I shall know fully, even as I have been fully known. —*1 CORINTHIANS 13:12 ESV

The LORD *will give strength to His people; the* LORD *will bless His people with peace. —*PSALM 29:11 NKJV

Precious Savior,

I come to You, needing to *find rest* in Your Presence. I'm sure this day will bring difficulties, and I've been trying to think my way through the trials I will face. Yet when I focus on anticipating what's ahead of me, I lose sight of the fact that *You are with me wherever I go—You will never leave me.*

I confess that I'm much too prone to rehearse my troubles over and over in my mind. This causes me to experience painful problems many times. But I know I'm supposed to endure them only once—when they actually occur. Please help me to stop multiplying my suffering in this way!

Instead of focusing on problems, I choose to come to You and relax in Your loving Presence. Lord, I ask You to strengthen me and prepare me for this day—transforming my fear into *confident trust*!

In Your trustworthy Name, Jesus, amen.

"Come to me, all you who are weary and burdened, and I will give you rest. Take my yoke upon you and learn from me, for I am gentle and humble in heart, and you will find rest for your souls. For my yoke is easy and my burden is light." —MATTHEW 11:28–30

"No man shall be able to stand before you all the days of your life; as I was with Moses, so I will be with you. I will not leave you nor forsake you. . . . Have I not commanded you? Be strong and of good courage; do not be afraid, nor be dismayed, for the LORD your God is with you wherever you go." —JOSHUA 1:5, 9 NKJV

For the LORD GOD, the Holy One of Israel has said this, "In returning [to Me] and rest you shall be saved, in quietness and confident trust is your strength." But you were not willing. —ISAIAH 30:15 AMP

Mighty Jesus,

All things are possible with You! These powerful words from Scripture light up my mind and encourage my heart. You are training me to *live by faith, not by sight.* So I refuse to be intimidated by the way things look at this moment.

I'm thankful for the sense of sight, a spectacular gift from You. But it's easy for me to be so mesmerized by the visual stimulation around me that You fade into the background of my mind. Help me instead to focus primarily on *You*—trusting in Your promises and trying to see things from Your perspective.

Teach me how to grow closer to You, Lord Jesus. I delight in knowing You as my Savior and Friend, but I want to relate to You also as Almighty God. When You lived as a Man in this world, *Your miraculous signs revealed Your Glory.* I know that You continue to do miracles according to Your will and purposes. Please train me to align my will with Yours and to *watch in hope for You* to work.

In Your powerful Name, amen.

*Jesus looked at them and said, "With man it is impossible, but not with God. For all things are possible with God." —*MARK 10:27 ESV

*We live by faith, not by sight. —*2 CORINTHIANS 5:7

*This, the first of his miraculous signs, Jesus performed at Cana in Galilee. He thus revealed his glory, and his disciples put their faith in him. —*JOHN 2:11

But as for me, I watch in hope for the LORD, *I wait for God my Savior; my God will hear me. —*MICAH 7:7

King of kings,

You are my Lord! I delight in relating to You as my Friend and the Lover of my soul. Yet I realize that You are also *Lord of lords and King of kings*—sovereign over all. I can make some plans as I gaze into the day that stretches out before me, but I need to hold my plans tentatively—anticipating that You may have other ideas. The most important thing to determine is what You want me to do *now*.

I often waste time scanning the horizon of my life, searching for things that have to be done *sometime*. Help me instead to concentrate on the task that is before me and on *You*—the One who never leaves my side. As I let everything else fade into the background, my mind becomes uncluttered—making room for You to occupy more and more of my thinking.

When I finish what I'm working on right now, I can ask You to show me what to do next. You guide me step by step as I walk along *the path of Peace* in trusting dependence on You. Thank You, Lord, for *giving me strength and blessing me with Peace.*

In Your exalted Name, Jesus, amen.

"They will make war against the Lamb, but the Lamb will overcome them because he is Lord of lords and King of kings —and with him will be his called, chosen and faithful followers." —REVELATION 17:14

Many are the plans in a man's heart, but it is the LORD's purpose that prevails. —PROVERBS 19:21

"To shine on those living in darkness and in the shadow of death, to guide our feet into the path of peace." —LUKE 1:79

The LORD will give strength to His people; the LORD will bless His people with peace. —PSALM 29:11 NKJV

February

*Then Jesus spoke to them again: "I am the light of the world. Anyone who follows Me will never walk in the darkness but will have the light of life." —*JOHN 8:12 HCSB

Ever-present God,

I want the Light of Your Presence to shine on everything I experience—enabling me to see things from Your perspective. Help me to stay mindful of You in each and every situation I encounter.

I'm encouraged by the biblical account of the patriarch Jacob who ran away from his enraged brother. He went to sleep on a stone pillow in a land that seemed desolate. But after dreaming about heaven and angels and promises of Your Presence, he awoke and said: *"Surely the Lord is in this place, and I was not aware of it."* I'm grateful that Jacob's wonderful discovery was not only for him but for everyone who seeks to know You better—and that definitely includes me.

Lord, I ask You to increase my awareness that You are with me—no matter where I am or what is happening. Whenever I'm feeling distant from You, please remind me that You are with me *in this place.* I'm so grateful that *nothing in all creation will ever be able to separate me from Your loving Presence*!

In Your magnificent Name, Jesus, amen.

When he reached a certain place, he stopped for the night because the sun had set. Taking one of the stones there, he put it under his head and lay down to sleep. He had a dream in which he saw a stairway resting on the earth. . . . There above it stood the LORD, and he said: "I am the LORD, the God of your father Abraham and the God of Isaac. I will give you and your descendants the land on which you are lying. . . . I am with you and will watch over you wherever you go, and I will bring you back to this land. I will not leave you until I have done what I have promised you." When Jacob awoke from his sleep, he thought, "Surely the LORD is in this place, and I was not aware of it." —GENESIS 28:11–16

No power in the sky above or in the earth below —indeed, nothing in all creation will ever be able to separate us from the love of God that is revealed in Christ Jesus our Lord. —ROMANS 8:39 NLT

My living Lord,

By day You direct Your Love; at night Your song is with me—for You are *the God of my life.* Knowing that You are in charge of everything is such a great comfort! During the day, You command Your Love to bless me in countless ways. So I'll be on the lookout for the many good things You place along my path—searching for Your blessings and thanking You for each one I find. Help me not to be discouraged by the hard things I encounter but to accept them as part of living in a deeply fallen world.

I rejoice that *Your song is with me* throughout the night as You lovingly watch over me. If I am wakeful, I can use this time to *seek Your Face* and enjoy Your peaceful Presence. A tender intimacy with You develops *when I remember You on my bed—meditating on You in the night watches.* Whether I am waking or sleeping, You are always present with me. For You are indeed the God of my life!

In Your blessed Name, Jesus, amen.

By day the LORD directs his love, at night his song is with me —a prayer to the God of my life. —PSALM 42:8

Therefore we do not lose heart. Though outwardly we are wasting away, yet inwardly we are being renewed day by day. —2 CORINTHIANS 4:16

My heart said to You, "Your face, LORD, I will seek." —PSALM 27:8 NKJV

When I remember You on my bed, I meditate on You in the night watches. Because You have been my help, therefore in the shadow of Your wings I will rejoice. —PSALM 63:6–7 NKJV

Dear Jesus,

I bring You my weakness—seeking to receive Your Peace. Help me to accept myself and my circumstances just as they are, remembering that You are sovereign over everything. Please protect me from wearing myself out with analyzing and planning. Instead, I want to let thankfulness and trust be my guides through this day—keeping me close to You.

The Bible tells me that You are not only *with* me but *for* me. How wonderful it is to realize that I face *nothing* alone! When I feel anxious, it's because I'm focusing on the visible world and leaving You out of the picture. The remedy is to *fix my eyes not on what is seen but on what is unseen*. I know I can trust You to get me safely through this day—and all my days.

As I live in the radiance of Your Presence, Your Peace shines upon me, and I stop thinking so much about how weak I am. While I continue this intimate journey with You, I'm blessed and strengthened by Your promise that the path I'm following is headed for heaven.

In Your radiant Name, amen.

What, then, shall we say in response to this? If God is for us, who can be against us? —ROMANS 8:31

So we fix our eyes not on what is seen, but on what is unseen. For what is seen is temporary, but what is unseen is eternal. —2 CORINTHIANS 4:18

"The LORD bless you and keep you; the LORD make His face shine upon you, and be gracious to you; the LORD lift up His countenance upon you, and give you peace." —NUMBERS 6:24–26 NKJV

The LORD will give strength to His people; the LORD will bless His people with peace. —PSALM 29:11 NKJV

Brilliant Jesus,

Help me to *cast off the works of darkness and put on the armor of Light*—wearing this bright, protective covering with a grateful heart. The darkness of this world is prevalent all around me. Your beautiful Light-armor enables me to see things more clearly; it protects me from being led astray by the worldliness that surrounds me.

I delight in *walking in the Light* with You—living close to You, aware of Your loving Presence. Just as I put clothes on my body each morning, I need to *clothe myself with You* every day. This nearness to You helps me make good decisions. Nonetheless, I sometimes make bad choices that lead me into sin. Whenever this happens, please remind me that Your sacrifice on the cross was sufficient for *all* my sins. Moreover, Your precious, sacrificial blood cleanses me so I can keep walking in the Light.

The Bible assures me that *if I confess my sins, You are faithful and just to forgive me and cleanse me from all unrighteousness.* I rejoice in You, my Savior!

In Your merciful Name, amen.

The night is far gone; the day is at hand. So then let us cast off the works of darkness and put on the armor of light. —ROMANS 13:12 ESV

But if we walk in the light as He is in the light, we have fellowship with one another, and the blood of Jesus Christ His Son cleanses us from all sin. —1 JOHN 1:7 NKJV

Rather, clothe yourselves with the Lord Jesus Christ, and do not think about how to gratify the desires of the sinful nature. —ROMANS 13:14

If we confess our sins, He is faithful and just to forgive us our sins and to cleanse us from all unrighteousness. —1 JOHN 1:9 NKJV

My great God,

Only in *You* can I find lasting Joy. There are many sources of happiness in this world, and sometimes they spill over into Joy—especially when I share my pleasure with You. You shower so many blessings on my life! I want to take note of each one—responding to Your goodness with a glad, thankful heart. As I draw near You with a grateful mindset, the Joy of Your Presence enhances the pleasure I receive from Your blessings.

On days when Joy seems a distant memory, I need to *seek Your Face* more than ever. Instead of letting circumstances or feelings weigh me down, I can encourage myself with biblical truth: *You are always with me; You hold me by my right hand. You guide me with Your counsel, and afterward You will take me into Glory.* I must hold on to these glorious truths with all my might as I make my way through the debris of this broken world. Help me remember that You Yourself are *the Truth.* You are also *the Way,* so it is wise to follow You. *The Light of Your Presence* is shining on me—illuminating the pathway before me.

In Your bright Name, Jesus, amen.

Seek the Lord *and His strength; seek His face*
continually. —Psalm 105:4 nasb 1995

Yet I am always with you; you hold me by my right hand. You guide me with
your counsel, and afterward you will take me into glory. —Psalm 73:23–24

Jesus said to him, I am the Way and the Truth and the Life; no one
comes to the Father except by (through) Me. —John 14:6 ampc

Blessed are those who have learned to acclaim you, who walk
in the light of your presence, O Lord. —Psalm 89:15

Merciful God,

Your steadfast Love never ceases, Your mercies never come to an end; they are new every morning. I desperately want to rest in this truth, but I'm struggling to do so. Today, the only things that seem endless are my problems and my pain. Yet I know You are *here*—tenderly present— ready to help me get safely through this day. Your loving Presence is my lifeline that keeps me from giving up in despair.

On some days, when things are going well, I readily trust in Your steadfast Love. But when new, unexpected problems arise, trusting You takes much more effort. At such times, I need to remember that Your ever-new mercies far outweigh my difficulties. *Great is Your faithfulness!*

While I'm dressing, I like to remind myself that *You have clothed me in garments of salvation.* Because I wear Your *robe of righteousness*, I am on my way to heaven! This is an incredible act of mercy— snatching me from the jaws of hell and putting me on the path to Glory. Nothing I face today can compare with Your amazing gift of *eternal Life*!

In Your victorious Name, Jesus, amen.

The steadfast love of the LORD never ceases, his mercies never come to an end; they are new every morning; great is your faithfulness. —LAMENTATIONS 3:22–23 NRSV

I will greatly rejoice in the LORD, my soul shall be joyful in my God; for He has clothed me with the garments of salvation, He has covered me with the robe of righteousness, as a bridegroom decks himself with ornaments, and as a bride adorns herself with her jewels. —ISAIAH 61:10 NKJV

"For God so loved the world, that he gave his only Son, that whoever believes in him should not perish but have eternal life." —JOHN 3:16 ESV

Delightful Jesus,

You are my Joy! I like to let these words reverberate in my mind and sink into my innermost being. You—my Companion who *will never leave me*—are a boundless source of Joy! Focusing on this wondrous truth makes it possible for me to approach each day of my life as a good day. So help me to refrain from using the label "a bad day," even when I'm struggling deeply. Though my circumstances may indeed be very hard, I know *You are continually with me; You hold me by my right hand.* There is good to be found in *this* day—and every day— because of Your constant Presence and Your steadfast Love.

I rejoice in *Your priceless, unfailing Love!* This Love guarantees that I can *find refuge in the shadow of Your wings* no matter what is happening. And it gives me access to *Your river of delights.* When my world seems anything but delightful, please draw me to this ravishing river—to drink deeply from Your loving Presence. In both difficult times *and* easy times, You are my Joy!

In Your matchless Name, amen.

"The LORD himself goes before you and will be with you; he will never leave you nor forsake you. Do not be afraid; do not be discouraged." —DEUTERONOMY 31:8

Nevertheless I am continually with You; You hold me by my right hand. —PSALM 73:23 NKJV

How priceless is your unfailing love! Both high and low among men find refuge in the shadow of your wings. They feast on the abundance of your house; you give them drink from your river of delights. —PSALM 36:7–8

Loving Savior,

You brought me out into a spacious place. You rescued me because You delighted in me. I know that Your delight in me wasn't based on any worthiness that was in me. You freely *chose* to lavish Your Love on me—bringing me out of *slavery to sin* into a spacious place of salvation. Since my best efforts were utterly insufficient to save myself, *You rescued me* and clothed me in Your own perfect righteousness. Help me to wear this *clothing of salvation* with overflowing Joy—*living as a child of Light*, secure in Your radiant righteousness.

Salvation is the greatest, most precious gift I could ever receive, and I'll never stop thanking You for it! In the morning when I awake, I'll rejoice that You have adopted me into Your royal family. Before I go to sleep at night, I'll praise You for Your glorious grace.

Lord, I want to live in ways that help other people see *You* as the Source of abundant, never-ending Life!

In Your righteous, royal Name, Jesus, amen.

He brought me out into a spacious place; he rescued me because he delighted in me. —PSALM 18:19

Jesus replied, "I tell you the truth, everyone who sins is a slave to sin." —JOHN 8:34

I am overwhelmed with joy in the LORD my God! For he has dressed me with the clothing of salvation and draped me in a robe of righteousness. I am like a bridegroom dressed for his wedding or a bride with her jewels. —ISAIAH 61:10 NLT

For you were once darkness, but now you are light in the Lord. Live as children of light. —EPHESIANS 5:8

Sovereign Lord,

You are *my Strength*! You know all about my weakness; You understand that my strength is insufficient to handle the challenges I face. Even though it feels uncomfortable to be so weak, I've learned that this can be a place of blessing. My awareness of my need reminds me to turn to You—clinging to Your promise that *You will supply my every need according to Your riches in Glory.*

When my energy is running low, it's vital for me to connect with You, *my Strength*. Sometimes You provide abundant stamina as I spend time in Your Presence. At other times You strengthen me only bit by bit, giving me just enough energy to keep moving slowly forward. This slower pace can be disappointing, but it gives me more time to focus on You. I realize this may be Your way of keeping me close to You on my life-path so I can hear You whispering, "I love you." To keep hearing these whispers, I need to trust that You, *Sovereign Lord*, are in charge of my life and that my journey—though difficult—is full of blessing. Help me trust You more and more!

In Your powerful Name, Jesus, amen.

The Sovereign Lord is my strength; he makes my feet like the feet of a deer, he enables me to go on the heights. —HABAKKUK 3:19

And my God will liberally supply (fill to the full) your every need according to His riches in glory in Christ Jesus. —PHILIPPIANS 4:19 AMPC

Splendor and majesty are before him; strength and glory are in his sanctuary. Ascribe to the Lord, O families of nations, ascribe to the Lord glory and strength. —PSALM 96:6–7

Precious Jesus,

Your Word assures me that *in Your Presence there is fullness of Joy.* As I rest in Your Presence—pondering who You are in all Your Power and Glory—I rejoice in Your eternal commitment to me. *Neither height nor depth nor anything else in all creation will be able to separate me from Your Love!* My relationship with You has been secure ever since I trusted You as my all-sufficient Savior. Help me remember that I am Your beloved child—*this* is my permanent identity.

You've shown me that I can find Joy even in this deeply broken world because *You are with me always.* I need to spend time refreshing myself in Your Presence—where I can relax and learn to *delight myself in You* above all else.

As the Love-bonds between us grow stronger, so does my desire to help others enjoy the blessings I have in You. I long for Your Love to flow freely through me into other people's lives. Please lead me along *the path of Life* and teach me how to show Your Love to others.

In Your cherished Name, amen.

You make known to me the path of life; in your presence there is fullness of joy; at your right hand are pleasures forevermore. —PSALM 16:11 ESV

Neither height nor depth, nor anything else in all creation, will be able to separate us from the love of God that is in Christ Jesus our Lord. —ROMANS 8:39

"Teach these new disciples to obey all the commands I have given you. And be sure of this: I am with you always, even to the end of the age." —MATTHEW 28:20 NLT

Delight yourself in the LORD; and He will give you the desires of your heart. —PSALM 37:4 NASB 1995

Beloved Jesus,

I come to You, seeking to rest in Your Peace. The Light of Your Face shines upon me, blessing me with *Peace that transcends all understanding.* Instead of trying to figure things out myself, I want to relax in Your Presence—trusting that You know and understand everything. As I lean on You in childlike dependence, I feel peaceful and complete. This is how You created me to live: in close communion with You. I delight in this time with You, enjoying awareness of Your loving Presence.

When I am around other people, I tend to cater to their expectations—real or imagined. As I focus on pleasing them, my awareness of Your Presence grows dim. I become exhausted by my efforts to gain the approval of others. When I live this way, I offer people dry crumbs rather than the *living water* of Your Spirit flowing through me. I know this is *not* Your way for me.

Please help me to stay in touch with You even during my busiest moments. As I live in the Light of Your Peace, may the Spirit give me words of grace to speak into the lives of others.

In Your gracious Name, amen.

Do not be anxious about anything, but in everything, by prayer and petition, with thanksgiving, present your requests to God. And the peace of God, which transcends all understanding, will guard your hearts and your minds in Christ Jesus. —PHILIPPIANS 4:6–7

"He who believes in Me, as the Scripture has said, out of his heart will flow rivers of living water." —JOHN 7:38 NKJV

Do not get drunk on wine, which leads to debauchery. Instead, be filled with the Spirit. Speak to one another with psalms, hymns and spiritual songs. Sing and make music in your heart to the Lord, always giving thanks to God the Father for everything, in the name of our Lord Jesus Christ. —EPHESIANS 5:18–20

Glorious God,

The Bible tells me *You created me in Your own image.* Moreover, *You made me a little lower than the heavenly beings and crowned me with Glory.* So please help me not to doubt my significance. You formed me with an amazing brain that can communicate with You, think rationally, create things, make decisions, and much more. You gave people *dominion over the fish of the sea, the birds of the air, and every living thing that moves on the earth.* Among all that You have created, only human beings are made in Your image. This is a wonderful privilege and responsibility—making every moment of my life meaningful.

I've learned that my chief purpose in life is to glorify You and enjoy You forever. *You crowned me with Glory* so that I can *reflect Your Glory*—lighting up this dark world and pointing others to You. Please teach me to enjoy You more and more. I'm grateful that You created me with boundless capacity for delighting in You. I know that the Joy I find in You here and now is just a foretaste of the vast eternal pleasures awaiting me in heaven!

In Your awesome Name, Jesus, amen.

*So God created man in His own image; in the image of God He created him; male and female He created them. Then God blessed them, and God said to them, "Be fruitful and multiply; fill the earth and subdue it; have dominion over the fish of the sea, over the birds of the air, and over every living thing that moves on the earth." —*Genesis 1:27–28 nkjv

*You made him a little lower than the heavenly beings and crowned him with glory and honor. —*Psalm 8:5

*And we, who with unveiled faces all reflect the Lord's glory, are being transformed into his likeness with ever-increasing glory, which comes from the Lord, who is the Spirit. —*2 Corinthians 3:18

Lord of Peace,

When something in my life or thoughts makes me anxious, I need to *come to You* and talk with You about it. So I come boldly into Your Presence today, bringing You my *prayer and petition with thanksgiving*. Lord, I thank You for this opportunity to trust You more. The lessons of trust You send me are usually wrapped in difficulties, but I've learned that their benefits far outweigh the cost.

You have taught me that well-developed trust brings many blessings—not the least of which is Your Peace. Your Word assures me *You will keep me in perfect Peace* to the extent that *my mind is stayed on You, trusting in You.*

The world has it all wrong—proclaiming that peace is the result of having enough money, possessions, insurance, and security systems. Thankfully, *Your* Peace is such an all-encompassing gift that it is independent of circumstances. I'm learning that no matter how much I may lose, I am rich indeed if I gain Your *perfect Peace*. Please help me trust You enough to receive this glorious gift!

In Your trustworthy Name, Jesus, amen.

Now may the Lord of peace himself give you peace at all times and in every way. The Lord be with all of you. —2 THESSALONIANS 3:16

"Come to Me, all of you who are weary and burdened, and I will give you rest." —MATTHEW 11:28 HCSB

Do not be anxious about anything, but in everything, by prayer and petition, with thanksgiving, present your requests to God. —PHILIPPIANS 4:6

You will keep him in perfect peace, whose mind is stayed on You, because he trusts in You. —ISAIAH 26:3 NKJV

Compassionate God,

You are the perfect antidote to loneliness. *For You are the Lord, my God, who takes hold of my right hand and says to me, "Do not fear; I will help you."* Sometimes I like to close my right hand as if I'm grasping *Your* hand. This symbolic gesture enables me to feel connected to You—to Your living Presence. I especially need this sense of connection when I'm feeling lonely or afraid.

I'm thankful I can tell You about my feelings and the struggles I face. You already know all about them, but it does me good to bring them to You. As I spend time basking in the Light of Your Presence, I realize how safe and secure I am. *You are with me* every nanosecond of my life, so I'm never alone!

The more I seek Your Face, the more I gain Your perspective on my life. At times I find it useful to write out my prayer-concerns. This clarifies my thinking and provides a record of my prayers. It's also a way to release my problems to You. I rejoice that *You are watching over me* continually.

In Your worthy Name, Jesus, amen.

"For I am the LORD, your God, who takes hold of your right hand and says to you, Do not fear; I will help you." —ISAIAH 41:13

"Teaching them to observe all things that I have commanded you; and lo, I am with you always, even to the end of the age." Amen. —MATTHEW 28:20 NKJV

One thing I have desired of the LORD, that will I seek: That I may dwell in the house of the LORD all the days of my life, to behold the beauty of the LORD, and to inquire in His temple. —PSALM 27:4 NKJV

He will not let your foot slip —he who watches over you will not slumber. —PSALM 121:3

My Shepherd,

I love to hear Your whisper in my heart: "I am taking care of you, My child." Sometimes I feel alone and vulnerable—exposed to the elements of this fallen world. When I'm feeling this way, I need to stop and remind myself that *You care for me.* This promise reassures me and draws me closer to You. As I relax in Your Presence, I quit trying to figure out the future and orchestrate what will happen.

Help me remember that I am always in Your watchcare—even when circumstances are confusing and I don't know which way to proceed. I'm thankful that *You* know everything about me and my situation. Also, Your perfect knowledge about the future encourages me and gives me hope.

Whenever I start to feel afraid, please remind me that *You are with me.* You have promised *You will never leave me or forsake me.* Moreover, *You Yourself go before me* wherever I go.

While *I'm walking through the deep valley* of adversity, I'll keep these comforting words flowing through my mind: *I will fear no evil, for You are with me.*

In Your vigilant Name, Jesus, amen.

Cast all your anxiety on him because he cares for you. —1 PETER 5:7

Yes, though I walk through the [deep, sunless] valley of the shadow of death, I will fear or dread no evil, for You are with me; Your rod [to protect] and Your staff [to guide], they comfort me. —PSALM 23:4 AMPC

"And the LORD, He is the One who goes before you. He will be with you, He will not leave you nor forsake you; do not fear nor be dismayed." —DEUTERONOMY 31:8 NKJV

Gentle Jesus,

You've been teaching me that there is no randomness about my life: *Here* and *Now* comprise the coordinates of my daily life. The present moment is not only the point at which time intersects eternity, it is the place where I encounter *You*—my eternal Savior. Every moment of every day is alive with Your glorious Presence! Help me to keep my thoughts focused on You—enjoying Your Presence here and now.

I confess that I let many moments slip through my fingers, half-lived. I neglect the present by worrying about the future or longing for a better time and place. Please open my eyes and awaken my heart so I can see all that this day contains! I want You to be involved in everything I do—equipping me to *do my work heartily.* Working collaboratively with You lightens my load and enables me to enjoy what I'm doing.

I find that the more time I spend communicating with You, the less I worry. This frees me to let Your Spirit direct my steps—*guiding my feet into the way of Peace.*

In Your guiding Name, amen.

"Who of you by worrying can add a single hour to his life? Since you cannot do this very little thing, why do you worry about the rest?" —LUKE 12:25–26

Whatever you do, do your work heartily, as for the Lord rather than for men. —COLOSSIANS 3:23 NASB 1995

"The thief comes only in order to steal and kill and destroy. I came that they may have and enjoy life, and have it in abundance (to the full, till it overflows)." —JOHN 10:10 AMPC

"To give light to those who sit in darkness and the shadow of death, to guide our feet into the way of peace." —LUKE 1:79 NKJV

49

Invincible Jesus,

You are the culmination of all my hopes and desires. *You are the Alpha and the Omega, the Beginning and the End, who is and who was and who is to come—the Almighty.* Before I knew You, I expressed my longing for You in harmful ways. I didn't realize that *You* were the One I was searching for, and I was ever so vulnerable to the evil around me in the world. But now Your Presence safely shields me, enfolding me in Your loving care. You have lifted me *out of darkness into Your marvelous Light.*

Though You have brought many pleasures into my life, not one of them is essential. Help me to receive Your blessings with open hands—enjoying Your good gifts while holding them lightly. I don't want to cling to anything but *You.*

As I keep turning my attention to the Giver of *every good and perfect gift,* I rest in the knowledge that in You I am complete. I rejoice that the one thing I absolutely need is the one thing I can never lose—Your Presence with me!

In Your magnificent Name, amen.

Find rest, O my soul, in God alone; my hope comes from him. —PSALM 62:5

I am the Alpha and the Omega, the Beginning and the End, says the Lord God, He Who is and Who was and Who is to come, the Almighty (the Ruler of all). —REVELATION 1:8 AMPC

But you are a chosen generation, a royal priesthood, a holy nation, His own special people, that you may proclaim the praises of Him who called you out of darkness into His marvelous light. —1 PETER 2:9 NKJV

Every good and perfect gift is from above, coming down from the Father of the heavenly lights, who does not change like shifting shadows. —JAMES 1:17

Cherished Lord Jesus,

While I sit quietly in Your Presence, please fill my heart and mind with thankfulness. This is a most delightful way to spend time with You. When my mind needs a focal point, I can gaze at Your Love poured out for me on the cross. I need to remember that *neither height nor depth nor anything else in all creation can separate me from Your Love.* This remembrance builds a foundation of gratitude in me—a foundation that circumstances cannot shake.

As I go through this day, I want to find all the treasures You have placed along my way. I know that You lovingly go before me and plant little pleasures to brighten my day. I'll look carefully for these blessings and pluck them one by one. Then when I reach the end of the day, I will have gathered a lovely bouquet. I'll offer it up to You, Lord, with gratitude in my heart. As I lie down to sleep, help me relax in Your Presence and receive Your Peace—with thankful thoughts playing a lullaby in my mind.

In Your soothing Name, amen.

For I am convinced that neither death nor life, neither angels nor demons, neither the present nor the future, nor any powers, neither height nor depth, nor anything else in all creation, will be able to separate us from the love of God that is in Christ Jesus our Lord. —ROMANS 8:38–39

For no one can lay any foundation other than the one already laid, which is Jesus Christ. —1 CORINTHIANS 3:11

You have filled my heart with greater joy than when their grain and new wine abound. I will lie down and sleep in peace, for you alone, O LORD, make me dwell in safety. —PSALM 4:7–8

Redeeming Savior,

I rejoice in You—knowing that Your sacrifice on the cross absorbed all my guilt: past, present, and future. *There is no condemnation for those who belong to You!*

My guilt-free status as Your child provides good reason to be joyful each day of my life. Ever since Adam and Eve's disobedience in the Garden of Eden, the world has been under the bondage of sin. I'm so grateful that Your sacrificial death provided the solution to this terrible problem. The gospel really is the best news imaginable! You took my sin—*You became sin for me*—and You gave me Your own perfect righteousness.

Please help me learn to fully enjoy my guilt-free status in Your kingdom. *Through You, the law of the Spirit of life has set me free.* I realize this is *not* an invitation to dive into a careless, sinful lifestyle. Instead, You enable me to live thankfully—celebrating the amazing privilege of belonging to You forever! It's such a wondrous blessing to know who I really am: a beloved *child of God*. This is my true identity, and it makes every moment of my life meaningful.

In Your precious Name, Jesus, amen.

There is now no condemnation for those who are in Christ Jesus, because through Christ Jesus the law of the Spirit of life set me free from the law of sin and death. —ROMANS 8:1–2

When the woman saw that the fruit of the tree was good for food and pleasing to the eye, and also desirable for gaining wisdom, she took some and ate it. —GENESIS 3:6

He made Him who knew no sin to be sin for us, that we might become the righteousness of God in Him. —2 CORINTHIANS 5:21 NKJV

He came to his own, and his own people did not receive him. But to all who did receive him, who believed in his name, he gave the right to become children of God. —JOHN 1:11–12 ESV

My loving Lord,

Satisfy me in the morning with Your unfailing Love, that I may sing for Joy and be glad all my days. I have sought satisfaction in a variety of ways, many of which were hurtful. I've discovered that even good things can fail to satisfy me if I elevate them above You. So I come to You this morning with my emptiness and my longings. As I sit quietly in Your Presence, communing with You, I ask You to fill me up to the full with Your limitless Love. I delight in pondering *how wide and long and high and deep* is this vast ocean of blessing!

Finding my satisfaction in You above all else provides a firm foundation for my life. By building on this solid foundation, I can be joyful and confident as I go through my days. I know I will continue to encounter hardships because I live in such a terribly broken world. Yet I can count on You to guide me along my way as I cling to You in trusting dependence. Lord, You make my life meaningful and satisfying while I'm traveling toward my ultimate goal—the gates of *Glory*!

In Your glorious Name, Jesus, amen.

Satisfy us in the morning with your unfailing love, that we may sing for joy and be glad all our days. —PSALM 90:14

So that Christ may dwell in your hearts through faith. And I pray that you, being rooted and established in love, may have power, together with all the saints, to grasp how wide and long and high and deep is the love of Christ. —EPHESIANS 3:17–18

I can do all things through Christ who strengthens me. —PHILIPPIANS 4:13 NKJV

You guide me with your counsel, and afterward you will take me into glory. —PSALM 73:24

Jesus, my Peace,

You are *the Lord of Peace; You give Peace at all times and in every way.* There is a deep, gaping hole within me that can be filled only by Your peaceful Presence. Before I knew You, I tried to fill that emptiness in many different ways—or simply pretend it wasn't there. Even now, I often fail to recognize the full extent of my need for Your Peace—at all times and in every situation. Moreover, You've been showing me that recognizing my neediness is only half the battle. The other half is to believe that You can—and will—*supply every need of mine.*

Shortly before Your death, You promised Peace to Your disciples—and to everyone who becomes Your follower. You made it clear that this is a gift, something You provide freely and lovingly. My part is just to *receive* this glorious gift—admitting my longing for it as well as my need. Please help me to wait patiently and expectantly in Your Presence, eager to receive Your Peace in full measure. I can express my openness to this gift by lifting my hands and saying, "Jesus, I receive Your Peace."

In Your comforting Name, amen.

Now may the Lord of peace himself give you peace at all times and in every way. The Lord be with all of you. —2 THESSALONIANS 3:16

And my God will supply every need of yours according to his riches in glory in Christ Jesus. —PHILIPPIANS 4:19 ESV

"Peace I leave with you, My peace I give to you; not as the world gives do I give to you. Let not your heart be troubled, neither let it be afraid." —JOHN 14:27 NKJV

Dearest Jesus,

Thank You for leading me, step by step, through my life. I ask You to guide me through *this* day as I hold Your hand in childlike dependence. My future looks uncertain and feels flimsy—even precarious. I know I need to *walk by faith, not by sight*, believing that You will open up the way before me.

Every time I affirm my trust in You, it's as if I put a coin into Your faith-treasury. In this way, I prepare for days of trouble. I'm thankful that You keep safely in Your heart all the trust I invest in You—with interest compounded continuously. I've seen that the more I endeavor to trust You, the more You empower me to do so.

I need to practice trusting You during quiet days, when nothing much seems to be happening. Then, when storms come, my faith-balance will be sufficient to get me through those tough times. Please remind me to affirm my trust in You—silently, in whispers, in shouts, in songs. This practice glorifies You and keeps me close to You, enjoying Your peaceful Presence.

In Your faithful Name, amen.

For we walk by faith, not by sight. —2 CORINTHIANS 5:7 NKJV

When I am afraid, I will trust in you. In God, whose word I praise, in God I trust; I will not be afraid. What can mortal man do to me? —PSALM 56:3–4

"But store up for yourselves treasures in heaven, where moth and rust do not destroy, and where thieves do not break in and steal." —MATTHEW 6:20

You will keep in perfect peace him whose mind is steadfast, because he trusts in you. —ISAIAH 26:3

My guiding God,

Help me to willingly follow Your lead—opening myself more fully to You and Your way for me. I don't want to be so focused on getting my own way that I miss the things You have prepared for me. Instead, I choose to relax with You while You *transform me by the renewing of my mind*—working Your newness into me. I need to *be still* in Your Presence, trusting You enough to let go of my expectations and demands.

Sometimes I obstruct the very things I desire by trying too hard to make them happen in my timing. Yet You know not only the desires of my heart but also the best way and time to reach those goals. So I'm learning to yield to *Your* will and timing. Rather than striving to be in control, I need to spend more time *seeking Your Face*—talking with You openly and resting in Your Presence. Once I'm feeling more refreshed, I can ask You to show me the way forward. I'm encouraged by Your words of promise: *"I will guide you along the best pathway for your life. I will advise you and watch over you."*

In Your transforming Name, Jesus, amen.

Do not conform any longer to the pattern of this world, but be transformed by the renewing of your mind. Then you will be able to test and approve what God's will is —his good, pleasing and perfect will. —ROMANS 12:2

"Be still, and know that I am God; I will be exalted among the nations, I will be exalted in the earth!" —PSALM 46:10 NKJV

Seek the LORD and His strength; seek His face continually. —1 CHRONICLES 16:11 NASB 1995

The LORD says, "I will guide you along the best pathway for your life. I will advise you and watch over you." —PSALM 32:8 NLT

Beautiful Savior,

I long to comprehend the depth and breadth of *Your Love that surpasses knowledge*! I've seen that there's an enormous difference between really knowing You and simply knowing *about* You. Instead of just knowing some facts about You, I want to enjoy the glorious experience of Your loving Presence. I realize that I need the help of Your Spirit—*strengthening me with Power in my inner being so I can grasp how wide and long and high and deep is Your Love* for me.

You have been alive in my heart since the moment of my salvation. I've discovered that the more room I make for You in my inner being, the more You fill me with Your Love. You've been teaching me to expand this space in my heart by spending ample time with You and absorbing Your Word. I want to learn to stay in communication with You more and more—*praying continually*. These are joyful disciplines, and they keep me close to You.

Lord, I ask that Your Love may flow through me into the lives of other people. This *makes Your Love in me complete.*

In Your loving Name, Jesus, amen.

I pray that out of his glorious riches he may strengthen you with power through his Spirit in your inner being, so that Christ may dwell in your hearts through faith. And I pray that you, being rooted and established in love, may have power, together with all the saints, to grasp how wide and long and high and deep is the love of Christ, and to know this love that surpasses knowledge —that you may be filled to the measure of all the fullness of God. —EPHESIANS 3:16–19

Pray continually. —1 THESSALONIANS 5:17

No one has ever seen God; but if we love one another, God lives in us and his love is made complete in us. —1 JOHN 4:12

My Savior-God,

Help me to rest deeply in You, forgetting about the worries of the world. May Your living Presence envelop me in Peace as I focus on You—*Immanuel*. I find comfort in Your eternal security, knowing that *You are the same yesterday, today, and forever.*

Sometimes I live too much on the surface of life—focusing on ever-changing phenomena. If I consistently live this way, I eventually reach the point where I echo the sentiment of Solomon: *"Meaningless! Meaningless! Everything is meaningless."*

I'm learning that the way to instill meaning into my days is to live in collaboration with You. I need to begin each day alone with You so I can experience the reality of Your Presence. As I spend time focusing on You and Your Word, I ask You to open up the way before me step by step. When I arise from this peaceful time of communion and begin my journey through the day, I'm aware that You go with me. I hold on to Your hand in deliberate dependence on You—and You smooth out the path before me. Thank You, Jesus!

In Your strong, dependable Name, Jesus, amen.

"The virgin will be with child and will give birth to a son, and they will call him Immanuel" —which means, "God with us." —MATTHEW 1:23

Jesus Christ is the same yesterday, today, and forever. —HEBREWS 13:8 NKJV

"Meaningless! Meaningless!" says the Teacher. "Utterly meaningless! Everything is meaningless." —ECCLESIASTES 1:2

In all your ways acknowledge Him, and He will make your paths straight. —PROVERBS 3:6 NASB 1995

Trustworthy Lord Jesus,

Please help me trust You enough to relax and enjoy Your Presence. I confess that I often live in a state of hypervigilance—feeling and acting as if I'm in the midst of an emergency. Your Word tells me that *I am remarkably and wonderfully made.* My body is carefully crafted to "gear up" when necessary and then "gear down" when the crisis is over. But because I live in a broken body and a broken world, I find it difficult to let down my guard and really relax.

I need to remember that You are continually with me and that You are worthy of all my confidence, all my trust. I can *pour out my heart to You*—committing into Your sovereign care everything that's troubling me.

Thank You for training me to *trust in You with all my heart and mind.* The more I *lean on You* in confident trust, the more fully I can enjoy Your Presence. As I relax in Your healing Light, You shine Peace into my mind and heart. While I spend time waiting with You, my awareness of Your Presence grows stronger and *Your unfailing Love* soaks into my inner being.

In Your holy, healing Name, amen.

I will praise You because I have been remarkably and wonderfully made. Your works are wonderful, and I know this very well. —PSALM 139:14 HCSB

Trust in him at all times, O people; pour out your hearts to him, for God is our refuge. —PSALM 62:8

But I am like an olive tree flourishing in the house of God; I trust in God's unfailing love for ever and ever. —PSALM 52:8

Lean on, trust in, and be confident in the Lord with all your heart and mind and do not rely on your own insight or understanding. —PROVERBS 3:5 AMPC

Regal Jesus,

You are my best Friend as well as my King. I want to walk hand in hand with You through my life. Please help me face whatever today brings—pleasures, hardships, adventures, disappointments—relying on You each step of the way. I know that nothing is wasted when it's shared with You. *You can bring a crown of beauty out of the ashes* of lost dreams. You can glean Joy out of sorrow, Peace out of adversity. Only a Friend who is also the King of kings could accomplish this marvelous metamorphosis. There is no other like You, Lord!

The friendship You offer me is practical and down-to-earth, yet it is saturated with heavenly Glory. Living in Your Presence involves living in two realms simultaneously—the visible world and unseen, eternal reality. Thank You, Lord, for giving me the ability to stay conscious of You while walking along dusty, earthbound paths. As Your Word declares, *I am fearfully and wonderfully made.*

In Your awesome Name, amen.

*"I no longer call you servants, because a servant does not know his master's business. Instead, I have called you friends, for everything that I learned from my Father I have made known to you." —*JOHN 15:15

And provide for those who grieve in Zion —to bestow on them a crown of beauty instead of ashes, the oil of gladness instead of mourning, and a garment of praise instead of a spirit of despair. They will be called oaks of righteousness, a planting of the LORD *for the display of his splendor. —*ISAIAH 61:3

*Sorrowful, yet always rejoicing; poor, yet making many rich; having nothing, and yet possessing everything. —*2 CORINTHIANS 6:10

*I will give thanks to You, for I am fearfully and wonderfully made; wonderful are Your works, and my soul knows it very well. —*PSALM 139:14 NASB 1995

Delightful Jesus,

Help me to *walk in the Light of Your Presence—acclaiming You, rejoicing in Your Name, and exulting in Your righteousness.* To acclaim You is to praise You in a strong and enthusiastic way, including shouts and applause. I rejoice in Your Name by delighting in all that You are—my Savior and Shepherd, my Lord and my God, my Sovereign King, my Friend who loves me with *unfailing Love.*

I exult in Your righteousness by reveling in the wondrous truth that You gave this priceless, holy gift to *me!* Your perfect righteousness is already credited to my account—even though I continue to battle sin in my life.

When I'm walking in Your glorious Light, *Your blood cleanses me from all sin.* As I seek to live near You, freely admitting I'm a sinner in need of forgiveness, Your radiant Presence purifies me. Moreover, this blessing of cleansing enables me to *have fellowship with* other believers.

Lord, I delight in walking in the Light with You—enjoying Your bright, loving Presence.

In Your brilliant Name, amen.

Blessed are those who have learned to acclaim you, who walk in the light of your presence, O LORD. They rejoice in your name all day long; they exult in your righteousness. —PSALM 89:15–16

Let your face shine on your servant; save me in your unfailing love. —PSALM 31:16

This righteousness from God comes through faith in Jesus Christ to all who believe. There is no difference. —ROMANS 3:22

But if we walk in the light as He is in the light, we have fellowship with one another, and the blood of Jesus Christ His Son cleanses us from all sin. —1 JOHN 1:7 NKJV

Gracious Lord,

Often I pray intensely for something and wait eagerly for the answer. If You grant my request, I respond joyfully and thankfully. But rather than lingering in a grateful attitude, I tend to move on too quickly to asking for the next thing. Lord, instead of experiencing only a short-lived burst of gratitude, I want to learn to remain in an attitude of thankful Joy—letting my gratefulness spill over into the future.

Help me to train myself to remember Your gracious responses to my requests. I find it beneficial to tell others about blessings I've received from You. Another way of being mindful of answered prayer is to write down the answers someplace where I'll see them frequently.

Please teach me to *remember Your marvelous works* with thankfulness. You've shown me that gratefulness blesses me doubly—with joyful memories of answered prayer and with the pleasure of sharing my happiness with You!

In Your jubilant Name, Jesus, amen.

Let us enter His presence with thanksgiving; let us shout triumphantly to Him in song. —PSALM 95:2 HCSB

But thanks be to God, who gives us the victory through our Lord Jesus Christ. —1 CORINTHIANS 15:57 ESV

Remember His marvelous works which He has done, His wonders, and the judgments of His mouth. —1 CHRONICLES 16:12 NKJV

March

*Jesus said to him, "I am the way, the truth, and the life. No one comes to the Father except through Me." —*JOHN 14:6 NKJV

Jesus, my Treasure,

Please give me Joy that is independent of circumstances—give me *Yourself*! Your Word tells me that *all the treasures of wisdom and knowledge are hidden in You.* You are infinitely wise and all-knowing. This means I will never run out of treasures to search for in You.

You are a wellspring of Joy overflowing into my life. So I open wide my heart, mind, and spirit—seeking to receive You in full measure. I'm thankful that Your Joy can coexist with the most difficult circumstances. No matter what is happening in my life, *the Light of Your Presence* continues to shine upon me. Help me to keep looking toward You with a trusting heart. When I persevere in searching for You, Joy-Light eventually breaks through the darkest storm clouds. As Your heavenly Light soaks into me, it brightens my perspective and fills me with sublime delight.

I'm so grateful to have *an inheritance in heaven that is imperishable, uncorrupted, and unfading.* Because I *believe in You,* I'm assured that *inexpressible and glorious Joy* is mine—now and forever!

In Your jubilant Name, amen.

All the treasures of wisdom and knowledge are hidden in Him. —COLOSSIANS 2:3 HCSB

Blessed are those who have learned to acclaim you, who walk in the light of your presence, O LORD. —PSALM 89:15

Praise the God and Father of our Lord Jesus Christ. According to His great mercy, He has given us a new birth into a living hope through the resurrection of Jesus Christ from the dead and into an inheritance that is imperishable, uncorrupted, and unfading, kept in heaven for you. . . . You love Him, though you have not seen Him. And though not seeing Him now, you believe in Him and rejoice with inexpressible and glorious joy. —1 PETER 1:3–4, 8 HCSB

Faithful God,

Morning by morning You awaken me and open my understanding to Your will. Thank You for always being mindful of me. It's comforting to know that You never sleep, so You're able to watch over me while I am sleeping. Then, *when I wake up, You are still with me.* As I become increasingly aware of Your Presence, You help me become more alert—combing out the tangles in my sleepy thoughts. I respond to Your Love-call by *drawing near to You.* I love to spend time enjoying Your Presence and nourishing my soul with Your Word.

I've found that time devoted to You blesses and strengthens me immensely. You open my understanding to Your Word—enabling me to comprehend Scripture better and apply it to my life. Please help me discern Your will clearly as I make plans for this day. When I walk alongside You, seeking to do Your will, You empower me to handle whatever comes my way.

Lord, teach me how to *trust in You at all times*—in all circumstances.

In Your trustworthy Name, Jesus, amen.

The Lord God has given me his words of wisdom so that I may know what I should say to all these weary ones. Morning by morning he wakens me and opens my understanding to his will. —ISAIAH 50:4 TLB

How precious are your thoughts about me, O God. They cannot be numbered! I can't even count them; they outnumber the grains of sand! And when I wake up, you are still with me! —PSALM 139:17–18 NLT

Draw near to God and He will draw near to you. Cleanse your hands, you sinners; and purify your hearts, you double-minded. —JAMES 4:8 NKJV

Trust in him at all times, O people; pour out your hearts to him, for God is our refuge. —PSALM 62:8

Precious Lord Jesus,

I love to hear You saying to me, *"I have called you by name; you are Mine!"* It's so comforting to know that I belong to You—no matter how isolated I sometimes feel. Thank You for redeeming me by paying the full penalty for my sins. I'm grateful that You called me to Yourself in the most personal way—reaching down into the circumstances of my life, speaking into the intricacies of my heart and mind. Even though You have vast numbers of followers, I am never just a number to You. You always speak to me *by name.* Scripture tells me I'm so precious to You that *You have inscribed me on the palms of Your hands. Nothing can separate me from Your loving Presence!*

When world events are swirling around me and my personal world feels unsteady, I don't want to let my thoughts linger on those stressors. Help me instead to focus my mind on the truth: Although this world is full of trouble, You are with me and You are in control. You're training me to change the subject from my problems to Your Presence by whispering, "But Jesus is with me," and then turning to You.

In Your victorious Name, amen.

"Do not fear, for I have redeemed you; I have called you by name; you are Mine!" —ISAIAH 43:1 NASB 1995

"See, I have inscribed you on the palms of My hands; your walls are continually before Me." —ISAIAH 49:16 NKJV

For I am convinced that neither death nor life, neither angels nor demons, neither the present nor the future, nor any powers, neither height nor depth, nor anything else in all creation, will be able to separate us from the love of God that is in Christ Jesus our Lord. —ROMANS 8:38–39

Dear Jesus,

I know that You are with me, so please help me not to be afraid. I love to hear You saying, *"Peace, be still!"* to my troubled heart. You have assured me that no matter what happens, *You will not leave me or forsake me.* When I let this assurance soak into my mind and heart, it fills me with confident trust.

The media relentlessly proclaims bad news—for breakfast, lunch, and dinner. I've found that a steady diet of its fare sickens me. Instead of focusing on fickle, ever-changing news, I choose to tune in to the living Word—*You*, the One who is always the same.

I want to let Scripture saturate my mind and heart so I can walk steadily along the path of Life with You. Your Word tells me that I need not fear *though the earth give way and the mountains fall into the heart of the sea.*

Although I don't know what will happen tomorrow, I can be absolutely sure of my ultimate destination. *You hold me by my right hand. You guide me with Your counsel, and afterward You will take me into Glory.* Hallelujah!

In Your magnificent Name, amen.

Then He arose and rebuked the wind, and said to the sea, "Peace, be still!" And the wind ceased and there was a great calm. —MARK 4:39 NKJV

"Be strong and courageous. Do not fear or be in dread of them, for it is the LORD your God who goes with you. He will not leave you or forsake you." —DEUTERONOMY 31:6 ESV

God is our refuge and strength, an ever-present help in trouble. Therefore we will not fear, though the earth give way and the mountains fall into the heart of the sea. —PSALM 46:1–2

Yet I am always with you; you hold me by my right hand. You guide me with your counsel, and afterward you will take me into glory. —PSALM 73:23–24

Sovereign Lord,

I want to learn to be joyful even when things don't go as I would like. My tendency is to begin each day striving to make things go my way. Yet I've found that every day I bump up against at least one thing that doesn't yield to my will. It can be as trivial as the reflection I see in the mirror or as massive as a loved one's serious illness.

I realize that Your purpose is *not* to grant my every wish or make my life easy. Help me to accept Your ways in my life and trust You in all circumstances.

On days when I'm intent upon trying to be in control, I feel frustrated much of the time—and I waste energy regretting things that have happened. But I know that the past cannot be changed. Please teach me to be grateful for Your help in the present and Your hope for the future.

Show me how to relax more—trusting in *Your* control over my life and remembering that You are always near. Your Word assures me there is *Joy in Your Presence*; moreover, *Your Face radiates with Joy* that shines upon me!

In Your radiant Name, Jesus, amen.

Trust in him at all times, O people; pour out your hearts to him, for God is our refuge. —PSALM 62:8

There is surely a future hope for you, and your hope will not be cut off. —PROVERBS 23:18

You have made known to me the paths of life; you will fill me with joy in your presence. —ACTS 2:28

"May the Lord bless and protect you; may the Lord's face radiate with joy because of you; may he be gracious to you, show you his favor, and give you his peace." —NUMBERS 6:24–26 TLB

Loving Lord Jesus,

I come into Your gracious Presence, asking You to *satisfy me with Your unfailing Love.* The best time for me to seek Your Face is *in the morning,* soon after I awaken. Connecting with You early prepares me for my day. Your endless Love satisfies me immensely: It enables me to believe I am treasured and significant. It reminds me that You and I together can handle the circumstances of this day. Knowing that I'm forever loved energizes me and gives me courage to persevere during difficulties.

Encountering Your loving Presence inspires me to *sing for Joy and be glad.* Meeting with the One who is *King of kings and Lord of lords*—in the privacy of my home—is an astonishing privilege! Moreover, I rejoice that my name is *written in the Lamb's Book of Life*—with indelible ink!

I want to take time to enjoy Your Presence: reading Scripture and praying, speaking and singing praises. I delight in the wondrous truth that *nothing in all creation can separate me from Your Love!*

In Your glorious Name, amen.

Satisfy us in the morning with your unfailing love, that we may sing for joy and be glad all our days. —PSALM 90:14

And on His robe and on His thigh He has a name written, "KING OF KINGS, AND LORD OF LORDS." —REVELATION 19:16 NASB 1995

Nothing impure will ever enter it, nor will anyone who does what is shameful or deceitful, but only those whose names are written in the Lamb's book of life. —REVELATION 21:27

Neither height nor depth, nor anything else in all creation, will be able to separate us from the love of God that is in Christ Jesus our Lord. —ROMANS 8:39

Compassionate Jesus,

I need to tell You about the things that have been weighing me down. I realize You already know all about them, but voicing them to You provides relief from the heavy load I've been carrying.

Whenever I'm feeling discouraged, it's essential for me to spend time *remembering You*. Thinking about who You are—*my Lord and my God*, my Savior and Shepherd, the Friend who *will never leave me*—lifts me up and brightens my perspective. I'm grateful that You are fully aware of every aspect of my life, including all my thoughts and feelings. Everything about me is important to You! As I relax in Your loving Presence, help me recall the many ways You've taken care of me, providing just what I need. I'll try to thank You for each blessing that comes to mind.

In the Light of Your Presence, I can see things more clearly and sort out what is important and what is not. As I linger with You, Your Face shines upon me—blessing, encouraging, and comforting me. *I will again praise You for the help of Your Presence.*

In Your mighty Name, amen.

O my God, my soul is cast down within me; therefore I will remember You from the land of the Jordan, and from the heights of Hermon, from the Hill Mizar. —PSALM 42:6 NKJV

Thomas responded to Him, "My Lord and my God!" —JOHN 20:28 HCSB

"The LORD himself goes before you and will be with you; he will never leave you nor forsake you. Do not be afraid; do not be discouraged." —DEUTERONOMY 31:8

Why are you in despair, O my soul? And why have you become disturbed within me? Hope in God, for I shall again praise Him for the help of His presence. —PSALM 42:5 NASB 1995

Lord Jesus,

I'm trying to trust that Your intentions for me are good even when they are radically different from what I'd hoped or expected. *You are Light; in You there is no darkness at all.* I will look for Your Light in my circumstances, for You are abundantly present in the moments of my life. I want to be open to You and all Your ways with me. Sometimes this requires relinquishing plans or dreams that are precious to me. At such times, I need to remember and wholeheartedly believe that *Your way is perfect*—no matter how hard it is.

You are a shield for all who take refuge in You. When I'm feeling disappointed or afraid, draw me closer to You—reminding me that You are my Refuge. I realize You don't shield me from absolutely everything. There are some trials You have prepared for me to handle. Thank You for giving me a significant part to play in this world. Please help me *lead the life You have assigned to me* in joyful dependence on You. Then *my soul will be satisfied as with the richest of foods; with singing lips my mouth will praise You!*

In Your supreme Name, amen.

This is the message we have heard from Him and announce to you, that God is Light, and in Him there is no darkness at all. —1 JOHN 1:5 NASB 1995

As for God, his way is perfect; the word of the LORD is flawless. He is a shield for all who take refuge in him. —PSALM 18:30

Only let each person lead the life that the Lord has assigned to him, and to which God has called him. This is my rule in all the churches. —1 CORINTHIANS 7:17 ESV

My soul will be satisfied as with the richest of foods; with singing lips my mouth will praise you. —PSALM 63:5

My ever-present Lord,

I've been looking ahead at uncertainties, letting them unnerve me. I see fear and discouragement waiting alongside my pathway into the future—ready to accompany me if I let them. Please keep reminding me that *You go before me and will be with me. You hold me by my right hand.* Because You live beyond time, You're able to be with me where I am *and* simultaneously be on the path up ahead. Through eyes of faith, I can see You shining brightly—beckoning me on, encouraging me to fix my gaze on You. So I will cling tightly to Your hand as I walk past those dark presences of dread and discouragement. Help me keep looking toward Your radiant Presence that beams out *unfailing Love* and endless encouragement.

My confidence comes from knowing *You are continually with me* and You are already in my future, preparing the way before me. If I listen carefully, I can hear You calling back to me from the trail up ahead—words of warning and wisdom, courage and hope: *"Do not fear, for I am with you. Do not anxiously look about you, for I am your God. I will strengthen you, surely I will help you."*

In Your powerful Name, Jesus, amen.

"The LORD himself goes before you and will be with you; he will never leave you nor forsake you." —DEUTERONOMY 31:8

Nevertheless I am continually with You; You hold me by my right hand. —PSALM 73:23 NKJV

May your unfailing love be my comfort. —PSALM 119:76

"Do not fear, for I am with you; do not anxiously look about you, for I am your God. I will strengthen you, surely I will help you." —ISAIAH 41:10 NASB 1995

My great God,

I don't want to let any set of circumstances intimidate me. Please keep reminding me that the more challenging my day is, the more of Your Power You provide.

I used to think that You empower me equally each day, but I've learned that this is not true. Still, my tendency upon awakening each morning is to assess the difficulties ahead of me—measuring them against my average strength. I realize these worry-thoughts are just an exercise in unreality, and I long to break free from them!

Lord, *You* know what each of my days will contain, and I can trust You to empower me accordingly. You've been showing me that the degree to which You strengthen me on a given day is based mainly on two variables: the difficulty of my circumstances and my willingness to depend on You as I'm dealing with those challenges.

Help me view difficult days as opportunities to receive more of Your Power than usual. Instead of panicking during tough times, I can look to You for all I need. Thank You for Your reassuring words: *"As your days, so shall your strength be."*

In Your strong Name, Jesus, amen.

But he said to me, "My grace is sufficient for you, for my power is made perfect in weakness." Therefore I will boast all the more gladly about my weaknesses, so that Christ's power may rest on me. —2 CORINTHIANS 12:9

Seek the LORD and His strength; seek His face continually. —PSALM 105:4 NASB 1995

"Your sandals shall be iron and bronze; as your days, so shall your strength be." —DEUTERONOMY 33:25 NKJV

My comforting Lord,

Help me *find rest in You alone; my hope comes from You.* I have a restless mind. It skips and scampers about—rarely taking time to be still. But Your Word instructs me to *be still and know that You are God.* When I sit quietly in Your Presence, I can hear You saying, *"Come to Me, and I will give you rest."*

You are the only resting place for my mind that truly satisfies and strengthens me. I need to take time to direct my thoughts to You—whispering Your Name and waiting in Your sacred Presence. This interlude with You provides refreshment for both my mind and my soul.

True hope comes from You. False hope comes from many sources, including persuasive advertising. Please give me discernment as I seek to walk along a hopeful path. Many voices call out to me: "This is the way!" Protect me from being deceived while I'm trying to process all the information clamoring for my attention. I've found that the best way to break free from information overload is to refocus my thoughts on *You.* As I rest in Your peaceful Presence, true hope grows within me.

In Your soothing Name, Jesus, amen.

Find rest, O my soul, in God alone; my hope comes from him. —PSALM 62:5

"Be still, and know that I am God." —PSALM 46:10

"Come to Me, all you who labor and are heavy laden, and I will give you rest. Take My yoke upon you and learn from Me, for I am gentle and lowly in heart, and you will find rest for your souls." —MATTHEW 11:28–29 NKJV

Hope in God, for I shall again praise Him for the help of His presence. —PSALM 42:5 NASB 1995

Cherished Jesus,

Sometimes I feel frazzled—pulled this way and that by people and circumstances around me. At such times, I need to stop and turn to You, but instead I tend to drive myself to get more and more done. Even if I manage to calm my body, my mind continues to race—anticipating future problems and searching for solutions.

Help me to focus on the wondrous truth that *all the treasures of wisdom and knowledge are hidden in You*. Please remind me often, whispering to my heart: "Beloved, I am your Treasure. In Me you are complete."

When I prize You above all else, delighting in You as *my First Love*, I'm protected from feeling fragmented. You are the One who completes me, and You're training me to bring my thoughts back to You whenever they wander from Your Presence. Thank You for Your patient work in me, Lord.

Living near You, enjoying Your Presence, includes seeking to obey Your commands. I confess that I fail frequently, and I'm eternally grateful that *You have clothed me with garments of salvation—the robe of Your righteousness*!

In Your holy Name, amen.

My purpose is that they may be encouraged in heart and united in love . . . in order that they may know the mystery of God, namely, Christ, in whom are hidden all the treasures of wisdom and knowledge. —COLOSSIANS 2:2–3

"Nevertheless I have this against you, that you have left your first love." —REVELATION 2:4 NKJV

I will greatly rejoice in the LORD; my soul shall exult in my God, for he has clothed me with the garments of salvation; he has covered me with the robe of righteousness. —ISAIAH 61:10 ESV

All-knowing God,

Please prepare me for the day that stretches out before me. You know *exactly* what this day will contain, whereas I have only vague ideas about it. I wish I could see a map that would show all the twists and turns of today's journey. I'd feel better prepared if I could somehow visualize what is on the road up ahead. But You've been teaching me a better way to prepare for *whatever* I will encounter today: spending quality time with You.

Even though I don't know what's awaiting me on the path ahead, I trust that You have equipped me well for the journey. I'm thrilled by the promise that You are my Companion each step of the way! And I'm learning to stay in better communication with You, whispering Your Name when I need to redirect my thoughts to You. This simple practice helps me walk through the day with my focus on You.

Lord, I rejoice in Your abiding Presence—the best possible road map!

In Your delightful Name, Jesus, amen.

The LORD replied, "My Presence will go with you,
*and I will give you rest." —*EXODUS 33:14

*Rejoice in the Lord always. I will say it again: Rejoice! —*PHILIPPIANS 4:4

"Abide in Me, and I in you. As the branch cannot bear fruit of itself unless
it abides in the vine, so neither can you unless you abide in Me. I am the
vine, you are the branches; he who abides in Me and I in him, he bears much
*fruit, for apart from Me you can do nothing." —*JOHN 15:4–5 NASB 1995

Glorious Lord,

You have been showing me that hope is like a golden cord connecting me to heaven. This cord helps me hold my head up high even when multiple trials are buffeting me. I know that You never leave my side, and You never let go of my hand. But without the cord of hope, my head sometimes slumps and my feet start to drag as I journey uphill with You. Hope lifts my perspective from my weary feet to the glorious view I can see from the high road!

Thank You, Lord, that You are always with me—and the road we're traveling together is ultimately the highway to heaven. When I contemplate this glorious destination, I stop worrying about the roughness or smoothness of the road ahead. Please train me to hold in my heart a dual focus: Your continual Presence and the hope of heaven.

In Your wonderful Name, Jesus, amen.

Be joyful in hope, patient in affliction, faithful in prayer. —Romans 12:12

But since we belong to the day, let us be self-controlled, putting on faith and love as a breastplate, and the hope of salvation as a helmet. —1 Thessalonians 5:8

We have this hope as an anchor for the soul, firm and secure. It enters the inner sanctuary behind the curtain, where Jesus, who went before us, has entered on our behalf. He has become a high priest forever, in the order of Melchizedek. —Hebrews 6:19–20

Now may the God of hope fill you with all joy and peace as you believe in Him so that you may overflow with hope by the power of the Holy Spirit. —Romans 15:13 HCSB

Beloved Jesus,

Your Word assures me that *if I walk in the Light*—living close to You—*Your blood cleanses me from all sin*. So I bring my sins to You, confessing them and asking You to help me make needed changes.

I'm thankful that my standing with You is not based on whether I confess my sins quickly enough or thoroughly enough. You've shown me that the only thing that keeps me right with You is *Your* perfect righteousness. Thank You, Lord, for giving me this priceless gift freely and permanently when I became a Christian. Since I am Yours—brilliantly *arrayed in Your robe of righteousness*—I can come confidently into Your glorious Presence.

I've found that *walking in the Light of Your Presence* blesses me in a multitude of ways. Good things are better and bad things become more bearable when I share them with You. As I delight in Your Love-Light, I'm able to love others more fully and *have fellowship* with them. Moreover, I'm less likely to stumble or fall because sins are glaringly evident in Your holy Light.

Lord, teach me to *rejoice in Your Name all day long*—enjoying Your Presence and *exulting in Your righteousness*!

In Your sacred Name, amen.

But if we walk in the Light as He Himself is in the Light, we have fellowship with one another, and the blood of Jesus His Son cleanses us from all sin. —1 JOHN 1:7 NASB 1995

I delight greatly in the LORD; my soul rejoices in my God. For he has clothed me with garments of salvation and arrayed me in a robe of righteousness. —ISAIAH 61:10

Blessed are those who have learned to acclaim you, who walk in the light of your presence, O LORD. They rejoice in your name all day long; they exult in your righteousness. —PSALM 89:15–16

Sovereign God,

I need to give up the illusion of being in control of my life. When things are going smoothly, it's easy for me to feel as if I'm the one in charge. Yet the longer I perceive myself as my own master, and the more comfortable I become in this role, the more at risk I am.

I can enjoy times of smooth sailing and be thankful for them. But I must not become addicted to a sense of mastery over my life—considering it the norm. I've learned from experience that storms *will* come and uncertainties *will* loom on the horizon. If I cling to control and feel entitled to having things go my way, I'm likely to sink when I encounter difficulties.

Help me to *trust in You at all times—pouring out my heart to You, for You are my Refuge.* Thank You for using adversity to set me free from the illusion of being in control. When my circumstances and my future are full of uncertainties, I can turn to You and take refuge in You. I want to find my security in *knowing You,* the Master who is sovereign over the storms of my life—over everything!

In Your great Name, Jesus, amen.

Now listen, you who say, "Today or tomorrow we will go to this or that city, spend a year there, carry on business and make money." Why, you do not even know what will happen tomorrow. What is your life? You are a mist that appears for a little while and then vanishes. —JAMES 4:13–14

Trust in him at all times, O people; pour out your hearts to him, for God is our refuge. —PSALM 62:8

And this is eternal life, that they may know You, the only true God, and Jesus Christ whom You have sent. —JOHN 17:3 NKJV

Precious Jesus,

You are the Resurrection and the Life. Whoever believes in You will live, even though he dies. You spoke this powerful truth to Martha when her brother Lazarus had been dead for four days, and she believed You. Then You commanded Lazarus to come out of his tomb, and he did!

I love pondering Your teaching that *You are the Way, the Truth, and the Life.* You are everything I could ever need—for this life and the next. *All the treasures of wisdom and knowledge are hidden in You.* Believing this truth simplifies my life and helps me stay focused on You. Please train me in the joyful discipline of treasuring You above all else.

You are the answer to all my struggles, the Joy that pervades all time and circumstances. You make my hard times bearable and my good times even better. So I *come to You* just as I am, desiring to share more and more of my life with You. I rejoice as I journey with You— *the Way* who guides me step by step and *the Resurrection* who gives me eternal Life.

In Your majestic Name, amen.

Jesus said to her, "I am the resurrection and the life. He who believes in me will live, even though he dies." . . . When he had said this, Jesus called in a loud voice, "Lazarus, come out!" —JOHN 11:25, 43

Jesus said to him, "I am the way, the truth, and the life. No one comes to the Father except through Me." —JOHN 14:6 NKJV

My purpose is that they may be encouraged in heart and united in love . . . in order that they may know . . . Christ, in whom are hidden all the treasures of wisdom and knowledge. —COLOSSIANS 2:2–3

"Come to me, all you who are weary and burdened, and I will give you rest." —MATTHEW 11:28

Dearest Jesus,

How wonderful it is to know that You are taking care of me! When I'm spending time with You—enjoying the warmth and security of Your loving Presence—it's easier to trust that every detail of my life is under Your control. The Bible affirms that *everything fits into a plan for good, for those who love You and are called according to Your design and purpose.*

Because the world is in such an abnormal, fallen condition, it sometimes feels as if chance is governing the universe. Events seem to happen randomly, with little or no apparent meaning. But You've shown me that when I view the world this way, I'm overlooking a most important fact: the limitations of my understanding. Submerged beneath the surface of the visible world, there are mysteries too profound for me to fathom!

If I could actually *see* how close You are to me and how constantly You work on my behalf, I would never again doubt Your wonderful care of me. But Your Word instructs me to *live by faith, not by sight.* Please help me to trust in Your mysterious, majestic Presence.

In Your magnificent Name, amen.

All things work together and are . . . for good to and for those who love God and are . . . called according to [His] design and purpose. —ROMANS 8:28 AMPC

You asked, "Who is this who hides counsel without knowledge?" Therefore I have uttered what I did not understand, things too wonderful for me, which I did not know. —JOB 42:3 NKJV

Cast all your anxiety on him because he cares for you. —1 PETER 5:7

We live by faith, not by sight. —2 CORINTHIANS 5:7

Exalted Jesus,

Help me to follow You one step at a time. I know this is all You require of me. In fact, I realize that the *only* way I can move through this space-time world is to take one step after another. But as I look ahead, I see huge mountains looming and I start wondering how I will ever be able to scale those heights. Meanwhile, because I'm not looking where I'm going, I stumble on the easy path where You're leading me right now. As You help me get back on my feet, I tell You how worried I am about the cliffs up ahead.

You lovingly remind me that I don't know what will happen *today*, much less tomorrow. Our path may take an abrupt turn, leading me away from those towering peaks. Or there may be an easier route up the mountains that is not visible from this distance. I know that if You do lead me up the steepest way, You will equip me thoroughly for that strenuous ascent. You will even *command Your angels to guard me in all my ways.*

I really want to stay focused on the present journey, enjoying Your Presence. Teach me to *walk by faith, not by sight*—trusting You to open up the way before me.

In Your compassionate Name, amen.

With your help I can advance against a troop; with my God I can scale a wall. —Psalm 18:29

For he will command his angels concerning you to guard you in all your ways; they will lift you up in their hands, so that you will not strike your foot against a stone. —Psalm 91:11–12

For we walk by faith, not by sight. —2 Corinthians 5:7 nkjv

Creator-God,

Your Word tells me that *You make my feet like the feet of a deer and enable me to stand on the heights.* You created deer with the ability to climb steep mountains effortlessly and to stand fearlessly on the heights. You also created me, and You redeemed me—making it possible for me to "stay on my feet" by trusting You. This gives me confidence to *walk and make progress upon my high places of trouble, responsibility, and suffering.*

It's crucial for me to remember that I live in a world where my spiritual enemies never declare a truce. Help me to *stay alert* and be ready for battle at all times—*putting on the full armor* You provide. No matter what happens, I want to *be able to stand my ground, and after I have done everything, to stand.*

Whenever I'm in the thick of battle, please remind me to assert my trust in You—my confidence that You are with me, fighting alongside me. Even when I feel as if I'm losing the battle, I know I must not give up. My assignment is to hold tightly to Your hand and just keep standing. This is victory!

In Your victorious Name, Jesus, amen.

He makes my feet like the feet of a deer; he enables me to stand on the heights. —2 SAMUEL 22:34

The Lord God ... will make me to walk ... and make [spiritual] progress upon my high places [of trouble, suffering, or responsibility]! —HABAKKUK 3:19 AMPC

Stay alert! Watch out for your great enemy, the devil. He prowls around like a roaring lion, looking for someone to devour. —1 PETER 5:8 NLT

Therefore put on the full armor of God, so that when the day of evil comes, you may be able to stand your ground, and after you have done everything, to stand. —EPHESIANS 6:13

Merciful Jesus,

Your Face is shining upon me—beaming out *Peace that transcends understanding*. I'm surrounded by a sea of problems, but I am face to Face with You, my Peace. As long as I keep my focus on You, I am safe. If I gaze too long at the myriad problems around me, I will sink under the weight of my burdens. I'm grateful that I can cry out, *"Lord, save me!"* if I start to sink, and You will lift me up.

The closer to You I live, the safer I feel. Circumstances around me are undulating, and I can see treacherous-looking waves in the distance. I need to keep *fixing my eyes on You*, the One who never changes. I know that by the time those faraway waves reach me, they will have shrunk to proportions of Your design. And I rejoice that You are always beside me—strengthening and encouraging me as I face *today's* waves.

You've been showing me that the future is a phantom, seeking to spook me. Help me to laugh at the future—and stay close to You.

In Your sheltering Name, amen.

And the peace of God, which transcends all understanding, will guard your hearts and your minds in Christ Jesus. —PHILIPPIANS 4:7

"Come," he said. Then Peter got down out of the boat, walked on the water and came toward Jesus. But when he saw the wind, he was afraid and, beginning to sink, cried out, "Lord, save me!" —MATTHEW 14:29–30

Let us fix our eyes on Jesus, the author and perfecter of our faith, who for the joy set before him endured the cross, scorning its shame, and sat down at the right hand of the throne of God. —HEBREWS 12:2

Jesus Christ is the same yesterday, today, and forever. —HEBREWS 13:8 NKJV

My loving God,

Sometimes I hear You whispering in my heart: "Relax, My child. I'm in control." I like to let these words wash over me repeatedly, like soothing waves on a beautiful beach—assuring me of Your endless Love.

I confess that I waste a lot of time and energy trying to figure things out before their time has come. All the while, You are working to prepare the way before me. So I ask You to open my eyes to Your wonderful surprises—circumstances that only *You* could have orchestrated. Please keep reminding me that I am Your beloved. You are on my side and You want what is best for me.

Someone who is loved by a generous, powerful person can expect to receive an abundance of blessings. I rejoice that I am loved by *You*, the King of the universe, and *You have good plans for me.* As I look ahead into the unknown future, help me to relax in Your assurance of who I am—*the one You love.* Then I can go forward with confidence, clinging to Your hand. While You and I walk together along *the path of Life*, You fill my heart with Joy and my mind with Peace.

In Your beautiful Name, Jesus, amen.

"For I know the plans I have for you," declares the LORD, "plans to prosper you and not to harm you, plans to give you hope and a future." —JEREMIAH 29:11

About Benjamin he said: "Let the beloved of the LORD rest secure in him, for he shields him all day long, and the one the LORD loves rests between his shoulders." —DEUTERONOMY 33:12

You will show me the path of life; in Your presence is fullness of joy; at Your right hand are pleasures forevermore. —PSALM 16:11 NKJV

Victorious Lord Jesus,

Help me to *rejoice in my sufferings*—really believing that *suffering produces perseverance, perseverance produces character, and character produces hope.* It's so encouraging to know that pain and problems can actually be blessings—increasing my hope. I realize, though, that this doesn't happen automatically. I need to cooperate with Your Spirit as He guides me through times of suffering.

Perseverance is such a rare quality these days. Like most people, I look for and long for a quick fix. But You've been showing me through Your Word that lengthy adversity—accepted with trust and confidence in You—transforms my character, making me more like You. This prepares me for an eternity of problem-free living with You.

The more I become like You, the more hope I experience. These changes in my character convince me that I really do belong to You! My closeness to You also helps me cope with problems—trusting that You and I *together* can handle them. And the radiant hope of heaven shines upon me, strengthening and encouraging me.

In Your glorious Name, amen.

Not only so, but we also rejoice in our sufferings, because we know that suffering produces perseverance; perseverance, character; and character, hope. —ROMANS 5:3–4

"I will ask the Father, and He will give you another Helper, that He may be with you forever; that is the Spirit of truth, whom the world cannot receive, because it does not see Him or know Him, but you know Him because He abides with you and will be in you." —JOHN 14:16–17 NASB 1995

I can do all things through Christ who strengthens me. —PHILIPPIANS 4:13 NKJV

Mighty God,

Though I walk in the midst of trouble, You will revive me. So I won't let problems intimidate me. Instead, I'll remember that You, *the Mighty One,* are *in my midst,* and You are greater than all the trouble in the world! The Bible assures me that *Your right hand will save me.* If I cling tightly to Your hand, I can walk confidently through my toughest times.

I'm grateful that You enable me not only to endure my hardships but to grow stronger through them. Even so, because I'm on an arduous journey, there are times when I feel weary and faint. Help me not to interpret this as a sign that You're displeased with me but to accept my weakness as part of living in a broken world. Please keep reminding me that I'm not alone in my struggles. You are with me, and *my brothers throughout the world are experiencing the same kind of sufferings.* As I go along this challenging path, I need to stay in communication with You. Your living Presence revives me—*strengthening me and blessing me with Peace.*

In Your matchless Name, Jesus, amen.

Though I walk in the midst of trouble, You will revive me; You will stretch out Your hand against the wrath of my enemies, and Your right hand will save me. —PSALM 138:7 NKJV

"The LORD your God in your midst, the Mighty One, will save; He will rejoice over you with gladness, He will quiet you with His love, He will rejoice over you with singing." —ZEPHANIAH 3:17 NKJV

Resist him, standing firm in the faith, because you know that your brothers throughout the world are undergoing the same kind of sufferings. —1 PETER 5:9

The LORD gives strength to his people; the LORD blesses his people with peace. —PSALM 29:11

My Refuge,

I come to You weak and weary—on the verge of feeling overwhelmed. It's comforting to know that You are perfectly aware of the depth and breadth of my difficulties. Nothing is hidden from You.

I *pour out my heart to You, for You are my Refuge.* It's such a relief to let down my guard and my pretense—to be real with You *and* with myself. Telling You all about my struggles enhances my relationship with You and creates a peaceful intimacy. Help me to rest in the safety of Your Presence, trusting that You understand me completely and *love me with an everlasting Love.*

While I relax in Your Presence, You refresh and renew me—showing me the best way to go forward. I'm thankful that You never leave my side; *You have a firm grip on me and You won't let go.* This knowledge gives me courage and confidence to continue my journey. As I walk along my path with You, I can hear You *telling me, "Don't panic. I'm right here to help you."*

In Your encouraging Name, Jesus, amen.

Trust in him at all times, O people; pour out your hearts to him, for God is our refuge. —PSALM 62:8

The LORD appeared to us in the past, saying: "I have loved you with an everlasting love; I have drawn you with loving-kindness." —JEREMIAH 31:3

"Be still, and know that I am God; I will be exalted among the nations, I will be exalted in the earth!" —PSALM 46:10 NKJV

"I, your God, have a firm grip on you and I'm not letting go. I'm telling you, 'Don't panic. I'm right here to help you.'" —ISAIAH 41:13 THE MESSAGE

Ever-present God,

The most important fact of my existence is that You are perpetually with me—taking care of me. I'm thankful that You are not limited by time or space and that Your Presence with me is a forever-promise. So I have good reason to face the future calmly, trusting that You are already there.

Your Word assures me that when I make the quantum leap into eternity, I will find You awaiting me in heaven. Since my future is in Your hands, I don't need to *worry about tomorrow*. Whenever I start to feel anxious, help me hear You saying: "My child, *do not worry.*"

Lord, I want to live this day abundantly—seeing all there is to see, doing all there is to do. Instead of being distracted by future concerns, I'll try to entrust them to You. Each day of life is a glorious gift from You, but I confess that I struggle to live within the confines of today. Often, my energy for abundant living spills over the timeline into tomorrow's worries or past regrets. When I waste my precious energy in this way, I limp through the day instead of living it *to the full*. But when I keep my focus on Your Presence in the present, I can walk confidently—living exuberantly.

In Your treasured Name, Jesus, amen.

Trust in the LORD with all your heart, and do not lean on your own understanding. In all your ways acknowledge him, and he will make straight your paths. —PROVERBS 3:5–6 ESV

"Therefore do not worry about tomorrow, for tomorrow will worry about itself. Each day has enough trouble of its own." —MATTHEW 6:34

"The thief comes only to steal and kill and destroy; I have come that they may have life, and have it to the full." —JOHN 10:10

Eternal God,

I realize that problems are inescapable—woven into the very fabric of this fallen world. Yet I confess that I go into problem-solving mode all too readily, acting as if I have the capacity to fix everything. This is a habitual response—so automatic that it usually bypasses my conscious thinking. This habit not only frustrates me, but it distances me from You.

I don't want to let fixing things be such a high priority in my life. I'm realizing more and more how limited I am in my ability to correct all that is wrong in this broken world. Instead of weighing myself down with matters that are not my responsibility, I yearn to make my relationship with You my primary focus. Please remind me to talk with You about whatever is on my mind, seeking Your perspective on the situation. Rather than trying to fix everything around me, I can ask You to show me what You want me to do today—and not worry about the rest.

Lord, I delight in pondering the wondrous truth that I am on my way to heaven. Help me to stay focused on You—letting my problems fade in the glorious Light of eternity.

In Your brilliant Name, Jesus, amen.

I will instruct you . . . in the way you should go. —PSALM 32:8

"Martha, Martha," the Lord answered, "you are worried and upset about many things, but only one thing is needed." —LUKE 10:41

Our citizenship is in heaven. And we eagerly await a Savior from there, the Lord Jesus Christ. —PHILIPPIANS 3:20

"In my Father's house are many rooms; if it were not so, I would have told you. I am going there to prepare a place for you." —JOHN 14:2

Gracious Lord,

Help me to *hope for what I do not see—eagerly waiting for it with perseverance.* Among the five senses, sight is the one I value the most. You created the world gloriously beautiful, and I delight in seeing the beauty of Your creation. However, I realize that hope, which is itself a kind of vision, is even more wonderful than sight. Hope enables me to see—through the eyes of my heart—things that are *not yet.* The most stunning example of this is the hope of heaven. Your Word tells me that my ultimate destination is to share in Your Glory! I can trust in this magnificent promise because it's based on Your finished work on the cross and Your miraculous resurrection.

I need to practice hoping for things I do not see—both for this life and the next. Please guide me into hopes and dreams that are in line with Your will. I want to train the eyes of my heart to "see" these blessings while praying for Your will to be done fully and only. Teach me to *wait eagerly with perseverance*—with my focus primarily on *You* but also on the longed-for outcome. You are my Hope!

In Your great Name, Jesus, amen.

But if we hope for what we do not see, we eagerly wait for it with perseverance. —ROMANS 8:25 NKJV

"And the glory which You gave Me I have given them, that they may be one just as We are one." —JOHN 17:22 NKJV

Now faith is the assurance (the confirmation, the title deed) of the things [we] hope for, being the proof of things [we] do not see and the conviction of their reality [faith perceiving as real fact what is not revealed to the senses]. —HEBREWS 11:1 AMPC

Lord Jesus,

Please help me to thank You for the very things that are troubling me. I confess that I'm on the brink of rebellion—precariously close to shaking my fist in Your Face. I'm feeling tempted to indulge in "just a little" complaining about Your treatment of me. But I've learned the hard way that torrents of anger and self-pity can sweep me away once I step over that line. You have shown me that the best protection against this hurtful behavior is *thanksgiving*. It's impossible for me to thank You and rebel against You at the same time.

When I thank You for difficult circumstances or terrible trials, my prayers feel awkward and contrived at first. But I've discovered that if I persist in these prayers, my thankful words will eventually make a difference in my heart. Thankfulness awakens my heart to Your abiding Presence, which overshadows all my problems. *In Your Presence there is fullness of Joy!*

In Your joyful Name, amen.

I will offer to You the sacrifice of thanksgiving, and will call upon the name of the LORD. —PSALM 116:17 NKJV

Rejoice in the Lord always. I will say it again: Rejoice! Let your gentleness be evident to all. The Lord is near. Do not be anxious about anything, but in everything, by prayer and petition, with thanksgiving, present your requests to God. And the peace of God, which transcends all understanding, will guard your hearts and your minds in Christ Jesus. —PHILIPPIANS 4:4–7

You will show me the path of life; in Your presence is fullness of joy; at Your right hand are pleasures forevermore. —PSALM 16:11 NKJV

My loving Savior,

Your unfailing Love is my comfort. Because I live in such a broken world, trouble is never far away. Although there are many sources of comfort available to me, only one of them is unfailing—Your Love! Other sources may help me *some* of the time, but Your consoling Presence is with me *all* the time.

The perfect, inexhaustible Love You provide is not just a *thing* that makes me feel less upset; it's also a *Person.* Your Love is inseparable from *You,* so *nothing in all creation can separate me from Your loving Presence.*

Help me to remember who I am—Your cherished follower. I can come to You for comfort as often as I need. Since You are a boundless Source of blessing to me, I want to be a blessing in the lives of other people—*comforting those in any trouble with the comfort I have received from You.*

In Your comforting Name, Jesus, amen.

May your unfailing love be my comfort, according to your promise to your servant. —PSALM 119:76

"These things I have spoken to you, that in Me you may have peace. In the world you will have tribulation; but be of good cheer, I have overcome the world." —JOHN 16:33 NKJV

For I am convinced that neither death nor life, neither angels nor demons, neither the present nor the future, nor any powers, neither height nor depth, nor anything else in all creation, will be able to separate us from the love of God that is in Christ Jesus our Lord. —ROMANS 8:38–39

Praise be to the God and Father of our Lord Jesus Christ, the Father of compassion and the God of all comfort, who comforts us in all our troubles, so that we can comfort those in any trouble with the comfort we ourselves have received from God. —2 CORINTHIANS 1:3–4

Precious Jesus,

I *rejoice that my name is written in heaven—in Your book of Life.* Because I am Yours, I have Joy that is independent of all circumstances. You have provided eternal Life that can *never* be taken away from me. Through faith in You as my risen Savior, I am *justified* and *also glorified.* Moreover, I have been *raised up with You and seated with You in the heavenly realms.*

Please help me remember that Joy is the birthright of all who belong to You, and it can coexist with the most difficult, painful circumstances. So I come to You this morning with open hands and open heart, saying, "Jesus, I receive Your Joy." While I wait with You, the Light of Your Presence shines upon me—soaking into the depths of my inner being. Thus You strengthen me, preparing me for the day that stretches out before me.

I'm grateful that I can return to You for fresh supplies of Joy as often as I need. Since You are a God of limitless abundance, You always have more than enough for me!

In Your bountiful Name, amen.

*"However, do not rejoice that the spirits submit to you, but rejoice that your names are written in heaven." —*LUKE 10:20

*But nothing unclean will ever enter it, nor anyone who does what is detestable or false, but only those who are written in the Lamb's book of life. —*REVELATION 21:27 ESV

*And those He predestined, He also called; and those He called, He also justified; and those He justified, He also glorified. —*ROMANS 8:30 HCSB

*And God raised us up with Christ and seated us with him in the heavenly realms in Christ Jesus. —*EPHESIANS 2:6

April

By grace you have been saved through faith. And this is not your own doing; it is the gift of God. —Ephesians 2:8 esv

Delightful Jesus,

Help me to live in joyful dependence on You! I used to view dependence as a weakness, so I would strive to be as self-sufficient as possible. But I know this is not *Your* way for me. You designed me to need You continually—and even to rejoice in my neediness. I want to live in harmony with Your intentions for me, trusting that Your way is best.

The Bible exhorts me to *be joyful always* and *pray continually*. There is always Joy to be found in Your Presence! You have promised *You will not leave me or forsake me*, so I can speak to You at all times— knowing that You hear and You care.

Praying continually is a way of demonstrating my deliberate dependence on You. Another powerful way of relying on You is studying Your Word, asking You to use it to transform me according to Your will. These delightful disciplines keep me close to You—living in joyous reliance on You. As I *delight myself in You* more and more, You are glorified and I am blessed.

In Your wonderful Name, amen.

Be joyful always; pray continually. —1 Thessalonians 5:16–17

"And the Lord, He is the One who goes before you. He will be with you, He will not leave you nor forsake you; do not fear nor be dismayed." —Deuteronomy 31:8 nkjv

I have hidden your word in my heart that I might not sin against you. Praise be to you, O Lord; teach me your decrees. —Psalm 119:11–12

Delight yourself in the Lord and he will give you the desires of your heart. —Psalm 37:4

Dear Lord Jesus,

Help me to *trust You and not be afraid.* You have been training me to view trials as exercises designed to develop my trust-muscles. I live in the midst of fierce spiritual battles, and fear is one of Satan's favorite weapons to use against me. Whenever I start to feel afraid, I need to affirm my trust in You—praying, "I trust You, Jesus." If circumstances permit, I can pray this affirmation out loud.

The Bible tells me that if I *resist the devil, standing firm against him, he will flee from me.* Then I can refresh myself in Your holy Presence. As I speak and sing praises to You, Your Face shines graciously upon me—blessing me with Peace.

Please keep reminding me that *there is no condemnation for those who belong to You.* Because You died on the cross for all my sins, I have been judged "NOT GUILTY!" for all eternity. *I will trust and not be afraid because You are my Strength, my Song, and my Salvation.*

In Your saving Name, amen.

*"Surely God is my salvation; I will trust and not be afraid. The LORD, the LORD, is my strength and my song; he has become my salvation." —*ISAIAH 12:2

*So be subject to God. Resist the devil [stand firm against him], and he will flee from you. —*JAMES 4:7 AMPC

*"The LORD bless you and keep you; the LORD make his face shine upon you and be gracious to you; the LORD turn his face toward you and give you peace." —*NUMBERS 6:24–26

*So now there is no condemnation for those who belong to Christ Jesus. —*ROMANS 8:1 NLT

Mighty God,

I delight in Your invitation: *"Cast your burden on Me, and I will sustain you."* Carrying my own burdens is exhausting! My shoulders aren't designed for heavy loads, so please teach me to *cast all my cares on You.* When I become aware that something is weighing me down, I'll examine the concern to determine whether or not it's my problem. If it isn't mine, I can simply let go of it. But if it *is* my problem, I need to talk with You about it—asking You to help me see it from Your perspective and take whatever action is needed.

I've been learning that I must not let problems become my focus and weigh me down. Instead, I want to bring You my concerns and *leave* them with You—trusting You to carry my burdens on Your amazingly strong shoulders.

I'm so thankful for Your promise to sustain me and provide everything I need. Your Word assures me that *You will meet all my needs according to Your glorious riches.*

In Your precious Name, Jesus, amen.

Cast your burden on the LORD, and He will sustain you; He will never allow the righteous to be shaken. —PSALM 55:22 HCSB

For a child will be born to us, a son will be given to us; and the government will rest on His shoulders; and His name will be called Wonderful Counselor, Mighty God, Eternal Father, Prince of Peace. —ISAIAH 9:6 NASB 1995

Casting all your cares [all your anxieties, all your worries, and all your concerns, once and for all] on Him, for He cares about you [with deepest affection, and watches over you very carefully]. —1 PETER 5:7 AMP

And my God will meet all your needs according to his glorious riches in Christ Jesus. —PHILIPPIANS 4:19

Magnificent Jesus,

You are the Light of the world! Because I am Your follower, *I will not walk in darkness but will have the Light of Life.* Although there is much darkness in this world, I always have access to You. So I am never in utter darkness.

The trail before me often looks shadowy, especially as it disappears into the future. I would love for it to be floodlit so I could anticipate what's ahead. But the truth is, You are enough! You are with me continually, and You also go before me—illuminating the way. All I need to do is trust You and follow the Light You provide. Even when the path before me is dimly lit, Your illumination is sufficient for me to find my way forward step by step.

Someday I will be with You in heaven, where I will see Your Light in all its Glory! Darkness will be a thing of the past, and I'll be able to see everything clearly. The Bible assures me *there will be no more night. I will not need the light of a lamp or of the sun, for You will give me Light*—beyond anything I can imagine!

In Your brilliant Name, amen.

Again Jesus spoke to them, saying, "I am the light of the world. Whoever follows me will not walk in darkness, but will have the light of life." —JOHN 8:12 ESV

The path of the righteous is like the first gleam of dawn, shining ever brighter till the full light of day. —PROVERBS 4:18

There will be no more night. They will not need the light of a lamp or the light of the sun, for the Lord God will give them light. And they will reign for ever and ever. —REVELATION 22:5

My strong Savior,

Help me *not to grow weary or lose heart.* When I'm dealing with difficulties that go on and on, it's easy to get so tired that I feel like giving up. Chronic problems tend to wear me out and wear me down. But I realize that if I focus too much on my troubles, I'm in danger of sliding into a black hole of self-pity or despair.

Unrelieved physical tiredness can make me vulnerable to emotional exhaustion and spiritual fatigue—*losing heart.* Thank You for equipping me to transcend my troubles by *fixing my eyes on You.* I know that You paid a terrible price to be my living Savior—*enduring the cross.* When I contemplate Your willingness to suffer so much for me, I gain strength to endure my own hardships.

I've found that worshiping You is a delightful way of renewing my strength! When I take steps of faith by praising You in the midst of adversity, Your glorious Light shines upon me. I ask that this Light may reflect to others as I live close to You, aware of Your loving Presence. And I rejoice that I am *being transformed into Your likeness with ever-increasing Glory*!

In Your beautiful Name, Jesus, amen.

Let us fix our eyes on Jesus, the author and perfecter of our faith, who for the joy set before him endured the cross, scorning its shame, and sat down at the right hand of the throne of God. Consider him who endured such opposition from sinful men, so that you will not grow weary and lose heart. —HEBREWS 12:2–3

For we walk by faith, not by sight. —2 CORINTHIANS 5:7 NKJV

And we, who with unveiled faces all reflect the Lord's glory, are being transformed into his likeness with ever-increasing glory, which comes from the Lord, who is the Spirit. —2 CORINTHIANS 3:18

Supreme Lord Jesus,

I want to trust You enough to let things happen without constantly striving to predict or control the outcome. Sometimes I just need to relax—and refresh myself in the Light of Your everlasting Love. Even though Your Love-Light never dims, I'm often unaware of Your radiant Presence. I realize that when I focus on the future, mentally rehearsing what I will do or what I will say, I'm seeking to be self-sufficient. This attempt to be adequate without Your help is a subtle sin—so common that it usually slips past me unnoticed.

Lord, teach me to live more fully in the present, depending on You moment by moment. I don't need to fear my inadequacy; instead, I can rejoice in Your abundant sufficiency! You are training me to *seek Your Face continually*, even when I feel competent to handle things by myself. Instead of dividing my life into things I can do by myself and things that require Your help, I want to learn to rely on You in *every* situation. As I live in trusting dependence on You, I can face each day confidently and enjoy Your loving Presence.

In Your loving Name, amen.

Commit your way to the Lord; trust in Him, and He will act. —Psalm 37:5 hcsb

And my God shall supply all your need according to His riches in glory by Christ Jesus. —Philippians 4:19 nkjv

Seek the Lord and His strength; seek His face continually. —Psalm 105:4 nasb 1995

For I can do everything through Christ, who gives me strength. —Philippians 4:13 nlt

My Savior-God,

I long for the absence of problems in my life, but I realize this is an unrealistic goal. Shortly before Your crucifixion, You told Your followers candidly: *"In this world you will have trouble."* I'm thankful I can look forward to an eternity of problem-free living, reserved for me in heaven. I rejoice in this glorious inheritance, which no one can take away from me. Teach me to wait patiently for this promised perfection rather than seeking my heaven here on earth.

Lord, help me to begin each day anticipating problems—asking You to equip me for whatever difficulties lie ahead. The best equipping is Your living Presence, Your hand that never lets go of mine.

Discussing my problems with You frees me to take a more light-hearted view of trouble—seeing it as a challenge that You and I together can handle. Please remind me again and again that You are on my side and *You have overcome the world*!

In Your conquering Name, Jesus, amen.

"I have told you these things, so that in me you may have peace. In this world you will have trouble. But take heart! I have overcome the world." —John 16:33

Nevertheless I am continually with You; You hold me by my right hand. —Psalm 73:23 NKJV

I can do all things through Christ who strengthens me. —Philippians 4:13 NKJV

What, then, shall we say in response to this? If God is for us, who can be against us? —Romans 8:31

Radiant Lord Jesus,

You are the Light that shines on in the darkness, for the darkness has never overpowered it—and it never will! Yet when multiple problems are closing in on me, the Light of Your Presence sometimes seems like a dim memory. Whenever I'm feeling distant from You, I need to stop everything and *pour out my heart to You.* Help me to carve out time and space to talk with You about my problems and feelings. As I unburden myself to You, please show me the way forward.

No matter how much darkness I see in the world around me, Your Light continues to *shine on*, for it is infinitely more powerful! Because I belong to You, this Light shines not only upon me but within me. I live *in the midst of a crooked and perverse generation*, and this is an opportunity for me to *shine as a light in the world.* To do this, I must take time to bask in Your radiant Presence, asking You to *transform me into Your likeness.* I am weak and sinful, but I long to live in ways that *reflect Your Glory.*

In Your glorious Name, amen.

And the Light shines on in the darkness, for the darkness has never overpowered it [put it out or absorbed it or appropriated it, and is unreceptive to it]. —JOHN 1:5 AMPC

Trust in him at all times, O people; pour out your hearts to him, for God is our refuge. —PSALM 62:8

Do all things without complaining and disputing, that you may become blameless and harmless, children of God without fault in the midst of a crooked and perverse generation, among whom you shine as lights in the world. —PHILIPPIANS 2:14–15 NKJV

And we all, with unveiled faces reflecting the glory of the Lord, are being transformed into the same image from one degree of glory to another, which is from the Lord, who is the Spirit. —2 CORINTHIANS 3:18 NET

Blessed Jesus,

Help me learn to live above my circumstances. I realize this requires focused time with You, *the One who has overcome the world*. Trouble and distress are woven into the very fabric of this perishing world. Only Your Life in me can empower me to face the endless flow of problems with *good cheer*.

As I relax in Your Presence—sitting quietly with You—You shine Peace into my troubled mind and heart. Little by little, through this time of focusing on You and Your Word, I am set free from earthly shackles and lifted above my circumstances. I gain Your perspective on my life—enabling me to distinguish between things that are important and things that are not. Moreover, resting in Your Presence blesses me with *Joy that no one will take away* from me.

In Your joyous Name, amen.

*"These things I have spoken to you, that in Me you may have peace. In the world you will have tribulation; but be of good cheer, I have overcome the world." —*JOHN 16:33 NKJV

*Why are you in despair, O my soul? And why have you become disturbed within me? Hope in God, for I shall again praise Him for the help of His presence. —*PSALM 42:5 NASB 1995

*"So with you: Now is your time of grief, but I will see you again and you will rejoice, and no one will take away your joy." —*JOHN 16:22

Beloved Jesus,

Your Word invites me to *taste and see that You are good*. I've discovered that the more fully I experience You, the more convinced I become of Your goodness. I rejoice that You are *the living One who sees me* and participates in every aspect of my life. You're training me to seek You in each moment, letting Your Love flow through me into the lives of others. Sometimes Your blessings come to me in mysterious ways—through pain and trouble. At such times I can know Your goodness only through my trust in You. My understanding fails me time after time, but trust keeps me close to You.

I thank You for the gift of Your Peace—a gift of such immense proportions that I can't begin to fathom its depth or breadth. When You appeared to Your disciples after Your resurrection, it was Peace that You communicated first of all. They desperately needed Your Peace—to calm their fears and clear their minds. You also speak Peace to me, for You know my anxious thoughts. Please help me tune out other voices so I can hear You more clearly. Lord, I come to You with open hands and an open heart, ready to receive Your Peace.

In Your peaceful Name, amen.

Taste and see that the Lord *is good.* —Psalm 34:8

She said, "Have I not even here [in the wilderness] remained alive after seeing Him [who sees me with understanding and compassion]?" Therefore the well was called Beer-lahai-roi (Well of the Living One Who Sees Me). —Genesis 16:13–14 amp

When the disciples were together, with the doors locked for fear of the Jews, Jesus came and stood among them and said, "Peace be with you!" —John 20:19

Let the peace of Christ rule in your hearts, since as members of one body you were called to peace. And be thankful. —Colossians 3:15

Dearest Jesus,

I believe in You—even though I do not see You with my eyes. I know You are far more real than the things I can see all around me. So when I believe in You, I'm trusting in rock-solid Reality! No matter what my circumstances may be, You are the indestructible *Rock* on which I stand. I'm thankful I can always *take refuge in You* because I belong to You forever.

You've been teaching me that believing in You has innumerable benefits. Of course, the most obvious one is *the eternal salvation of my soul*—a gift of infinite value! My belief in You also enhances my present life immensely, enabling me to know Whose I am and who I am. You help me find my way through this broken world with hope in my heart as I stay in close communication with You.

Lord, You have been enlarging my capacity for Joy. The more I seek You and the more fully I come to know You, the more You fill me with *inexpressible and glorious Joy*!

In Your Name above all names, amen.

Though you have not seen him, you love him; and even though you do not see him now, you believe in him and are filled with an inexpressible and glorious joy, for you are receiving the goal of your faith, the salvation of your souls. —1 PETER 1:8–9

The LORD is my rock, my fortress and my deliverer; my God is my rock, in whom I take refuge. He is my shield and the horn of my salvation, my stronghold. —PSALM 18:2

But if we hope for what we do not see, we eagerly wait for it with perseverance. —ROMANS 8:25 NKJV

Worthy God,

The Bible assures me that *Your blessing is on those who trust in You, who put their confidence in You.* Please help me to trust You in every detail of my life. I know that nothing is random in Your kingdom. *All things work together and are fitting into a plan for good—for those who love You and are called according to Your purpose.*

Instead of trying to figure everything out, I want to focus my energy on trusting and thanking You. I'm learning that nothing is wasted when I walk close to You. You've shown me that even my mistakes and sins can be recycled into something good—through Your transforming grace.

While I was still living in darkness, You began shining the Light of Your holy Presence into my sin-stained life. At the right time, *You lifted me out of the slimy pit, out of the mud and mire. You set my feet on a rock and gave me a firm place to stand.*

Thank You for *calling me out of darkness into Your marvelous Light.* Because of all You have done, I'm convinced that You can be trusted in every facet of my life!

In Your splendid Name, Jesus, amen.

"My blessing is on those people who trust in me, who put their confidence in me." —JEREMIAH 17:7 NET

All things work together and are [fitting into a plan] for good to and for those who love God and are called according to [His] design and purpose. —ROMANS 8:28 AMPC

He lifted me out of the slimy pit, out of the mud and mire; he set my feet on a rock and gave me a firm place to stand. —PSALM 40:2

You are a chosen generation, a royal priesthood. —1 PETER 2:9 NKJV

Mighty Jesus,

When things don't go as I would like, help me to accept the situation immediately. I realize that fantasizing about how things might have gone is a waste of time and energy. Moreover, I've learned that if I indulge in feelings of regret, they can easily spill over into resentment. I need to remember that You are sovereign over all my circumstances—and *humble myself under Your mighty hand, casting all my anxiety on You*. I can rejoice in what You are doing in my life, even though it's beyond my understanding.

You are the Way, the Truth, and the Life. In You I have everything I need—for this life and for the life yet to come. I don't want to let the impact of the world shatter my thinking or draw my attention away from You. The challenge I face each moment is to *keep my eyes on You*—no matter what is going on around me. When You are central in my thinking, I can view circumstances from Your perspective. This enables me to walk with You along *the path of life*, experiencing *Joy in Your Presence*.

In Your matchless Name, amen.

Therefore humble yourselves under the mighty hand of God, that He may exalt you at the proper time, casting all your anxiety on Him, because He cares for you. —1 PETER 5:6–7 NASB 1995

Jesus said to him, "I am the way, the truth, and the life. No one comes to the Father except through Me." —JOHN 14:6 NKJV

We do this by keeping our eyes on Jesus, the champion who initiates and perfects our faith. Because of the joy awaiting him, he endured the cross, disregarding its shame. Now he is seated in the place of honor beside God's throne. —HEBREWS 12:2 NLT

You have made known to me the path of life; you will fill me with joy in your presence, with eternal pleasures at your right hand. —PSALM 16:11

Prince of Peace,

I *come to You*, feeling *weary and burdened*. I want to spend time resting in Your Presence. I need Your Peace continually, just as I need *You* each moment.

When things are going smoothly in my life, it's easy to forget how dependent on You I really am. Then, when I encounter bumps in the road, I tend to become anxious and upset. Eventually, this revives my awareness of my need for You, and I return to You—seeking Your Peace. I'm thankful that You give me this glorious gift, but it's hard for me to receive it until I calm down. How much better it would be to stay close to You at all times!

Please help me remember that You, my Prince, are *Mighty God*! *All authority in heaven and on earth has been given to You*. Whenever I'm experiencing hard times, I can come to You and tell You my troubles. But I need to come humbly, acknowledging how great and wise You are. Rather than shaking my fist at You or insisting that You do things my way, I can pray these wonderful words of David: "*I trust in You, O Lord; I say, 'You are my God.' My times are in Your hands.*"

In Your majestic Name, Jesus, amen.

For to us a Child is born . . . and His name shall be called Wonderful
Counselor, Mighty God . . . Prince of Peace. —ISAIAH 9:6 AMPC

"Come to me, all you who are weary and burdened,
*and I will give you rest." —*MATTHEW 11:28

Then Jesus came to them and said, "All authority in heaven and
*on earth has been given to me." —*MATTHEW 28:18

But I trust in you, O LORD; *I say, "You are my God." My times are in your hands;*
*deliver me from my enemies and from those who pursue me. —*PSALM 31:14–15

Precious Jesus,

Through reading Your Word, I've seen that waiting, trusting, and hoping are intricately connected—like golden strands woven together to form a strong chain. I think of *trusting* as the central strand because this attitude is taught so frequently throughout the Bible. Waiting and hoping embellish the central strand and strengthen the chain that connects me to You.

Waiting for You to work, with my eyes fixed on You, shows that I really do trust You. But if I simply mouth the words "I trust You" while anxiously trying to make things go my way, my words ring hollow.

Hoping is future-directed, connecting me to my glorious inheritance in heaven. However, as You have shown me, the benefits of hope fall fully on me in the present.

Because I belong to You, I don't just pass time in my waiting. I can wait expectantly, in hopeful trust. Please help me stay alert so I can pick up even the faintest glimmer of Your Presence.

In Your trustworthy Name, amen.

"Do not let your hearts be troubled. Trust in God; trust also in me." —JOHN 14:1

When I am afraid, I will put my trust in You. In God, whose word I praise, in God I have put my trust; I shall not be afraid. What can mere man do to me? —PSALM 56:3–4 NASB 1995

Wait for the LORD; be strong, and let your heart take courage; wait for the LORD! —PSALM 27:14 ESV

And everyone who has this hope in Him purifies himself, just as He is pure. —1 JOHN 3:3 NKJV

My loving Lord,

Thank You for loving me regardless of how well I'm performing. Sometimes I feel uneasy—questioning whether I'm doing enough to be worthy of Your Love. But I realize that no matter how exemplary my behavior may be, the answer to that question will always be *no*. You've been showing me that my performance and Your Love are completely different issues. *You have loved me with an everlasting Love* that flows outward from eternity without limits or conditions. *You have clothed me in Your robe of righteousness*, and this is an eternal transaction. Nothing and no one can reverse it! This means that my successes and failures have no bearing on Your Love for me.

I've discovered that even my ability to evaluate how well I'm doing is flawed. My limited human perspective and the condition of my body, with its mercurial variations, distort my assessment of my behavior.

Lord, I bring my performance anxiety to You, and I ask You to replace it with *Your unfailing Love*. Help me to stay aware of Your loving Presence with me in everything I do. Please direct my steps as I go through this day.

In Your precious Name, Jesus, amen.

The LORD appeared to us in the past, saying: "I have loved you with an everlasting love; I have drawn you with loving-kindness." —JEREMIAH 31:3

I will greatly rejoice in the LORD, my soul shall be joyful in my God; for He has clothed me with the garments of salvation, He has covered me with the robe of righteousness, as a bridegroom decks himself with ornaments, and as a bride adorns herself with her jewels. —ISAIAH 61:10 NKJV

Let your face shine on your servant; save me in your unfailing love. —PSALM 31:16

Compassionate Jesus,

You have been teaching me that anxiety is a result of envisioning the future without You. So my best defense against worry is staying in communication with You. When I turn my thoughts toward You, I can *give all my worries and cares to You,* knowing that *You care about me.* Help me remember to read Your Word and listen as I'm praying—making my thoughts a dialogue with You.

Thank You for providing guidelines for me to follow whenever I'm considering upcoming events: First, I must not linger in the future because anxieties sprout up like mushrooms when I wander there. Second, I need to remember the promise of Your continual Presence—and include You in my thoughts as I plan future events. I confess that this mental discipline is challenging for me; my mind easily slips into daydreaming while I'm making plans. But I'm learning that the glorious reality of Your Presence with me, now and forevermore, outshines any daydream I could ever imagine!

In Your brilliant Name, amen.

And he said to his disciples, "Therefore I tell you, do not be anxious about your life, what you will eat, nor about your body, what you will put on. For life is more than food, and the body more than clothing. Consider the ravens: they neither sow nor reap, they have neither storehouse nor barn, and yet God feeds them. Of how much more value are you than the birds! And which of you by being anxious can add a single hour to his span of life?" —LUKE 12:22–25 ESV

Give all your worries and cares to God, for he cares about you. —1 PETER 5:7 NLT

Now to him who is able to do immeasurably more than all we ask or imagine, according to his power that is at work within us, to him be glory in the church and in Christ Jesus throughout all generations, for ever and ever! Amen. —EPHESIANS 3:20–21

Steadfast Jesus,

Help me to keep my focus on You. You created me with the amazing ability to choose the focal point of my thoughts. This is a sign of being *made in Your image*. Yet I've seen that if my mind gets stuck on worries, they can develop into idols. Anxiety gains a life of its own, infesting my mind like a parasite. Thankfully, I can break free from this bondage by affirming my trust in You and refreshing myself in Your Presence.

What goes on in my mind is invisible to other people, but *You* read my thoughts continually—You know everything about me. I want to guard my thinking carefully since good thought-choices honor You and keep me close to You.

My goal is to *take captive every thought to make it obedient to You.* When my mind wanders from You, I need to capture those thoughts and bring them into Your Presence. In Your radiant Light, anxious thoughts shrink and shrivel up. Judgmental thinking is unmasked as I bask in Your merciful Love. Confused ideas are untangled while I rest in the simplicity of Your Peace. Your Word assures me that *You will keep in perfect Peace all who trust in You—whose thoughts are fixed on You!*

In Your comforting Name, amen.

So God created man in His own image; in the image of God He created him; male and female He created them. —GENESIS 1:27 NKJV

We take captive every thought to make it obedient to Christ. —2 CORINTHIANS 10:5

He will have no fear of bad news. —PSALM 112:7

You will keep in perfect peace all who trust in you, all whose thoughts are fixed on you! —ISAIAH 26:3 NLT

All-knowing God,

You have searched me and known me. You understand my thoughts from afar, and You are intimately acquainted with all my ways. How thankful I am to be *fully known* by You! Everything about me is visible to You—including my most secret thoughts and feelings. This transparency would terrify me if I were not Your beloved child. But I have nothing to fear because Your perfect righteousness has been credited to me *through my faith in You.* I'm so grateful to be a permanent member of Your royal family!

I've been learning that my intimate relationship with You is a powerful antidote to feelings of loneliness. Please remind me to voice my prayers to You whenever I'm feeling alone or afraid. I know that You hear my silent prayers too, but I think more clearly when I whisper my words or speak them out loud. Because You understand me *and* my circumstances perfectly, I don't need to explain things to You. I can dive right in, asking You to help me cope with the things I'm facing. And I can spend time just relaxing with You—breathing in *the Joy of Your Presence.*

In Your royal Name, Jesus, amen.

O LORD, You have searched me and known me. You know when I sit down and when I rise up; You understand my thought from afar. You scrutinize my path and my lying down, and are intimately acquainted with all my ways. —PSALM 139:1–3 NASB 1995

For now we see indistinctly, as in a mirror, but then face to face. Now I know in part, but then I will know fully, as I am fully known. —1 CORINTHIANS 13:12 HCSB

This righteousness from God comes through faith in Jesus Christ to all who believe. There is no difference. —ROMANS 3:22

Surely you have granted him eternal blessings and made him glad with the joy of your presence. —PSALM 21:6

Almighty God,

Your Word tells me that *You will fight for me; I need only to be still.* Lord, You know how weary I am. I've been struggling just to keep my head above water, and my strength is running low. I need to stop trying so hard—and just let You fight for me.

This is very difficult for me to do because my feelings tell me I must keep striving in order to survive. But I know You're working on my behalf, and You are calling me to rest in You. So please help me to *be still and know that You are God.*

Trying to calm my mind is even more challenging than quieting my body. In my battle to feel secure, I have relied too heavily on my own thinking. As I've struggled to feel in control, I've unwittingly elevated my mind to a position of self-reliance. Forgive me, Lord! I desperately need Your Spirit to work within me—controlling my mind more and more, soothing me from the inside out. While I spend time *resting in the shadow of Your Almighty Presence*, I'll rejoice that You are fighting for me.

In Your invincible Name, Jesus, amen.

"The LORD will fight for you; you need only to be still." —EXODUS 14:14

"Be still, and know that I am God; I will be exalted among the nations, I will be exalted in the earth!" —PSALM 46:10 NKJV

The mind of sinful man is death, but the mind controlled by the Spirit is life and peace. —ROMANS 8:6

He who dwells in the shelter of the Most High will rest in the shadow of the Almighty. —PSALM 91:1

Refreshing Lord Jesus,

I come to You for rest and refreshment. My journey has been a strenuous, uphill climb, and I am bone-weary. Help me not to be ashamed of my exhaustion but to see it as an opportunity to rely more fully on You.

Please keep reminding me that You can *fit everything into a plan for good*, including the things I wish were different. I need to just start with where I am right now—accepting that this is where You intend for me to be. As I lean on You for support, I can get through this day— one step, one moment at a time.

My main responsibility is to remain attentive to You, asking You to guide me through the many decisions I must make. This sounds like an easy assignment, but I find it quite challenging. My desire to live in awareness of Your Presence goes against the grain of the world, the flesh, and the devil. Much of my weariness results from my constant battle with these opponents. But I won't give up! Instead, I will *hope in You*—trusting that *I will again praise You for the help of Your Presence.*

In Your worthy Name, amen.

We are assured and know that [God being a partner in their labor] all things work together and are [fitting into a plan] for good to and for those who love God and are called according to [His] design and purpose. —ROMANS 8:28 AMPC

Lean on, trust in, and be confident in the Lord with all your heart and mind and do not rely on your own insight or understanding. —PROVERBS 3:5 AMPC

Why are you in despair, O my soul? And why have you become disturbed within me? Hope in God, for I shall again praise Him for the help of His presence. —PSALM 42:5 NASB 1995

Dear God,

Help me to *be strong and courageous*—trusting that *You will be with me* no matter what happens. I've learned that I can *choose* to be strong and courageous even when I'm feeling very weak. However, the weaker I feel, the more effort it takes for me to make this choice. It all depends on where I look. If I focus on myself and my problems, my courage melts away. But if, through eyes of faith, I see *You* on the path ahead—beckoning me on, one step at a time—I am strengthened. The choice to be bold rests in my confidence that You are *with* me and *for* me.

Even when everything seems to be going wrong, I can fight discouragement through my trust in You. I know that You are a God of surprises—not limited by the way things are or by the paltry possibilities I can see. *With You all things are possible* because You are infinitely creative and powerful! The longer I wait for my prayers to be answered, the closer I am to a breakthrough. Meanwhile, I've found that waiting for You—aware of Your loving Presence—is a blessed way to live. Your Word assures me that *You are good to those who wait for You.*

In Your breathtaking Name, Jesus, amen.

*"Have I not commanded you? Be strong and courageous. Do not be terrified; do not be discouraged, for the LORD your God will be with you wherever you go." —*JOSHUA 1:9

*Jesus looked at them and said, "With man this is impossible, but with God all things are possible." —*MATTHEW 19:26

*The LORD is good to those who wait for Him, to the soul who seeks Him. It is good that one should hope and wait quietly for the salvation of the LORD. —*LAMENTATIONS 3:25–26 NKJV

Treasured Lord Jesus,

Help me to trust in *Your unfailing Love*—thanking You for the good I cannot see. When evil seems to be flourishing in the world around me, it feels as if things are spinning out of control. But I know *You* are not wringing Your hands helplessly, wondering what to do next. You are completely in control, working behind-the-scenes goodness in the midst of the turmoil. So, in faith, I thank You not only for the blessings I can see but for the ones I can't see.

Your *wisdom and knowledge* are deeper and richer than my words could ever express. *Your judgments are unsearchable, and Your paths beyond tracing out!* So my wisest choice is to *trust in You at all times*— even when my world feels unsteady and I don't understand Your ways.

I need to remember that *You are always with me, holding me by my right hand. And afterward You will take me into Glory.* As I ponder this hidden treasure—my heavenly inheritance—I thank You for this glorious blessing I cannot yet see!

In Your sacred Name, amen.

"Though the mountains be shaken and the hills be removed, yet my unfailing love for you will not be shaken nor my covenant of peace be removed," says the LORD, who has compassion on you. —ISAIAH 54:10

Oh, the depth of the riches of the wisdom and knowledge of God! How unsearchable his judgments, and his paths beyond tracing out! —ROMANS 11:33

Trust in Him at all times, you people; pour out your heart before Him; God is a refuge for us. Selah. —PSALM 62:8 NKJV

Yet I am always with you; you hold me by my right hand. You guide me with your counsel, and afterward you will take me into glory. —PSALM 73:23–24

Ever-present Jesus,

I rejoice that You are with me in all that I do—even in the most menial task. It's so comforting to know that You are always aware of me, concerned with every detail of my life. Nothing about me escapes Your notice—not even *the number of hairs on my head*. However, I confess that my awareness of Your Presence falters and flickers; as a result, my life experience often feels fragmented. When my focus is wide enough to include You in my thoughts, I feel safe and complete. But when my focus narrows so that problems and details fill my mind, I lose sight of You. As a result, I feel empty and incomplete.

Lord, please teach me how to look steadily at You in all my moments and all my circumstances. Though this world is unstable and in flux, I can experience continuity by staying aware of Your steadfast Presence. Help me to *fix my eyes on what is unseen*—especially on *You*—even as the visible world parades before my eyes.

In Your faithful Name, amen.

"Are not two sparrows sold for a penny? Yet not one of them will fall to the ground apart from the will of your Father. And even the very hairs of your head are all numbered. So don't be afraid; you are worth more than many sparrows." —MATTHEW 10:29–31

By faith he left Egypt behind, not being afraid of the king's anger, for Moses persevered as one who sees Him who is invisible. —HEBREWS 11:27 HCSB

So we fix our eyes not on what is seen, but on what is unseen. For what is seen is temporary, but what is unseen is eternal. —2 CORINTHIANS 4:18

Trustworthy Jesus,

Help me to welcome challenging times as opportunities to trust You. I have You beside me and Your Spirit within me, so no set of circumstances is really too much for me to handle. However, I confess that when the path before me is dotted with difficulties, I usually start measuring my strength against those challenges. Of course, that calculation invariably fills me with anxiety. Without Your help, I couldn't make it past the first hurdle!

You have been teaching me the *right* way to walk through demanding days—gripping Your hand tightly and staying in close communication with You. Also, I've learned that I cope much better with the demands of my day when my thoughts and words are richly flavored with thankfulness and trust.

Instead of worrying about all my problems, I want to put my energy into *thinking carefully about You*. Your Word assures me that *You will keep me in perfect peace* to the extent that *my mind is focused on You— trusting in You*.

In Your great Name, amen.

Consider it pure joy, my brothers, whenever you
face trials of many kinds. —James 1:2

I can do all things through Christ who strengthens me. —Philippians 4:13 NKJV

And so, dear brothers and sisters who belong to God and are partners
with those called to heaven, think carefully about this Jesus whom we
declare to be God's messenger and High Priest. —Hebrews 3:1 NLT

"You will keep in perfect and constant peace the one whose
mind is steadfast [that is, committed and focused on You —in
both inclination and character.]" —Isaiah 26:3 AMP

Faithful Savior,

I want to live as close to You as I can—moment by moment. But sometimes I let difficulties distract me from Your Presence with me.

I used to think that my circumstances determined the quality of my life. So I poured my energy into trying to control those situations. I felt happy when things were going well—and sad or upset when things didn't go my way. I didn't question this correlation between my circumstances and my feelings. But the Bible tells me that it's possible to *be content in any and every situation.*

Help me to put more of my energy into trusting You and enjoying Your Presence. Instead of letting my happiness depend on my circumstances, I long to connect my joy to You and Your precious promises—as You speak to me through Your Word:

I am with you and will watch over you wherever you go.
I will meet all your needs according to My glorious riches.
Nothing in all creation can separate you from My Love.

In Your beloved Name, Jesus, amen.

I know what it is to be in need, and I know what it is to have plenty. I have learned the secret of being content in any and every situation, whether well fed or hungry, whether living in plenty or in want. —Philippians 4:12

"Look, I am with you and will watch over you wherever you go. I will bring you back to this land, for I will not leave you until I have done what I have promised you." —Genesis 28:15 hcsb

And my God will meet all your needs according to his glorious riches in Christ Jesus. —Philippians 4:19

Neither height nor depth, nor anything else in all creation, will be able to separate us from the love of God that is in Christ Jesus our Lord. —Romans 8:39

Merciful Jesus,

I come gladly into Your Presence—basking in the luxury of being fully understood and perfectly loved. Help me to see myself as You see me: radiant in Your righteousness, cleansed by Your blood. I'm grateful that You view me as the one You created me to be, the one I will *actually* be when heaven becomes my home. It is Your Life within me that is changing me *from Glory to Glory*! I rejoice in this mysterious miracle.

As I sit quietly in Your Presence, my awareness of Your Life within me is heightened. You are *Christ in me, the hope of Glory*. I'm grateful that You—the One who walks beside me, holding me by my hand—are the same One who lives within me. This is a glorious, unfathomable mystery. The Light of Your Presence shines within me as well as upon me. You and I are intertwined in an intimacy that involves every fiber of my being. You are in me, and I am in You. This means that nothing in heaven or on earth can separate me from You. Hallelujah!

In Your magnificent Name, amen.

Those who look to him are radiant; their faces are never covered with shame. —Psalm 34:5

He made the One who did not know sin to be sin for us, so that we might become the righteousness of God in Him. —2 Corinthians 5:21 hcsb

But we all, with unveiled face, beholding as in a mirror the glory of the Lord, are being transformed into the same image from glory to glory, just as by the Spirit of the Lord. —2 Corinthians 3:18 nkjv

To them God chose to make known how great among the Gentiles are the riches of the glory of this mystery, which is Christ in you, the hope of glory. —Colossians 1:27 esv

Supreme Savior,

Help me to give up the illusion that I deserve a problem-free life. Part of me still hungers for the resolution of all my difficulties, but I realize this is a false hope. Your Word states clearly that *in this world I will have trouble.* I must link my hope not to problem solving in this life but to the promise of an eternity of trouble-free life with You in heaven. Instead of seeking perfection in this fallen world, I want to pour my energy into seeking *You*—the Perfect One.

You've shown me that it's possible to glorify You in the midst of adverse circumstances. Your Light shines brightly through believers who trust You in the dark. This is supernatural trust, produced by Your indwelling Spirit.

Lord, I invite You to transform me more and more into the one You designed me to be. I want to yield to Your creative work in me, neither resisting it nor trying to speed it up. I long to enjoy the tempo of a God-breathed life—with *You* setting the pace. I'm grateful that *You hold me by my right hand, You guide me with Your counsel, and afterward You will take me into Glory.*

In Your triumphant Name, Jesus, amen.

"I have told you these things, so that in me you may have peace. In this world you will have trouble. But take heart! I have overcome the world." —JOHN 16:33

And we all, with unveiled face, beholding the glory of the Lord, are being transformed into the same image from one degree of glory to another. For this comes from the Lord who is the Spirit. —2 CORINTHIANS 3:18 ESV

Yet I am always with you; you hold me by my right hand. You guide me with your counsel, and afterward you will take me into glory. —PSALM 73:23–24

Glorious Jesus,

Help me to lay down my problems long enough to gaze at You. Sometimes I picture myself standing at the edge of a magnificent ocean, on a beach covered with pebbles. The pebbles represent problems—mine, my family's, my friends', the world's. When I pick up these small stones and hold them close to my eyes, examining their details, my view of the grandeur all around me is blocked. Usually, as soon as I put down one pebble-problem, I pick up another. Thus I fail to enjoy the beauty of Your Presence and the blessing of *Your unfailing Love.*

The ocean represents *You*—endlessly glorious and continually present with me. I want to put down *all* the pebbles so I can experience Your loving Presence. As I wait with You, I can almost hear You whispering: "Choose *Me*, beloved. Choose to see Me—to find Me—in your moments."

I long for the day when seeking You continually will be a habit—a delightful habit that keeps me close to You on *the path of Life.*

In Your exquisite Name, amen.

Looking to Jesus, the founder and perfecter of our faith, who for the joy that was set before him endured the cross, despising the shame, and is seated at the right hand of the throne of God. —HEBREWS 12:2 ESV

The LORD loves righteousness and justice; the earth is full of his unfailing love. —PSALM 33:5

By faith he left Egypt, not fearing the king's anger; he persevered because he saw him who is invisible. —HEBREWS 11:27

You will show me the path of life; in Your presence is fullness of joy; at Your right hand are pleasures forevermore. —PSALM 16:11 NKJV

My great God,

You are my Strength and my Shield! I'm grateful that You're continually at work in my life—sometimes in wondrous ways—to strengthen and protect me. I'm finding that the more fully I trust You, the more *my heart leaps for Joy!*

Help me to trust You wholeheartedly, resting in Your sovereign control over the universe. When circumstances seem to be spinning out of control, I need to grab on to You—clinging to the truth that You know what You are doing. While I'm in the throes of adversity, my greatest challenge is to keep trusting that You are both sovereign and good. But I realize I can't expect to understand Your ways, *for as the heavens are higher than the earth, so are Your ways higher than mine.*

I want to please You by responding to trouble with thanksgiving, trusting that You can bring good out of the most difficult situations. When I respond in this way, You are glorified and I am strengthened. O Lord, I *give thanks to You in song.*

In Your joyful Name, Jesus, amen.

The LORD is my strength and my shield; my heart trusts in him, and I am helped. My heart leaps for joy and I will give thanks to him in song. —PSALM 28:7

I love you, O LORD, my strength. The LORD is my rock, my fortress and my deliverer; my God is my rock, in whom I take refuge. He is my shield and the horn of my salvation, my stronghold. —PSALM 18:1–2

"For as the heavens are higher than the earth, so are My ways higher than your ways, and My thoughts than your thoughts." —ISAIAH 55:9 NKJV

And we know that for those who love God all things work together for good, for those who are called according to his purpose. —ROMANS 8:28 ESV

May

"Come to Me, all who are weary and burdened, and I will give you rest." —MATTHEW 11:28 NASB

Precious Jesus,

Help me to find Joy even in the most unlikely places. I know this requires effort on my part—searching for the good and refusing to let my natural responses blind me to what is there. Please open my eyes to see beyond the obvious so that I can discover treasures hidden in my troubles.

You've been teaching me that living joyously is a choice. Because I inhabit such a sinful, broken world, I must make the effort to choose gladness many times a day. This is especially true during my difficult times. Your Word tells me to *consider it pure joy whenever I face trials of many kinds.* This verse shows me that when I encounter various difficulties, I'm being put to the test. Such trials can strengthen my faith—which is *much more precious than gold*—and prove that it is genuine.

Thank You, Jesus, for making the excruciating decision to *endure the cross for the Joy set before You*—the eternal pleasure of *bringing many sons and daughters to Glory.* Please enable me to choose Joy by *fixing my eyes on You* and looking for treasures in my trials.

In Your courageous Name, amen.

In this you greatly rejoice . . . that . . . your faith, being much more precious than gold . . . may be found to praise, honor, and glory at the revelation of Jesus Christ. —1 PETER 1:6–7 NKJV

Consider it pure joy, my brothers, whenever you face trials of many kinds, because you know that the testing of your faith develops perseverance. —JAMES 1:2–3

Let us fix our eyes on Jesus . . . who for the joy set before him endured the cross, scorning its shame, and sat down at the right hand of the throne of God. —HEBREWS 12:2

In bringing many sons to glory, it was fitting that God, for whom and through whom everything exists, should make the author of their salvation perfect through suffering. —HEBREWS 2:10

Gracious God,

Sometimes I hear You whispering in my heart, *"I take great delight in you."* It's hard for me to receive this blessing, but I know it's based on the unconditional Love You have for all Your children. Please help me to relax in the Light of Your Presence—taking time to soak in Your luminous Love. I long to sit quietly with You while You *renew me by Your Love.*

I find it terribly challenging to live in a fallen world. There is so much brokenness all around me, as well as within me. But I can choose—moment by moment—to focus on what is wrong or to *seek Your Face* and enjoy your approval.

I need to remember that Your delight in me is based on Your finished work on the cross. This remembrance protects me from falling into the trap of trying to earn Your Love. Teach me to live as the one I truly am—Your beloved child, *saved by grace through faith.* Then my gratitude will keep me close to You, eager to follow wherever You lead.

In Your wondrous Name, Jesus, amen.

"The LORD your God is in your midst; he is a warrior who can deliver. He takes great delight in you; he renews you by his love; he shouts for joy over you." —ZEPHANIAH 3:17 NET

When You said, "Seek My face," my heart said to You, "Your face, LORD, I will seek." —PSALM 27:8 NKJV

"The LORD make His face shine upon you [with favor], and be gracious to you [surrounding you with lovingkindness]." —NUMBERS 6:25 AMP

For you are saved by grace through faith, and this is not from yourselves; it is God's gift. —EPHESIANS 2:8 HCSB

Compassionate Lord,

Your Word tells me *You broaden the path beneath me so that my ankles do not turn.* This shows me how intricately You are involved in my life-journey. You know exactly what is ahead of me, and You can alter the hazardous parts of my path before I get there—making my way easier. Sometimes You enable me to see what You have done on my behalf. At other times You spare me hardships without showing me Your protective work. Either way, Your watchful work on my behalf demonstrates Your loving involvement in my life.

From my limited human perspective, Your ways are often mysterious. You do not protect me—or anyone—from *all* adversity. Neither were *You* shielded from hardship during Your thirty-three years of living in this world. On the contrary, You willingly suffered unimaginable pain, humiliation, and agony on the cross—for my sake! When Your Father turned away from You, You experienced unspeakable suffering. But because You were willing to endure that excruciating isolation from Him, I *never* have to suffer alone. Please help me to remember and rejoice in the glorious truth that *You are with me always*—and be thankful!

In Your marvelous Name, Jesus, amen.

You broaden the path beneath me, so that my ankles do not turn. —PSALM 18:36

And about the ninth hour Jesus cried out with a loud voice, saying, "Eli, Eli, lama sabachthani?" that is, "My God, My God, why have You forsaken Me?" —MATTHEW 27:46 NKJV

He will not let your foot slip —he who watches over you will not slumber. —PSALM 121:3

"Teach these new disciples to obey all the commands I have given you. And be sure of this: I am with you always, even to the end of the age." —MATTHEW 28:20 NLT

Dear Jesus,

Help me to be willing to go out on a limb with You. If that's where You are leading, I know it's the safest place for me to be.

You've been showing me that my desire to live a risk-free life is really a form of unbelief. More and more, I recognize that my longing to live close to You is at odds with my attempts to minimize risks. I seem to be approaching a crossroads in my life-journey. In order to follow You wholeheartedly, I must relinquish my tendency to play it safe. As I seek to step outside my comfort zone, I need to cling tightly to Your hand for support and guidance.

Lord, please lead me step by step through this day—and all my days. I've discovered that when I keep my focus on You, I can walk along perilous paths without being frightened. I hope that eventually I'll learn to relax and really enjoy the adventure of our journey together. The Bible tells me that Your protective Presence *will watch over me wherever I go*. So my part in this adventure is to keep looking to You in confident trust.

In Your vigilant Name, amen.

Even though I walk through the valley of the shadow of death, I will fear no evil, for you are with me; your rod and your staff, they comfort me. —Psalm 23:4

"If anyone serves Me, he must follow Me. Where I am, there My servant also will be. If anyone serves Me, the Father will honor him." —John 12:26 hcsb

Those who know your name will trust in you, for you, Lord, have never forsaken those who seek you. —Psalm 9:10

"I am with you and will watch over you wherever you go, and I will bring you back to this land. I will not leave you until I have done what I have promised you." —Genesis 28:15

131

Glorious Savior,

Help me to live in the present, *giving my entire attention to what You are doing right now*. I don't want to *get worked up about what may or may not happen tomorrow*. Yet I confess that entrusting my tomorrows to You goes against the grain of my human nature—against my strong desire to feel in control. The truth is, I waste a lot of time thinking about the future.

I've found that trying not to think about something is usually ineffective and counterproductive. My effort to stop thinking about the matter keeps me chained to those thoughts. However, I can break free by focusing my attention on You and on what You're doing in my life. You are my living Lord, and You're always doing *new things*.

The main thing that keeps me chained to future thoughts is my fear of what tomorrow may bring—wondering whether or not I'll be able to cope with it. But Your Word reassures me: *You will help me deal with whatever hard things come up—when the time comes.*

In Your merciful Name, Jesus, amen.

"Give your entire attention to what God is doing right now, and don't get worked up about what may or may not happen tomorrow. God will help you deal with whatever hard things come up when the time comes." —MATTHEW 6:34 THE MESSAGE

Let us fix our eyes on Jesus, the author and perfecter of our faith, who for the joy set before him endured the cross, scorning its shame, and sat down at the right hand of the throne of God. —HEBREWS 12:2

"See, the former things have taken place, and new things I declare; before they spring into being I announce them to you." —ISAIAH 42:9

My loving Lord,

You continually invite me to draw near You, whispering in my heart: "*Come to Me,* beloved. *I have loved you with an everlasting Love. I have drawn you with lovingkindness.*" I respond to Your beautiful invitation by being still in Your Presence—relaxing and *fixing my thoughts on You.* And I meditate on the glorious truth that *You are continually with me.* This rock-solid reality provides a firm foundation for my life.

The world I inhabit is constantly in flux—I can find no solid ground here. So I desperately need to stay aware of *You* as I go about my day. I know I won't be able to do this perfectly, but I can return to You time after time, praying: "Jesus, keep me aware of Your loving Presence." I like to let this prayer continually echo in my heart and mind—drawing me back to You when my thoughts start to wander away.

I've found that the more of You I have in my life through living close to You, the more joyful I am. This blesses not only me but others—as Your Joy flows through me to them.

In Your blessed Name, Jesus, amen.

*"Come to me, all you who are weary and burdened, and I will give you rest." —*MATTHEW 11:28

The LORD *has appeared of old to me, saying: "Yes, I have loved you with an everlasting love; Therefore with lovingkindness I have drawn you." —*JEREMIAH 31:3 NKJV

*Therefore, holy brothers, who share in the heavenly calling, fix your thoughts on Jesus, the apostle and high priest whom we confess. —*HEBREWS 3:1

*Nevertheless I am continually with You; You hold me by my right hand. —*PSALM 73:23 NKJV

All-sufficient Savior,

Help me to accept and embrace my inadequacy. It's the perfect link to Your infinite sufficiency. When my resources seem lacking, my natural inclination is to worry. The best way I've found to resist this temptation is to openly acknowledge my insufficiencies and thank You for them. This protects me from trying to be what I am not: my own savior and provider. Because I'm weak and sinful, I need a Savior who is strong and perfect—a Provider who can *meet all my needs.*

You've been teaching me to access Your boundless resources by being both still and active. Spending time alone with You, waiting in Your Presence, enhances my connection with You. Moreover, *You work for those who wait for You*—doing for me what I cannot do for myself. But I realize there are many things I *can* do. When I go about my activities relying on *the strength that You provide, You are glorified*—and I am blessed.

Please remind me to turn to You whenever I'm feeling inadequate. This place of neediness is where You graciously and lovingly meet me.

In Your redeeming Name, Jesus, amen.

And my God will meet all your needs according to his glorious riches in Christ Jesus. —PHILIPPIANS 4:19

For since the world began, no ear has heard and no eye has seen a God like you, who works for those who wait for him! —ISAIAH 64:4 NLT

If anyone serves, it should be from the strength God provides, so that God may be glorified through Jesus Christ in everything. —1 PETER 4:11 HCSB

He said to me, "My grace is sufficient for you, for my power is made perfect in weakness." Therefore I will boast all the more gladly about my weaknesses, so that Christ's power may rest on me. —2 CORINTHIANS 12:9

Mighty God,

You give strength to the weary and increase the power of the weak. Please help me not to be discouraged by my frailty. I have various kinds of weaknesses—spiritual, emotional, and physical. You use them to humble me and train me to wait for You in trusting dependence. Your Word assures me that *those who wait for You will gain new strength.*

I realize that this dependent way of living isn't something I should practice only sometimes. You designed me to look to You continually—experiencing You as *the Living One who sees me.*

Waiting for You is closely related to trusting You. The more time I spend focusing on You, the more I grow to trust You. And the more I trust You, the more I want to spend time with You. *Waiting for You* in the midst of my moments also increases my hope in You. This hope blesses me in countless ways—lifting me above my circumstances, enveloping me in *Your unfailing Love.*

In Your hopeful Name, Jesus, amen.

He gives strength to the weary and increases the power of the weak. —ISAIAH 40:29

> *Though youths grow weary and tired, and vigorous young men stumble badly, yet those who wait for the LORD will gain new strength; they will mount up with wings like eagles, they will run and not get tired, they will walk and not become weary.* —ISAIAH 40:30–31 NASB 1995

> *Therefore the well was called Beer-lahai-roi (Well of the Living One Who Sees Me); it is between Kadesh and Bered.* —GENESIS 16:14 AMP

> *We wait in hope for the LORD; he is our help and our shield. In him our hearts rejoice, for we trust in his holy name. May your unfailing love rest upon us, O LORD, even as we put our hope in you.* —PSALM 33:20–22

Beloved Jesus,

I want to live in continual awareness of Your Presence and Your Peace. I know that these are gifts of supernatural proportions. Ever since Your resurrection, You have comforted Your followers with these wonderful messages: *"Surely I am with you always"* and *"Peace be with you."* Please help me to be increasingly receptive to You, Lord, as You offer me these glorious gifts. I'm learning that the best way to receive Your Presence and Peace is to thank You for them.

I am delighted that You created me first and foremost to glorify You. This means it's impossible for me to spend too much time thanking and praising You. I've found that thanksgiving and praise put me in proper relationship with You—opening the way for Your Joy to flow into me as I draw near You in worship.

Thanking You for Your Presence and Your Peace is a wise investment of time, enabling me to receive more of You and Your precious gifts.

In Your glorious Name, amen.

"And teaching them to obey everything I have commanded you. And surely I am with you always, to the very end of the age." —MATTHEW 28:20

While they were still talking about this, Jesus himself stood among them and said to them, "Peace be with you." —LUKE 24:36

Through Jesus, therefore, let us continually offer to God a sacrifice of praise —the fruit of lips that confess his name. —HEBREWS 13:15

Thanks be to God for His indescribable gift! —2 CORINTHIANS 9:15 NKJV

Faithful God,

My relationship with You transcends all my circumstances! So I desire to praise You and enjoy Your Presence even during my times of deepest struggle. But to find You at such times, I have to make the effort to exercise my faith.

I find it challenging to live on two planes simultaneously: the natural world, where adverse situations abound, and the supernatural world, where You reign supreme. To experience Your Presence with me even in my hardest times, I need strong trust-muscles. I'm thankful that trials can both strengthen my faith and show me how much—or how little—I actually trust You.

I realize that I have to work on strengthening my trust-muscles—filling my mind and heart with Scripture, *seeking Your Face continually.* Please remind me to keep turning my thoughts toward You and affirming my faith in You, whether I'm feeling confident or inadequate. And help me really believe—in the depths of my being—that my adequacy rests in my relationship with You, Lord. You make me *ready for anything and equal to anything by infusing me with inner strength*!

In Your trustworthy Name, Jesus, amen.

Consider it pure joy, my brothers, whenever you face trials of many kinds, because you know that the testing of your faith develops perseverance. —JAMES 1:2–3

Seek the LORD and His strength; seek His face continually. —PSALM 105:4 NASB 1995

I can do all things [which He has called me to do] through Him who strengthens and empowers me [to fulfill His purpose —I am self-sufficient in Christ's sufficiency; I am ready for anything and equal to anything through Him who infuses me with inner strength and confident peace.] —PHILIPPIANS 4:13 AMP

Merciful God,

I don't want to be *fearful of bad news*. Please help me to have *a steadfast heart, trusting in You*. In this world there is certainly an abundance of bad news. But instead of being afraid of what's happening, I want to rely confidently on You. Pondering Your sacrificial death on the cross and Your miraculous resurrection fills me with hope and gratitude. I rejoice that You, my living Savior, are Almighty God! And I find comfort in the truth that You are *sovereign* over global events—You are in control.

When things around me or things in the world look as if they're spinning out of control, I can come to You and *pour out my heart*. Instead of fretting and fuming, I can put that worry-energy into communicating with You.

Lord, I come to You not only for comfort but for direction. When I spend time waiting in Your Presence, You show me the right way to go.

Because I belong to You, I don't have to dread bad news or let it spook me. Instead, I can keep my heart steadfast and calm by boldly trusting in You.

In Your steadfast Name, Jesus, amen.

He will have no fear of bad news; his heart is steadfast, trusting in the LORD. —PSALM 112:7

Yes, the Sovereign LORD is coming in power. He will rule with a powerful arm. See, he brings his reward with him as he comes. —ISAIAH 40:10 NLT

Trust in him at all times, O people; pour out your hearts to him, for God is our refuge. —PSALM 62:8

For a child will be born to us, a son will be given to us; and the government will rest on His shoulders. —ISAIAH 9:6 NASB 1995

Jesus, my Hope,

Whenever I'm tempted to indulge in self-pity or escape into unreality, trusting You wholeheartedly is my only hope. In the midst of adversity, I find it hard to think clearly and make wise choices. Sometimes it seems as if a dizzying array of choices is swirling around me—waiting for me to grab on to the right one. But I know there is *one* choice that's always appropriate and effective: the decision to *trust You with all my heart and mind.*

If I find myself sliding down into discouragement or self-pity, I can put on the brakes by declaring my trust in You—whispering, speaking, even shouting it! As I think about the many reasons I have for *being confident in You*, I rejoice in Your *unfailing Love.*

When I'm feeling tempted to numb my pain by escaping into unreality, help me instead to come close to You—expressing my confidence in You. This brings me into contact with *ultimate* Reality! I love confiding in You because You know everything about me *and* my circumstances. O Lord, You are infinitely wise and understanding.

In Your encouraging Name, amen.

Lean on, trust in, and be confident in the Lord with all your heart and mind and do not rely on your own insight or understanding. —PROVERBS 3:5 AMPC

But I am like an olive tree flourishing in the house of God; I trust in God's unfailing love for ever and ever. —PSALM 52:8

Oh, the depth of the riches of the wisdom and knowledge of God! How unsearchable his judgments, and his paths beyond tracing out! —ROMANS 11:33

Cherished Jesus,

I'm so thankful that You are committed to *the renewing of my mind.* I confess that when my thoughts flow freely, they often move toward problems. My focus gets snagged on a pesky problem, and I circle round and round it in futile attempts to resolve it. Meanwhile, this negative focus drains away my energy from other matters that need my attention. Worst of all, I lose sight of *You.*

I've learned that a renewed mind is Presence-focused. Please help me remember that You are always near—and train my mind to *seek You* in every moment, every situation. Sometimes I find reminders of Your Presence in my surroundings: a lilting birdsong, a loved one's smile, golden sunlight. At other times, I draw inward to find You in my spirit, where Your Spirit dwells. I know the most important place to *search for You* is in Your Word. As I seek You and communicate with You, You renovate my mind—transforming me!

In Your magnificent Name, amen.

Do not conform any longer to the pattern of this world, but be transformed by the renewing of your mind. Then you will be able to test and approve what God's will is —his good, pleasing and perfect will. —ROMANS 12:2

Therefore, holy brothers, who share in the heavenly calling, fix your thoughts on Jesus, the apostle and high priest whom we confess. —HEBREWS 3:1

Look to the LORD and his strength; seek his face always. —PSALM 105:4

"And you will seek Me and find Me, when you search for Me with all your heart." —JEREMIAH 29:13 NKJV

My Savior-God,

When many things seem to be going wrong and my life feels increasingly out of control, help me to trust You and thank You. These are supernatural responses that can lift me above my circumstances. If I do what comes *naturally* in the face of difficulties, I tend to fall prey to negativism.

Even a few complaints can darken my perspective and set me on a downward spiral. With this negative attitude controlling me, complaints flow more and more readily from my mouth. Each one moves me further down the slippery slope, and the lower I go, the faster I slide. But it's always possible to apply the brakes by crying out to You in Your Name—affirming my trust in You and *giving thanks for everything*. Though this feels unnatural, I've learned that if I persist in these responses, I will gradually move back up the slope.

Once I've recovered all my lost ground, I can face my circumstances from a humble perspective. If I choose supernatural responses this time—trusting and thanking You—*Your Peace that surpasses understanding will guard my heart and my mind*.

In Your unsurpassed Name, Jesus, amen.

But I trust in your unfailing love; my heart rejoices in your salvation. —PSALM 13:5

And give thanks for everything to God the Father in the name of our Lord Jesus Christ. —EPHESIANS 5:20 NLT

Do not be anxious about anything, but in everything by prayer and supplication with thanksgiving let your requests be made known to God. And the peace of God, which surpasses all understanding, will guard your hearts and your minds in Christ Jesus. —PHILIPPIANS 4:6–7 ESV

Dearest Lord Jesus,

Whenever plans and problems are preoccupying my mind, I need to turn to You and whisper Your Name. As I rest in You and rejoice in *Your unfailing Love*, the Light of Your Presence shines upon me. Thank You for watching over me always and for loving me eternally. I love You, Jesus, and I trust You to illuminate the way forward—showing me what needs to be done today and what does not. Help me to deal with problems as needed while refusing to let worry or fear become central in my thoughts.

You light up my perspective as I keep turning my attention to You. A wonderful way to focus on You is to saturate my mind and heart with Scripture—reading it, studying it, and memorizing verses that are especially meaningful to me. *Your Word is a lamp to my feet and a light for my path.*

As I persevere in these practices, my preoccupation with problems and plans diminishes. This leaves room in my life for more of *You.* Lord, I ask You to *fill me with the Joy of Your Presence*!

In Your delightful Name, amen.

May your unfailing love rest upon us, O LORD, even as we put our hope in you. —PSALM 33:22

Casting all your cares [all your anxieties, all your worries, and all your concerns, once and for all] on Him, for He cares about you [with deepest affection, and watches over you very carefully]. —1 PETER 5:7 AMP

Your word is a lamp to my feet and a light for my path. —PSALM 119:105

You have shown me the way of life, and you will fill me with the joy of your presence. —ACTS 2:28 NLT

Jesus, my Shepherd,

Your Word assures me that *there is no condemnation for those who belong to You.* Through Your glorious work of salvation, *the law of the Spirit of Life has set me free from the law of sin and death.* This radical freedom is my birthright as a Christian, but I admit that I struggle to live free.

To walk along the path of freedom, I must keep my mind firmly fixed on You. Many voices proclaim, "This is the way for you to go," but only *Your* voice tells me the true way. If I follow the ways of the world with all its glitter and glamour, I will descend deeper and deeper into an abyss. Even Christian voices can lead me astray, saying: "Do this!" "Don't do that!" "Pray this way!" "Don't pray that way!"

When I listen to all those voices, I become increasingly confused. Please help me be content to be a simple "sheep," listening for Your voice and following You—my faithful Shepherd. *You lead me beside quiet waters and make me lie down in green pastures. You guide me in paths of righteousness.*

In Your lovely Name, amen.

Therefore, there is now no condemnation for those who are in Christ Jesus, because through Christ Jesus the law of the Spirit of life set me free from the law of sin and death. —ROMANS 8:1–2

And your ears shall hear a word behind you, saying, "This is the way, walk in it," when you turn to the right or when you turn to the left. —ISAIAH 30:21 ESV

"My sheep listen to my voice; I know them, and they follow me." —JOHN 10:27

The LORD is my shepherd, I shall not be in want. He makes me lie down in green pastures, he leads me beside quiet waters, he restores my soul. He guides me in paths of righteousness for his name's sake. —PSALM 23:1–3

Comforting God,

I love to hear You whispering in my mind: *"Don't be afraid, for I am with you. Don't be discouraged, for I am your God."* These loving words are like a warm blanket wrapped around me—sheltering me from the coldness of fear and discouragement.

When trouble is stalking me, remind me to grip Your hand tightly and stay in communication with You. I can *trust and not be afraid because You are my Strength and Song.* Your powerful Presence is with me always: I face *nothing* alone! I'm grateful that You have promised to *strengthen me and help me.*

Your strong hand supports me in both good and bad times. When things are going smoothly in my life, I may be less attentive to Your faithful Presence. But when I'm *walking through the valley of the shadow of death*, I'm profoundly aware of my need for You. At such times, holding on to Your hand keeps me standing—and enables me to put one foot in front of the other.

As I seek to endure adversity in trusting dependence on You, please bless me with Peace and Joy in Your Presence.

In Your dependable Name, Jesus, amen.

"Don't be afraid, for I am with you. Don't be discouraged, for I am your God. I will strengthen you and help you. I will hold you up with my victorious right hand." —ISAIAH 41:10 NLT

"Behold, God is my salvation, I will trust and not be afraid; for the LORD GOD is my strength and song, and He has become my salvation." —ISAIAH 12:2 NASB 1995

Yea, though I walk through the valley of the shadow of death, I will fear no evil; for You are with me; Your rod and Your staff, they comfort me. —PSALM 23:4 NKJV

My Creator,

This is the day that You have made! Help me to *rejoice and be glad in it.* I begin this day holding up empty hands of faith—ready to receive all that You are pouring into this brief portion of my life. Since You are the Author of my circumstances, I need to be careful not to complain about anything, even the weather.

I've found that the best way to handle unwanted circumstances is to thank You for them. This act of faith frees me from resentment and enables me to look for blessings emerging from the problems. Sometimes You show me the good that You're bringing out of the difficulties. At *all* times, You offer me the glorious gift of Yourself!

I realize that living within the boundaries of this day is vital for finding Joy in it. You knew what You were doing when You divided time into twenty-four-hour segments. You have perfect understanding of human frailty, and You know that I can only handle the trouble of one day at a time.

I don't want to *worry about tomorrow* or get stuck in the past. Instead, I seek to enjoy abundant Life in Your Presence today!

In Your joyful Name, Jesus, amen.

This is the day the LORD has made; let us rejoice and be glad in it. —PSALM 118:24

But encourage one another daily, as long as it is called Today, so that none of you may be hardened by sin's deceitfulness. —HEBREWS 3:13

For we do not have a high priest who cannot sympathize with our weaknesses, but One who has been tempted in all things as we are, yet without sin. —HEBREWS 4:15 NASB 1995

"Therefore do not worry about tomorrow, for tomorrow will worry about itself. Each day has enough trouble of its own." —MATTHEW 6:34

Precious Jesus,

Every time something thwarts my plans or desires, I face an important choice: to flounder in frustration or to communicate with You. When I choose to talk with You about the situation, I'm blessed in several ways. First, communicating with You—in all circumstances—strengthens my relationship with You. Also, my disappointments, instead of dragging me down, can be transformed into opportunities for good. This transformation removes the sting from difficult circumstances, making it possible for me to be joyful in the midst of adversity.

Please help me to practice this discipline in all the little disappointments of daily life. It is often these minor setbacks that draw me away from Your Presence. Yet I've discovered that when I reframe *setbacks* as *opportunities*, I gain much more than I have lost. Someday I hope to reach the place where I can accept major losses in this positive way. My goal is to attain the perspective of the apostle Paul, who wrote that he considered everything he'd lost to be *rubbish compared to the surpassing greatness of knowing You*!

In Your marvelous Name, amen.

Many are the plans in a man's heart, but it is the LORD's purpose that prevails. —PROVERBS 19:21

Devote yourselves to prayer with an alert mind and a thankful heart. —COLOSSIANS 4:2 NLT

But whatever was to my profit I now consider loss for the sake of Christ. What is more, I consider everything a loss compared to the surpassing greatness of knowing Christ Jesus my Lord, for whose sake I have lost all things. I consider them rubbish, that I may gain Christ. —PHILIPPIANS 3:7–8

Blessed Jesus,

I delight in hearing You whisper to my heart: *"I am with you. I am with you. I am with you."* These comforting words are like a safety net to my spirit, protecting me from falling into despair. Because I am human, I have lots of ups and downs in my life experience. But the promise of Your Presence limits how far down I can fall. So please increase my awareness of Your loving Presence that is with me always.

I admit that sometimes I feel as if I'm in a free fall—especially when people or things I had counted on let me down. Yet as soon as I remember that You are with me, my perspective changes radically. Instead of bemoaning my circumstances and wallowing in them, I turn to You for help. I recall that not only are You *with me*, but *You are holding me by my right hand. You guide me with Your counsel, and afterward You will take me into Glory.* This is exactly the perspective I need: the assurance of Your abiding Presence and the promise of heaven's eternal Glory!

In Your exalted Name, amen.

"Teach these new disciples to obey all the commands I have given you. And be sure of this: I am with you always, even to the end of the age." —MATTHEW 28:20 NLT

The LORD your God is with you, he is mighty to save. He will take great delight in you, he will quiet you with his love, he will rejoice over you with singing. —ZEPHANIAH 3:17

Yet I am always with you; you hold me by my right hand. You guide me with your counsel, and afterward you will take me into glory. —PSALM 73:23–24

My steadfast Savior,

Protect me from the trap of looking at myself through other people's eyes. I realize that this practice is hurtful in several ways. First of all, it's nearly impossible to discern what others actually think of me. Moreover, their views of me are variable—subject to each person's spiritual, emotional, and physical state at the time. But the main problem with letting others define me is that it's a form of idolatry. Seeking to please people dampens my desire to please You, my Creator. Forgive me for this idolatrous preoccupation with others' views of me.

You've been showing me that it's much more real to see myself through *Your* eyes. Your gaze upon me is steady and sure—absolutely untainted by sin or a changeable nature. Lord, help me to view both myself and others from Your perspective. Through spending time in Your Presence, I can experience the reality of being perfectly, eternally loved. As I rest in Your loving gaze, you fill me with deep Peace. I want to respond to Your glorious Presence by *worshiping You in spirit and in truth.*

In Your great Name, Jesus, amen.

Fear of man will prove to be a snare, but whoever trusts in the Lord is kept safe. —PROVERBS 29:25

And without faith it is impossible to please God, because anyone who comes to him must believe that he exists and that he rewards those who earnestly seek him. —HEBREWS 11:6

Now hope does not disappoint, because the love of God has been poured out in our hearts by the Holy Spirit who was given to us. —ROMANS 5:5 NKJV

"Yet a time is coming and has now come when the true worshipers will worship the Father in spirit and truth, for they are the kind of worshipers the Father seeks. God is spirit, and his worshipers must worship in spirit and in truth." —JOHN 4:23–24

Jesus, my Rock,

I rejoice in my dependence on You! I've discovered that this is a place of wonderful security. I found out the hard way that depending on myself, others, or circumstances was like building my life on a foundation of sand. When storms came, I realized how flimsy my foundation was; it was totally inadequate to support me. Now I'm seeking to build my life *on the rock*—a foundation that is more than sufficient to support me during life's storms.

Lord, help me to depend on You not only in stormy circumstances but also when the sky is clear and my life is calm. This is a daily discipline—preparing me for *whatever* lies ahead. I've found that it's also a source of great Joy! Relying on You involves staying in communication with You—an extraordinary privilege! This rich blessing provides me with strength, encouragement, and guidance. When I stay in touch with You, I can cope with difficulties because I *know* I'm not alone. As I *walk in the Light of Your Presence*, You empower me to *rejoice in Your Name all day long*. Depending on You is a joyful, blessed way to live.

In Your joyous Name, amen.

"Everyone who hears these words of mine and puts them into practice is like a wise man who built his house on the rock. The rain came down, the streams rose, and the winds blew and beat against that house; yet it did not fall, because it had its foundation on the rock. But everyone who hears these words of mine and does not put them into practice is like a foolish man who built his house on sand. The rain came down . . . and [that house] fell with a great crash." —MATTHEW 7:24–25

Blessed are those who . . . walk in the light of your presence, O LORD. They rejoice in your name all day long. —PSALM 89:15–16

Always be joyful. —1 THESSALONIANS 5:16 NLT

My strong Shepherd,

I come to You with all my weaknesses: spiritual, emotional, and physical. As I rest in the comfort of Your Presence, I remember that *nothing is impossible with You*—and I *rejoice in You!*

Help me pry my mind away from my problems so I can focus my attention more fully on You. Lord, You are the One *who is able to do immeasurably more than all I ask or imagine!* Instead of trying to direct You to do this and that, I want to attune myself to what You are *already* doing.

Whenever anxiety attempts to wedge its way into my thoughts, please remind me that *You are my Shepherd.* Since You are taking care of me, I don't need to be afraid of anything! Rather than trying to maintain control over my life, I want to abandon myself to You. Even though this feels scary and precarious, I know that the most secure place to be is right beside You.

In Your comforting Name, Jesus, amen.

"For nothing is impossible with God." —LUKE 1:37

Rejoice in the Lord always. Again I will say, rejoice! —PHILIPPIANS 4:4 NKJV

Now to him who is able to do immeasurably more than all we ask or imagine, according to his power that is at work within us, to him be glory in the church and in Christ Jesus throughout all generations, for ever and ever! Amen. —EPHESIANS 3:20–21

The Lord is my Shepherd [to feed, guide, and shield me], I shall not lack. —PSALM 23:1 AMPC

Gentle, loving Jesus,

Help me to *rejoice in You always—letting my gentleness be evident to all.* I've found that rejoicing in You protects me from the temptation to complain. When my circumstances are stressful, it's all too easy for me to become irritable. But You are teaching me to demonstrate gentleness—not irritability—to others. This is possible to the extent that I find Joy in You. There is always much for me to rejoice about because *You are the same yesterday, today, and forever.*

I can be especially joyful in the knowledge that *You are near.* When a man and a woman are deeply in love, they tend to bring out the best in each other. Just being with the beloved can soothe irritations and increase happiness. *You* are the Lover who is always near—unseen yet tenderly present. When I take time to tune in to Your loving Presence, You soothe my frustrations and fill me with Joy.

Please remind me to thank You frequently for Your continual Presence and Your unfailing Love. When circumstances are getting me down, I need to turn my attention to You and *consider Your great Love* for me!

In Your glorious Name, amen.

Rejoice in the Lord always. I will say it again: Rejoice! Let your gentleness be evident to all. The Lord is near. —PHILIPPIANS 4:4–5

But the fruit of the Spirit is love, joy, peace, patience, kindness, goodness, faithfulness, gentleness, self-control; against such things there is no law. —GALATIANS 5:22–23 ESV

Jesus Christ is the same yesterday, today, and forever. —HEBREWS 13:8 NKJV

Whoever is wise, let him heed these things and consider the great love of the LORD. —PSALM 107:43

My delightful Lord,

This is the day that You have made! As I rejoice in this day of life, it will yield precious gifts and beneficial training. I want to walk with You along the high road of thanksgiving—discovering all the delights You have prepared for me.

To protect my thankfulness, I need to remember that I reside in a fallen world where blessings and sorrows intermingle freely. When I'm too focused on troubles, I walk through a day that's brimming with beauty and brightness while seeing only the grayness of my thoughts. Neglecting the practice of giving thanks darkens my mind and dims my vision.

Lord, please clear up my vision by helping me remember to thank You at all times. When I'm grateful, I can walk through the darkest days with Joy in my heart because I know that *the Light of Your Presence* is still shining on me. So *I rejoice in You*—my delightful, steadfast Companion.

In Your bright, shining Name, Jesus, amen.

This is the day that the LORD has made; let us rejoice and be glad in it. —PSALM 118:24 ESV

Devote yourselves to prayer, being watchful and thankful. —COLOSSIANS 4:2

Blessed are those who have learned to acclaim you, who walk in the light of your presence, O LORD. They rejoice in your name all day long; they exult in your righteousness. —PSALM 89:15–16

Give thanks to the LORD, for He is good; His faithful love endures forever. —PSALM 118:1 HCSB

King Jesus,

The Light of the gospel of Your Glory is an astonishingly rich treasure! What makes the gospel such amazingly good news is that it opens the way for me to know *You* in Your majestic Glory.

When I trusted You as my Savior, You set my feet on a pathway to heaven. Forgiveness of sins and a future in heaven are wondrous gifts, but You provided even more! *You made Your Light shine in my heart to give me the Light of the knowledge of the Glory of Your Face.* Help me to *seek Your Face* wholeheartedly—delighting in the radiant knowledge of Your glorious Presence.

One of the meanings of *knowledge* is "awareness acquired by experience or study." Knowing You involves awareness of You—experiencing Your Presence through the Holy Spirit. It also involves studying the Bible to learn more and more about You. Though *the god of this age has blinded the minds of unbelievers*, I can perceive You clearly through searching the Scriptures and enjoying *the Light of the gospel of Your Glory.*

In Your wonderful Name, amen.

The god of this age has blinded the minds of unbelievers, so that they cannot see the light of the gospel of the glory of Christ, who is the image of God. —2 CORINTHIANS 4:4

For God, who said, "Let light shine out of darkness," made his light shine in our hearts to give us the light of the knowledge of the glory of God in the face of Christ. —2 CORINTHIANS 4:6

When You said, "Seek My face," my heart said to You, "Your face, LORD, I will seek." —PSALM 27:8 NKJV

My ever-near God,

Sometimes I feel as if I'm in a desolate place—devoid of Your loving companionship. But whether I sense Your Presence or not, I can call out to You and *know* that You are with me. The Bible promises that *You are near to all who call on You.* As I whisper Your Name in tender trust, help me cast my doubts to the wind!

I need to spend some time telling You about my troubles and seeking Your guidance. Then I'll change the subject to *You*—praising You for Your greatness and majesty, Your Power and Glory. I'll thank You for the many good things You have done and are doing in my life. Lord, You are richly present in my praise and thanksgiving!

Your Word instructs me to *taste and see that You are good.* The more I focus on You and Your blessings, the more fully I can taste Your goodness. The sweetness of *Your unfailing Love* delights me. The heartiness of Your mighty strength encourages me. You satisfy the hunger of my heart with the Joy and Peace of Your Presence, assuring me: *"I am with you and will watch over you wherever You go."*

In Your generous Name, Jesus, amen.

The Lord is near to all who call on him. —Psalm 145:18

Oh, taste and see that the Lord is good; blessed is the man who trusts in Him! —Psalm 34:8 nkjv

"Though the mountains be shaken and the hills be removed, yet my unfailing love for you will not be shaken nor my covenant of peace be removed," says the Lord, who has compassion on you. —Isaiah 54:10

"I am with you and will watch over you wherever you go, and I will bring you back to this land. I will not leave you until I have done what I have promised you." —Genesis 28:15

Treasured Jesus,

Help me remember that challenging circumstances come and go, but *You are continually with me.* The constancy of Your Presence is a glorious treasure!

It comforts me to know that You are writing the storyline of my life—through good times *and* hard times. You can see the big picture: from before my birth to beyond the grave. And You know exactly what I will be like when heaven becomes my forever-home. Moreover, You're constantly at work in me—changing me into the person You designed me to be. Your Word assures me that I am royalty in Your kingdom.

One of my favorite ways to draw near You is to lovingly speak Your Name. This simple prayer expresses my trust that You are indeed with me and You're taking care of me. You, *the God of hope, fill me with all Joy and Peace as I trust in You.*

No matter how heavy my burdens are, the reality of Your Presence with me outweighs all my difficulties. When I wait quietly with You, I can hear You whisper: *"Come to Me, all you who are weary and burdened, and I will give you rest."*

In Your refreshing Name, amen.

Nevertheless I am continually with You; You hold me by my right hand. —PSALM 73:23 NKJV

You are a chosen people . . . a people belonging to God. —1 PETER 2:9

May the God of hope fill you with all joy and peace as you trust in him. —ROMANS 15:13

"Come to me, all you who are weary and burdened, and I will give you rest." —MATTHEW 11:28

My loving Lord,

Let the morning bring me word of Your unfailing Love. Help me to *put my trust in You* and enjoy Your Love shining upon me—even in the midst of my troubles. When I'm struggling with discouragement, I need to affirm my trust in You and remember who You are: Creator and Sustainer of the universe, as well as my Savior, Lord, and Friend. I know I can count on You because Your Love is boundless and steadfast. It never runs out or grows dim, and it doesn't depend on how well I'm performing. Your perfect Love never changes because *You are the same yesterday, today, and forever.*

I'm blessed when I take time to *lift up my soul to You*—waiting in Your Presence with no pretense and no demands. As I devote time to worshiping and waiting, You work within me and prepare me for the day. Then You *show me the way I should go*—step by step. I'm grateful that You are *my God forever and ever; You will be my Guide even to the end!*

In Your guiding Name, Jesus, amen.

Let the morning bring me word of your unfailing love, for I have put my trust in you. Show me the way I should go, for to you I lift up my soul. —PSALM 143:8

And now in these final days, he has spoken to us through his Son. God promised everything to the Son as an inheritance, and through the Son he created the universe. The Son radiates God's own glory and expresses the very character of God, and he sustains everything by the mighty power of his command. When he had cleansed us from our sins, he sat down in the place of honor at the right hand of the majestic God in heaven. —HEBREWS 1:2–3 NLT

Jesus Christ is the same yesterday, today, and forever. —HEBREWS 13:8 NKJV

For this God is our God for ever and ever; he will be our guide even to the end. —PSALM 48:14

Majestic Jesus,

Your unfailing Love is better than life itself! I'm grateful that there's no limit to Your Love—in quality, quantity, or duration. *How priceless is Your unfailing Love!* It is infinitely better than anything this world can offer, and it will never run out. This Love is so precious that it's worth losing everything else to secure it.

Though gaining Your Love is worth losing my life, this glorious gift greatly *enriches* my life. Your steadfast Love provides a firm foundation for me to build on. Knowing I'm perfectly, eternally loved improves my relationships with others and helps me grow into the person You designed me to be. Moreover, *grasping how wide and long and high and deep is Your Love* for me leads me into worship. *This* is where my intimacy with You grows by leaps and bounds—as I joyously celebrate Your magnificent Presence!

My heart echoes the words of the psalmist: *Let everything that has breath praise You, Lord.* Hallelujah!

In Your praiseworthy Name, amen.

Your unfailing love is better than life itself; how I praise you! —PSALM 63:3 NLT

How priceless is your unfailing love! Both high and low among men find refuge in the shadow of your wings. —PSALM 36:7

I pray that out of his glorious riches he may strengthen you with power through his Spirit in your inner being, so that Christ may dwell in your hearts through faith. And I pray that you, being rooted and established in love, may have power, together with all the saints, to grasp how wide and long and high and deep is the love of Christ. —EPHESIANS 3:16–18

Let everything that has breath praise the LORD. Praise the LORD! —PSALM 150:6 NKJV

157

Splendid Savior,

Your Word tells me: *If anything is excellent or praiseworthy, think about such things.* This sounds easy, but putting it into practice is really hard for me.

I've seen how countercultural it is to focus on admirable things. People who work in the media almost always shine their spotlights on negative news. They rarely bother to report good things that are happening—especially the many good things Your people are doing.

I admit that having a positive focus is not only countercultural but counter to my fallen nature. When Adam and Eve rebelled against You, *everything* was damaged by the Fall—including my mind. As a result, focusing on excellent, admirable things is not at all natural to me. It requires persistent effort, trying to make the right choice over and over again. Lord, please help me choose to look for what is good—daily, moment by moment.

In spite of the massive problems in this world, there is much that is worthy of praise. I rejoice that You, the One who is the *most* praiseworthy, are *continually with me*—closer than my thoughts!

In Your excellent, admirable Name, Jesus, amen.

Finally, brothers, whatever is true . . . whatever is admirable —if anything is excellent or praiseworthy —think about such things. —PHILIPPIANS 4:8

When the woman saw that the fruit of the tree was good for food . . . and also desirable for gaining wisdom, she took some and ate it. —GENESIS 3:6

Rejoice in the Lord always. I will say it again: Rejoice! —PHILIPPIANS 4:4

Nevertheless I am continually with You; You hold me by my right hand. —PSALM 73:23 NKJV

June

This God is our God for ever and ever; he will be our guide even to the end. —Psalm 48:14

Jesus, my faithful Guide,

I delight in spending time with You—*meditating on Your unfailing Love. For You are my God forever and ever.* Please help me, through Your Spirit, to bring my mind back to You whenever it wanders.

I find great encouragement in the words of Jacob: *"Surely the Lord is in this place."* No matter where I am, You are with me. I'm so grateful that You are my God forevermore—today, tomorrow, and throughout all eternity!

You are also *my Guide.* It's easy for me to be spooked by the future when I forget that You're leading me each step along my life-path. Yet Your guiding Presence has been available to me ever since I trusted You as my Savior. You've been training me to be increasingly aware of You as I go about my daily activities. One way I'm learning to draw near You is by whispering Your Name. This reminds me that You are close beside me. Instead of *worrying about anything,* I can bring You my requests *through prayer and petition with thanksgiving.* How I rejoice in the wondrous assurance that *You will be my Guide even to the end*!

In Your blessed, eternal Name, amen.

Within your temple, O God, we meditate on your unfailing love. Like your name, O God, your praise reaches to the ends of the earth; your right hand is filled with righteousness. . . . For this God is our God for ever and ever; he will be our guide even to the end. —PSALM 48:9–10, 14

When Jacob awoke from his sleep, he thought, "Surely the LORD is in this place, and I was not aware of it." —GENESIS 28:16

Don't worry about anything, but in everything, through prayer and petition with thanksgiving, let your requests be made known to God. —PHILIPPIANS 4:6 HCSB

Gentle Jesus,

Sometimes I need Your help even to ask for help. As I try to do several things at once, I find myself moving faster and faster—interrupting one thing to do another. If my phone rings at such a time, my stress level rises even higher. Only when I *stop* everything, take a few deep breaths, and whisper Your Name do I begin to calm down. Then I can acknowledge my need for You to guide me through the day. You have promised to *lead me in paths of righteousness for Your Name's sake.*

When I'm preparing to do something challenging, I usually take time to ask for Your help. But when I do everyday tasks, I tend to dive in unassisted—acting as if I can handle these matters alone. Yet it's so much better to approach *everything* in humble dependence on You. Whenever I'm feeling tempted to just dive in, I need to stop and turn to You—asking You to show me the way forward. As I wait in Your loving Presence, I delight in hearing You speak these words of assurance: *"I will guide you along the best pathway for your life."*

In Your reassuring Name, amen.

*He restores my soul. He leads me in paths of righteousness
for his name's sake.* —PSALM 23:3 ESV

*"God did this so that men would seek him and perhaps reach out for him
and find him, though he is not far from each one of us."* —ACTS 17:27

*The LORD says, "I will guide you along the best pathway for your
life. I will advise you and watch over you."* —PSALM 32:8 NLT

God of grace,

I come to You for understanding since You know me far better than I know myself. You comprehend me in all my complexity; no detail of my life is hidden from You. Yet I don't need to fear Your intimate awareness of me because I know that You view me through eyes of grace. Lord, I want the Light of Your healing Presence to shine into the deepest recesses of my being—cleansing, healing, refreshing, and renewing me.

Help me to trust You enough to accept the full forgiveness that You offer me continually. This glorious gift cost You Your Life, and it is mine for all eternity! I'm grateful that forgiveness is at the very core of Your abiding Presence. You assure me through Your Word: *"I will never leave you nor forsake you."*

When no one else seems to understand me, I can simply draw nearer to You—rejoicing in the One who understands me completely and loves me perfectly. As You fill me with Your Love, I long to become a reservoir of love that overflows into the lives of other people.

In Your lovely Name, Jesus, amen.

O LORD, you have searched me and you know me. You know when I sit and when I rise; you perceive my thoughts from afar. You discern my going out and my lying down; you are familiar with all my ways. Before a word is on my tongue you know it completely, O LORD. —PSALM 139:1–4

For from his fullness we have all received, grace upon grace. For the law was given through Moses; grace and truth came through Jesus Christ. —JOHN 1:16–17 ESV

"No one will be able to stand up against you all the days of your life. As I was with Moses, so I will be with you; I will never leave you nor forsake you." —JOSHUA 1:5

Compassionate Savior,

I *come to You* feeling *weary and burdened,* so I ask You to *give me rest.* Only You know the depth and breadth of my weariness. Nothing is hidden from You! You've been showing me that there's a time to keep pushing myself and there's a time to stop working—and just rest. Even You, who have infinite energy, rested on the seventh day after completing Your work of creation.

I want to spend time lingering in Your loving Presence while *Your Face shines upon me.* As favorite scriptures amble through my brain, they refresh my heart and spirit. When something comes to mind that I don't want to forget, I'll jot it down and then return my attention to You. As I'm relaxing with You, may Your Love soak into the depths of my being. I delight in expressing my love to *You*—in whispers, spoken words, and song.

Help me to believe that You approve of me and You approve of rest. While I relax in Your Presence, trusting in Your finished work on the cross, I am deeply refreshed.

In Your invigorating Name, Jesus, amen.

"Come to me, all you who are weary and burdened, and I will give you rest." —MATTHEW 11:28

And on the seventh day God ended His work which He had done, and He rested on the seventh day from all His work which He had done. —GENESIS 2:2 NKJV

"The LORD make His face shine upon you [with favor], and be gracious to you [surrounding you with lovingkindness]; the LORD lift up His countenance (face) upon you [with divine approval], and give you peace [a tranquil heart and life]." —NUMBERS 6:25–26 AMP

Precious Jesus,

Sometimes I sense the Light of Your Glory shining on me. As I look up to You with worship in my heart, the radiance of Your Love falls upon me, soaking into the depths of my being. How I treasure these moments with You! Please use them to make me more like You. I'm learning that the more I *fix my eyes on You*—in quiet times *and* busy times—the better I can *reflect Your Glory* to other people.

I admit that staying conscious of You when I'm busy is very challenging for me. Thankfully, You have created me with a mind that can function on more than one "track" at a time. Help me to remain mindful of You by dedicating one of those tracks to Your Presence with me. This practice benefits me in various ways: When I'm aware that You are present with me, I'm less likely to do or say something that's displeasing to You. Whenever I'm struggling with difficult circumstances or painful feelings, awareness of Your Presence brings me comfort and encouragement.

I know You can use *everything* in my life for good—*transforming me into Your likeness with ever-increasing Glory*!

In Your glorious Name, amen.

Let us fix our eyes on Jesus, the author and perfecter of our faith, who for the joy set before him endured the cross, scorning its shame, and sat down at the right hand of the throne of God. —HEBREWS 12:2

And we, who with unveiled faces all reflect the Lord's glory, are being transformed into his likeness with ever-increasing glory, which comes from the Lord, who is the Spirit. —2 CORINTHIANS 3:18

And we know that God causes everything to work together for the good of those who love God and are called according to his purpose for them. —ROMANS 8:28 NLT

My great God,

On days when my primary goal is pleasing myself, my life is filled with frustration. The attitude that things should go my way is based on a faulty premise: that I am the center of my world. The truth is, *You* are the Center—and everything revolves around You. So I need to make my plans tentatively, *seeking Your Face* and Your will in all that I do. This is actually a win-win situation. If things go according to my plans, I can thank You and rejoice. When my desires are thwarted, I can stay in communication with You and subordinate my will to Yours—trusting that *Your way is perfect*.

Please help me remember that *I am not my own*; I belong to You. This awareness that I am Yours—Your beloved—is a great relief. It shifts my focus away from myself and what I want. Instead of striving to make things go my way, my primary goal becomes pleasing *You*. This sounds as if it could be burdensome, but it's really quite freeing because *Your yoke is easy and Your burden is light*. Moreover, knowing that I belong to You provides deep, satisfying *rest for my soul*.

In Your refreshing Name, Jesus, amen.

Seek the LORD and His strength; seek His face
continually. —PSALM 105:4 NASB 1995

As for God, his way is perfect; the word of the LORD is flawless. He
is a shield for all who take refuge in him. —PSALM 18:30

Don't you know that your body is a sanctuary of the Holy Spirit who is in you,
whom you have from God? You are not your own. —1 CORINTHIANS 6:19 HCSB

"Take my yoke upon you and learn from me, for I am gentle and
humble in heart, and you will find rest for your souls. For my yoke
is easy and my burden is light." —MATTHEW 11:29–30

Joyous Lord Jesus,

In You I have found *Joy inexpressible and full of Glory*! This amazing Joy is available nowhere else; I find it only in my relationship with You. Lord, help me to trust You wholeheartedly and walk confidently with You along my life-path. As we journey together, I know I will encounter many obstacles—and some of them will be quite difficult to overcome.

Your Word teaches me that *each day has enough trouble of its own.* So I must expect daily difficulties and not let them throw me off course—refusing to let adversity keep me from enjoying Your Presence. My life with You is an adventure, and there are always some dangers involved in adventurous journeys. Please give me courage to face trouble with confidence and perseverance.

My hope needs to be fastened on You and on the heavenly reward that You have prepared for me. I know that my Joy will expand exponentially—beyond anything I can imagine—when I reach my eternal home. There I will see You *face to Face*, and my Joy will know no bounds!

In Your triumphant Name, amen.

Though now you do not see Him, yet believing, you rejoice with joy inexpressible and full of glory. —1 PETER 1:8 NKJV

"So do not worry about tomorrow; for tomorrow will care for itself. Each day has enough trouble of its own." —MATTHEW 6:34 NASB 1995

Now we see but a poor reflection as in a mirror; then we shall see face to face. Now I know in part; then I shall know fully, even as I am fully known. —1 CORINTHIANS 13:12

My living Lord,

You are everything I could possibly need in a Savior-God, and *You live in me*! You fill me with radiant Life and Love. I want Your Life in me to overflow and impact other people. Please live through me and love through me as I interact with others. I ask that Your Love will grace my words and Your Light will reflect from my demeanor as I live in joyful dependence on You.

In this world I often feel insufficient, but I know *I am complete in You*, Lord. All that I need for my salvation and spiritual growth is found in You. Through *Your divine Power* I have everything necessary to persevere in my journey toward heaven. You bless me with intimate *knowledge of You*, and You invite me to open up and share with You at the deepest levels—both my struggles and my delights.

Your finished work on the cross provides deep rest for my soul, Lord Jesus. I'm so grateful that I am eternally secure in You—my living Savior and my forever-Friend.

In Your victorious Name, Jesus, amen.

My old self has been crucified with Christ. It is no longer I who live, but Christ lives in me. So I live in this earthly body by trusting in the Son of God, who loved me and gave himself for me. —GALATIANS 2:20 NLT

For in Him dwells all the fullness of the Godhead bodily; and you are complete in Him, who is the head of all principality and power. —COLOSSIANS 2:9–10 NKJV

His divine power has given us everything we need for life and godliness through our knowledge of him who called us by his own glory and goodness. —2 PETER 1:3

Trustworthy Jesus,

I bring You all my feelings, including the ones I wish I didn't have. I confess that fear and anxiety often plague me—tempting me to focus on myself instead of trusting in You. Blazing missiles of fear fly at me day and night; these attacks from the evil one come at me relentlessly. Teach me to use my *shield of faith* effectively—*extinguishing those flaming arrows.*

Lord, please enable me to keep affirming my faith, regardless of how I feel. I've seen that when I persist in declaring my trust in You, my feelings eventually fall in line with my faith.

I don't want to hide from my fear or pretend it isn't there. If I hide anxiety in the recesses of my heart, it gives birth to fear of fear—a monstrous mutation. Instead, I choose to bring my anxieties into the Light of Your loving Presence, where You can show me how to deal with them. Help me to persevere in trusting You and living close to You; then fearfulness will gradually lose its foothold in me.

In Your faithful Name, amen.

In addition to all this, take up the shield of faith, with which you can extinguish all the flaming arrows of the evil one. —EPHESIANS 6:16

This is the message we have heard from him and declare to you: God is light; in him there is no darkness at all. If we claim to have fellowship with him yet walk in the darkness, we lie and do not live by the truth. But if we walk in the light, as he is in the light, we have fellowship with one another, and the blood of Jesus, his Son, purifies us from all sin. —1 JOHN 1:5–7

"Behold, God is my salvation, I will trust and not be afraid; for the LORD GOD is my strength and song, and He has become my salvation." —ISAIAH 12:2 NASB 1995

Delightful Jesus,

Your Word tells me to *cast all my care on You, for You care for me.* I know You're an excellent Catcher, so I want to just throw all my cares—my anxieties and concerns—to You. As I release those worrisome things, I relax in Your Presence and breathe a sigh of relief. I need to keep doing this throughout the day—and sometimes during the night too. Thankfully, You are always awake, ready to catch my cares and *bear my burdens.*

Because You are infinitely powerful, carrying my burdens does not weigh You down at all. I've found that "playing catch" with You has a buoyant effect on me—lightening my load and lifting my spirit. No matter how much I throw at You, You never miss a catch! So instead of letting worries weigh me down, I'll rejoice that You are with me—ready to help me with whatever I'm facing.

Whenever I realize that I'm mulling over a problem, I can look to You lightheartedly and fling my concern into Your strong, waiting hands. Thank You, Jesus, for always *watching over me* and catching my cares!

In Your watchful, caring Name, amen.

Casting all your care upon Him, for He cares for you. —1 PETER 5:7 NKJV

Search me, O God, and know my heart; try me, and know my anxieties. —PSALM 139:23 NKJV

Praise be to the Lord, to God our Savior, who daily bears our burdens. —PSALM 68:19

The LORD watches over you —the LORD is your shade at your right hand; the sun will not harm you by day, nor the moon by night. —PSALM 121:5–6

Jesus, my constant Companion,

I want to walk joyously with You through today, holding Your hand in trusting dependence. With You beside me, I can savor the pleasures and endure the difficulties this day will bring. Help me to appreciate everything You've prepared for me: beautiful scenery, bracing winds of adventure, sheltered nooks for resting when I'm weary, and much more. I'm thankful that You are not only my constant Companion but also my Guide. You know every step of the journey ahead of me—all the way to heaven.

I don't have to choose between staying close to You and staying on course. Since *You are the Way*, being close to You *is* being on course. As I *fix my thoughts on You*, I trust You to guide me moment by moment along today's journey. Help me not to worry about what I'll encounter on the road ahead. And please keep reminding me that You are always by my side. This sets me free to focus on enjoying Your Presence and staying in step with You.

In Your joyful Name, amen.

I can do all things through Christ who strengthens me. —Philippians 4:13 nkjv

"The Lord will guide you always; he will satisfy your needs in a sun-scorched land and will strengthen your frame. You will be like a well-watered garden, like a spring whose waters never fail." —Isaiah 58:11

Jesus said to him, "I am the way, the truth, and the life. No one comes to the Father except through Me." —John 14:6 nkjv

Therefore, holy brothers, who share in the heavenly calling, fix your thoughts on Jesus, the apostle and high priest whom we confess. —Hebrews 3:1

Cherished God,

I draw near to You in this quiet moment—seeking to enjoy Your Presence in the present. I've learned that trust and thankfulness are excellent allies in this quest.

If I wallow in the past or worry about the future, my awareness of You grows dim. The more I trust You, the more fully I can live in the present—where Your Presence awaits me.

You've been training me to communicate with You continually. Short prayers such as "I trust You, Jesus" and *"I love You, O Lord, my strength"* keep me close to You. They also increase my confidence that You are lovingly watching over me.

You've shown me that having a thankful attitude is essential for intimacy with You. An ungrateful attitude dishonors You and weakens my relationship with You. Help me remember that *I am receiving a kingdom that cannot be shaken*—no matter what is happening in my life or in the world. This gives me a constant, unshakable reason to *be thankful.* I want to stay close to You and enjoy Your loving Presence by *giving thanks in all circumstances.*

In Your precious Name, Jesus, amen.

"*I love You, O Lord, my strength.*" —Psalm 18:1 nasb 1995

Therefore, since we are receiving a kingdom that cannot be shaken, let us be thankful, and so worship God acceptably with reverence and awe, for our "God is a consuming fire." —Hebrews 12:28–29

Give thanks in all circumstances; for this is the will of God in Christ Jesus for you. —1 Thessalonians 5:18 esv

Faithful God,

Help me to *learn the secret of being content in any and every situation.* I realize that contentment-training is a challenging process— learned through enduring a wide range of difficulties. I thought I was fairly advanced in this training, but then the circumstances of my life got harder. On some days I'm able to cope fairly well with all the stress. On other days I just want *out*! Please teach me how to handle the "other days."

I am so grateful that I can *pour out my heart to You*—acknowledging how frustrated and upset I'm feeling. Just releasing those pent-up feelings in Your Presence does me a world of good. Knowing that You completely understand me *and* my circumstances encourages me even more.

Lord, would You please deepen my awareness of Your continual Presence with me? I know I need to stay in communication with You—talking with You, bathing my mind and heart in scriptures that speak to my situation. And singing praises to You lifts my spirits like nothing else! *It is good to sing praises to Your Name—declaring Your lovingkindness in the morning and Your faithfulness every night.*

In Your loving Name, Jesus, amen.

I know what it is to be in need, and I know what it is to have plenty. I have learned the secret of being content in any and every situation, whether well fed or hungry, whether living in plenty or in want. —PHILIPPIANS 4:12

Trust in him at all times, O people; pour out your hearts to him, for God is our refuge. —PSALM 62:8

It is good to give thanks to the LORD, and to sing praises to Your name, O Most High; to declare Your lovingkindness in the morning, and Your faithfulness every night. —PSALM 92:1–2 NKJV

Powerful Savior,

You tell me in Your Word that *You are able to do immeasurably more than all I ask or imagine.* So I come to You with positive expectations, knowing there is no limit to what You can accomplish!

I confess, though, that I sometimes feel discouraged because so many of my long-term prayers are still unanswered. Please help me to wait patiently—trusting You in the midst of uncertainty. You have promised that *those who wait for You will gain new strength*, and I definitely need more strength.

Instead of letting difficulties draw me into worry, I'm trying to view them as setting the scene for Your glorious intervention. You've shown me that the more extreme my circumstances, the more likely I am to see Your *Power and Glory* at work in the situation. Lord, I long to live with my eyes and my mind fully open—beholding all that You are doing in my life!

In Your holy Name, Jesus, amen.

Now to him who is able to do immeasurably more than all we ask or imagine, according to his power that is at work within us, to him be glory in the church and in Christ Jesus throughout all generations, for ever and ever! Amen. —EPHESIANS 3:20–21

Though youths grow weary and tired, and vigorous young men stumble badly, yet those who wait for the LORD will gain new strength; they will mount up with wings like eagles, they will run and not get tired, they will walk and not become weary. —ISAIAH 40:30–31 NASB 1995

So I have looked upon you in the sanctuary, beholding your power and glory. —PSALM 63:2 ESV

My loving God,

You are *my Strength*! I begin this day feeling weak and weary, but that's okay. My weakness is a reminder of my dependence on You. I need to remember that You are continually with me, and *You will help me* as I go along my way. So I take hold of Your hand in joyful trust—asking You to *strengthen me* and guide me. I delight in Your loving Presence!

Whenever I'm feeling inadequate for the task ahead, it's crucial for me to stop and think about my resources. You, my Strength, are infinite: You never run out of anything! So when I work in collaboration with You, I must not set limits on what can be accomplished. Instead, I will depend on You to give me everything I need for this endeavor. Whether I reach the goal quickly or gradually, I know I'll get there in Your perfect timing. Thus, I can refuse to let delays or detours discourage me.

Help me to keep moving forward step by step—and to trust wholeheartedly that You know what You are doing. I'm learning that perseverance and trust make a potent combination!

In Your strong Name, Jesus, amen.

But I will sing of your strength, in the morning I will sing of your love; for you are my fortress, my refuge in times of trouble. O my Strength, I sing praise to you; you, O God, are my fortress, my loving God. —PSALM 59:16–17

"For I am the LORD, your God, who takes hold of your right hand and says to you, Do not fear; I will help you." —ISAIAH 41:13

I can do all things through Him who strengthens me. —PHILIPPIANS 4:13 NASB 1995

Do you not know? Have you not heard? The LORD is the everlasting God, the Creator of the ends of the earth. He will not grow tired or weary, and his understanding no one can fathom. —ISAIAH 40:28–29

Sovereign Lord,

Teach me to trust You—really trust You—with my whole being! If I learn this vital lesson, then nothing will be able to separate me from Your Peace. I know that You are sovereign over every detail of my life. This means that *everything* I endure can be put to good use: training me to trust You more. *This* is how I can foil the works of evil, growing in grace through the very adversity that was meant to harm me. I love the story of Joseph in the Old Testament. He was a prime example of this divine reversal—declaring to his brothers who had sold him into slavery, *"You meant evil against me, but God meant it for good."*

I realize that the more I trust You, the less afraid I will be. As I concentrate on trusting You, please help me relax in Your sovereignty—remembering that You go before me, as well as with me, into each day. So I don't need to fear what this day, or *any* day, may bring my way.

I will fear no evil, for I know You can bring good out of every situation that I will ever encounter!

In Jesus' exalted Name, amen.

Trust in the LORD forever, for the LORD, the LORD,
is the Rock eternal. —ISAIAH 26:4

As for you, you meant evil against me, but God meant it for
good in order to bring about this present result, to preserve
many people alive. —GENESIS 50:20 NASB 1995

For momentary, light affliction is producing for us an eternal weight of
glory far beyond all comparison. —2 CORINTHIANS 4:17 NASB 1995

Even though I walk through the valley of the shadow of death, I will fear no evil,
for you are with me; your rod and your staff, they comfort me. —PSALM 23:4

My Shepherd,

I long to *lie down in green pastures* of Peace. Please help me to unwind, resting in the Presence of my Shepherd—You! This electronic age keeps me "wired" much of the time, too tense to find You in the midst of my moments. Yet You built into my very being the need for rest.

The world is so twisted and broken that it's easy for me to feel guilty about meeting my inborn need for rest. As a result, I waste time and energy staying busy rather than spending time with You—finding refreshment in Your Presence and seeking Your guidance for my life.

Lord Jesus, I want to walk with You down the path of Peace—blazing a trail for others who desire to live in Your peaceful Presence. I know it is not my strengths that have prepared me for this adventure but my weaknesses, which amplify my need for You. I've discovered that the more I depend on You, the more You shower Peace on my path. Thank You, Lord!

In Your tender Name, Jesus, amen.

The LORD is my shepherd, I shall not be in want. He makes me lie down in green pastures, he leads me beside quiet waters, he restores my soul. He guides me in paths of righteousness for his name's sake. —PSALM 23:1–3

And on the seventh day God ended His work which He had done, and He rested on the seventh day from all His work which He had done. Then God blessed the seventh day and sanctified it, because in it He rested from all His work which God had created and made. —GENESIS 2:2–3 NKJV

"To shine on those living in darkness and in the shadow of death, to guide our feet into the path of peace." —LUKE 1:79

My Savior-God,

I rejoice that *You have clothed me with garments of salvation*: Your *robe of righteousness* is mine eternally! Because You are my Savior forever, Your perfect righteousness can never be taken away from me. This means I don't need to be afraid of facing my sins—or dealing with them. As I become aware of sin in my life, I can confess it and receive Your forgiveness in full measure.

Help me also to forgive myself. I know that self-hatred is very unhealthy for me—and it is *not* pleasing to You. To avoid this hurtful snare, I'm learning to take many looks at *You* for every look I take at my sins and failures.

I delight in Your assurances that I am precious in Your sight. I'm so thankful I don't have to prove my worth by trying to be good enough. You lived a perfect life on my behalf because You knew I could not do so. Now I want to live in this glorious freedom of being Your fully forgiven follower—remembering that *there is no condemnation for those who belong to You*!

In Your forgiving Name, Jesus, amen.

I delight greatly in the Lord; my soul rejoices in my God. For he has clothed me with garments of salvation and arrayed me in a robe of righteousness, as a bridegroom adorns his head like a priest, and as a bride adorns herself with her jewels. —Isaiah 61:10

And she will bring forth a Son, and you shall call His name Jesus, for He will save His people from their sins. —Matthew 1:21 nkjv

If we confess our sins, He is faithful and just to forgive us our sins and to cleanse us from all unrighteousness. —1 John 1:9 nkjv

So now there is no condemnation for those who belong to Christ Jesus. —Romans 8:1 nlt

Valiant Jesus,

You are *the Champion who perfects my faith*. You've been teaching me that the more problem-filled my life becomes, the more important it is for me to *keep my eyes on You*. If I gaze too long at my problems or at world events that trouble me, I'm likely to become discouraged. Whenever I'm feeling weighed down or disheartened, please remind me to turn to You. I'm grateful that You are continually with me and You always hear my prayers. Instead of just letting my thoughts run freely, I want to keep directing them to You. This gives traction to my thinking and draws me nearer to You.

Help me to rest in Your embrace, enjoying the nurturing protection of Your Presence. As I survey the landscape of this broken world, I rejoice in Your promise that *nothing can separate me from Your Love*! No matter how bleak things look, I'm comforted by knowing You are still in control. Moreover, You—my Champion who fights for me—*scoff at* those who think they can defeat You.

Lord, I praise You for *Your unfailing Love that surrounds those who trust in You*. I trust You, Jesus!

In Your invincible Name, amen.

Let us strip off every weight that slows us down, especially the sin that so easily trips us up. And let us run with endurance the race God has set before us. We do this by keeping our eyes on Jesus, the champion who initiates and perfects our faith. —HEBREWS 12:1–2 NLT

I am convinced that neither death nor life . . . nor anything else in all creation, will be able to separate us from the love of God that is in Christ Jesus our Lord. —ROMANS 8:38–39

The One enthroned in heaven laughs; the Lord scoffs at them. —PSALM 2:4

Many are the woes of the wicked, but the LORD's unfailing love surrounds the man who trusts in him. —PSALM 32:10

Jesus, my Peace,

Help me to live close to You, remembering that You are my resting place. Since You—my *Prince of Peace*—are both with and within me, I can dwell in this peaceful haven with You.

I long to be able to stay calm in the midst of stressful situations, centering myself in You. We can deal with my problems together, You and I, so there's no need for me to panic when things seem out of control. But I confess that the more difficult my circumstances, the more likely I am to anxiously shift into high gear—forgetting Your steadfast Presence that *strengthens me.*

As soon as I realize I've wandered from Your Presence, I need to return to You immediately. Whispering Your Name reconnects me with You and calms me down. Sometimes I get discouraged because I seem to wander away from You so frequently. However, I'm striving to form a new habit, and I know this takes time and persistent effort. Thank You for showing me that the rewards of this strenuous training are well worth all the effort. I'm finding that the more I return to You—my resting place—the more peaceful and joyful my life becomes.

In Your wonderful Name, amen.

For to us a child is born, to us a son is given, and the government will be on his shoulders. And he will be called Wonderful Counselor, Mighty God, Everlasting Father, Prince of Peace. —ISAIAH 9:6

I can do all things through Christ who strengthens me. —PHILIPPIANS 4:13 NKJV

The name of the LORD is a strong tower; the righteous run to it and are safe. —PROVERBS 18:10

"Come to Me, all who are weary and heavy-laden, and I will give you rest." —MATTHEW 11:28 NASB 1995

Glorious God,

Your Word teaches that *I am being transformed into Your image from Glory to Glory.* I find this verse both comforting and thrilling! I'm grateful that Your Spirit is orchestrating this massive work in me. When I face difficulties in my life, I don't want to waste those challenging circumstances. Instead, I can invite You to use them to transform me more and more into Your likeness. This may be a painful process, but I know that Your wisdom, ways, and will are perfect. I need to be willing to *suffer with You so I may also be glorified with You.*

Even though my troubles sometimes seem heavy and endless, I realize they're really just *light and momentary*—compared to the *eternal Glory they are achieving for me.* I'm learning to thank You for my hard times and praise You for ongoing troubles, regardless of how I'm feeling. I want to glorify You by *always giving thanks,* even in the midst of adversity—because of who You are and all that You've done for me. Moreover, a thankful attitude helps me make progress in my transformation from Glory to Glory!

In Your beautiful Name, Jesus, amen.

But we all . . . beholding as in a mirror the glory of the Lord, are being transformed into the same image from glory to glory, just as by the Spirit of the Lord. —2 Corinthians 3:18 nkjv

And if children, then heirs (namely, heirs of God and also fellow heirs with Christ) —if indeed we suffer with him so we may also be glorified with him. —Romans 8:17 net

For our light and momentary troubles are achieving for us an eternal glory that far outweighs them all. —2 Corinthians 4:17

Sing and make music in your heart to the Lord, always giving thanks to God the Father for everything. —Ephesians 5:19–20

Mighty God,

Help me to trust You by relinquishing control into Your hands—letting go, *knowing that You are God*. This is *Your* world: You made it and You control it. My part in the litany of Love is to be responsive to You. You have planted in my soul a gift of receptivity to Your Presence. I want to guard this gift and nurture it with the Light of Your Love.

I rejoice that You encourage me to speak candidly to You—*pouring out my heart* as I express my concerns and bring You my requests. After opening up to You, I like to thank You for answering my prayers even though I don't yet see results. When the problems come to mind again, please remind me to continue thanking You for the answers that are on the way.

I've found that when I tell You about my concerns over and over again, I live in a state of tension. But if I thank You for how You *are* answering my prayers, my mind-set becomes much more positive and peaceful. Thankful prayers keep my focus on Your Presence and on *Your great and precious promises*.

In Your excellent Name, Jesus, amen.

"Cease striving and know that I am God." —PSALM 46:10 NASB 1995

Pour out your hearts to him, for God is our refuge. —PSALM 62:8

Devote yourselves to prayer, being watchful and thankful. —COLOSSIANS 4:2

His divine power has given us everything we need for life and godliness through our knowledge of him who called us by his own glory and goodness. Through these he has given us his very great and precious promises, so that through them you may participate in the divine nature and escape the corruption in the world caused by evil desires. —2 PETER 1:3–4

All-knowing God,

When my spirit grows faint within me, it is You who know my way. This is one of the benefits of weakness; it highlights the reality that I cannot find my way without Your guidance. Whenever I'm feeling weary or confused, I can choose to look away from these feelings and turn wholeheartedly toward You. As I pour out my heart to You, I find rest in the Presence of the One who knows my way perfectly—all the way to heaven.

Help me to continue this practice of gazing at You even during the times when I'm feeling confident and strong. This is when I am most at risk of going in the wrong direction. Instead of assuming that I know the next step of my journey, I'm learning to make my plans in Your Presence—asking You to guide me.

Please remind me often that *Your ways and thoughts are higher than mine, as the heavens are higher than the earth.* Remembering this great truth draws me into worshiping You, *the High and Lofty One who inhabits eternity.* I rejoice that even though *You dwell in the high and holy place,* You reach down to show me the way I should go.

In Your exalted Name, Jesus, amen.

When my spirit grows faint within me, it is you who know my way. In the path where I walk men have hidden a snare for me. —PSALM 142:3

"As the heavens are higher than the earth, so are my ways higher than your ways and my thoughts than your thoughts." —ISAIAH 55:9

For thus says the High and Lofty One who inhabits eternity, whose name is Holy: "I dwell in the high and holy place, with him who has a contrite and humble spirit, to revive the spirit of the humble, and to revive the heart of the contrite ones." —ISAIAH 57:15 NKJV

Beloved Jesus,

Your Word tells me to *sing to You because You have dealt bountifully with me.* I confess that sometimes singing praises is the last thing I feel like doing, but that's when I need it the most. You have indeed dealt bountifully with me—even when it doesn't seem that way. I've been on an uphill journey with You, and I'm growing weary. I yearn for some easy days, for a path that is not so steep. But I realize it is the strenuous climbs that take me ever upward—closer and closer to the summit.

Help me remember that the difficulty of my circumstances is *not* a mistake. It's a matter of Your sovereign will and—to some extent—my own goals. I desire to live close to You and to grow more fully into the one You created me to be. Pursuing these goals has put me on an adventurous trail where difficulties and dangers abound.

Sometimes I compare my life-path with those of people whose lives seem easier than mine. But I don't fully comprehend the problems they face, nor do I know what the future holds for them. Instead of comparing my circumstances with those of others, I need to turn to You and listen as You instruct me, *"You follow Me!"*

In Your bountiful Name, amen.

I will sing to the Lord, because He has dealt
bountifully with me. —Psalm 13:6 nkjv

It is God who arms me with strength and makes my way perfect. He makes my feet
like the feet of a deer; he enables me to stand on the heights. —2 Samuel 22:33–34

Jesus said to him, "If I want him to remain until I come, what is
that to you? You follow Me!" —John 21:22 nasb 1995

Merciful Jesus,

I want to lean on You more and more. Only *You* know the full extent of my weakness, and Your powerful Presence meets me at that very place. Your strength and my weakness fit together perfectly—in a beautiful pattern designed long before my birth. In fact, Your Word tells me that *Your Power shows itself most effectively in weakness.*

Whenever I'm feeling inadequate or overwhelmed, I love being able to lean on You, Lord. You remind me that I am more than adequate when I rely on You to *strengthen me.* I rejoice in Your encouraging words from Scripture: *"I take hold of your right hand and say to you, 'Do not fear; I will help you.'"*

Even when I feel competent to handle something myself, I need to depend on You. I know You are infinitely wise! Please guide my thinking as I make plans and decisions. I'm thankful that leaning on You builds bonds of intimacy with You—the One who *will never leave me or forsake me.*

In Your wise, comforting Name, amen.

But He has said to me, "My grace is sufficient for you [My lovingkindness and My mercy are more than enough —always available —regardless of the situation]; for [My] power is being perfected [and is completed and shows itself most effectively] in [your] weakness." Therefore, I will all the more gladly boast in my weaknesses, so that the power of Christ [may completely enfold me and] may dwell in me. —2 CORINTHIANS 12:9 AMP

I can do all things through Christ who strengthens me. —PHILIPPIANS 4:13 NKJV

"For I am the LORD, your God, who takes hold of your right hand and says to you, Do not fear; I will help you." —ISAIAH 41:13

"Be strong and courageous. Do not be afraid or terrified because of them, for the LORD your God goes with you; he will never leave you nor forsake you." —DEUTERONOMY 31:6

Compassionate Lord Jesus,

You've been teaching me to *rejoice always*—connecting my Joy to You first and foremost. It comforts me to remember that You love me at all times and in all circumstances. As Your Word assures me: *Though the mountains be shaken and the hills be removed, yet Your unfailing Love for me will not be shaken.* So I must not give in to the temptation to doubt Your Love when things don't go as I would like or when I've failed in some way. Your loving Presence is the solid rock on which I can *always* stand—knowing that in You I am eternally secure. I'm grateful that You are *the Lord who has compassion on me!*

I've found that *giving thanks in all circumstances* increases my Joy immensely. Please help me to view my life through a grid of gratitude more and more. Even during my toughest times, I can search for Your blessings scattered along my path—and thank You for each one that I find. To look steadily through a lens of thankfulness, I need to *think about excellent and praiseworthy things—true, noble, right, pure, lovely, admirable things.*

In Your exquisite Name, amen.

Rejoice always, pray without ceasing, give thanks in all circumstances; for this is the will of God in Christ Jesus for you. —1 THESSALONIANS 5:16–18 ESV

"Though the mountains be shaken and the hills be removed, yet my unfailing love for you will not be shaken nor my covenant of peace be removed," says the LORD, *who has compassion on you.* —ISAIAH 54:10

Finally, brothers, whatever is true, whatever is noble, whatever is right, whatever is pure, whatever is lovely, whatever is admirable —if anything is excellent or praiseworthy —think about such things. —PHILIPPIANS 4:8

Glorious Lord,

You are training me not only to endure my difficulties but to collaborate with You as You transform them into Glory. This is a supernatural feat—requiring the help of Your Spirit. When problems are weighing heavily on me, my natural tendency is to speed up my pace, frantically searching for answers. But what I really need at such times is to slow down, *seek Your Face*, and discuss my difficulties with You. Your Word instructs me to *lay my requests before You and wait in expectation.*

Even though I'm waiting expectantly, I realize You may not answer my prayers for a long time. You are always doing something important in my life—far beyond simply solving my problems. You've been showing me that my struggles are part of a much larger battle, and the way I handle them can contribute to significant outcomes. I want to glorify You by trusting You and *praying with thanksgiving.* Moreover, this practice of praying persistently will eventually make a difference in *me*, as Your Spirit works to *transform me into Your image with ever-increasing Glory*!

In Your wondrous Name, Jesus, amen.

Seek the LORD and His strength; seek His face
continually. —PSALM 105:4 NASB 1995

In the morning, O LORD, you hear my voice; in the morning I lay
my requests before you and wait in expectation. —PSALM 5:3

Do not be anxious about anything, but in everything, by prayer and petition,
with thanksgiving, present your requests to God. —PHILIPPIANS 4:6

And we, who with unveiled faces all reflect the Lord's glory, are being
transformed into his likeness with ever-increasing glory, which comes
from the Lord, who is the Spirit. —2 CORINTHIANS 3:18

Dear Jesus,

You are the Risen One—my *living God*. I celebrate the Joy of serving a Savior who is so exuberantly alive! I rejoice also in Your promise to be with me continually—throughout time and eternity. These truths can sustain me through my worst trials and deepest disappointments. So help me to walk boldly with You along the path of Life, trusting confidently that You will never let go of my hand.

I delight in thinking about all that You offer me: Your loving Presence, complete forgiveness of my sins, and forever-pleasures in heaven. This is all so extravagant and lavish that I can't even begin to comprehend it! That is why worshiping You is so important to me. It's a powerful way of connecting with You that transcends my ever-so-limited understanding.

I enjoy worshiping You in a variety of ways—singing hymns and praise songs, studying and memorizing Your Word, praying individually and with others, glorying in the wonders of Your creation. Another way I worship You is by serving others and loving them with Your Love. *Whatever I do*, Lord, I want to *do it all for Your Glory*!

In Your victorious Name, amen.

The angel said to the women, "Do not be afraid, for I know that you are looking for Jesus, who was crucified. He is not here; he has risen, just as he said. Come and see the place where he lay." —MATTHEW 28:5–6

My soul thirsts for God, for the living God. When can I go and meet with God? —PSALM 42:2

All the treasures of wisdom and knowledge are hidden in Him. —COLOSSIANS 2:3 HCSB

So whether you eat or drink or whatever you do, do it all for the glory of God. —1 CORINTHIANS 10:31

Triumphant God,

Your Word poses the rhetorical question: *"If God is for us, who can be against us?"* I trust that You are indeed *for me* since I am Your follower. I realize this verse does not mean that no one will ever oppose me. It does mean that having *You* on my side is the most important fact of my existence.

Regardless of what losses I experience, I am on the winning side. You have already won the decisive victory through Your death and resurrection! You are the eternal Victor, and I share in Your triumph because I belong to You forever. No matter how much adversity I encounter on my journey to heaven, nothing can ultimately prevail against me!

Knowing that my future is utterly secure is changing my perspective dramatically. Instead of living in defensive mode—striving to protect myself from suffering—I am learning to follow You confidently, wherever You lead. You are teaching me not only to *seek Your Face* and follow Your lead but to enjoy this adventure of abandoning myself to You. I rejoice that You are with me continually and *You are always ready to help me in times of trouble.*

In Your magnificent Name, Jesus, amen.

What, then, shall we say in response to this? If God is for us, who can be against us? —ROMANS 8:31

When You said, "Seek My face," my heart said to You, "Your face, LORD, I will seek." —PSALM 27:8 NKJV

God is our refuge and strength, always ready to help in times of trouble. —PSALM 46:1 NLT

All-satisfying God,

My soul thirsts for You—for the living God. The deepest yearnings of my heart are for intimacy with You, Lord. I'm thankful You designed me to desire You, and I delight in *seeking Your Face.* Help me not to feel guilty about taking so much time to be still in Your Presence. I'm simply responding to the tugs of Your Spirit within me. You made me in Your image, and You hid heaven in my heart. My longing for You is a form of homesickness—a yearning for my true home in heaven.

I realize my journey is different from that of other people, and I need courage to persevere. Yet I trust that the path You have called me to travel with You is exquisitely right for me. I've found that the more closely I follow Your leading, the more fully You develop my gifts. In order to follow You wholeheartedly, I need to relinquish my desire to please others. Still, my closeness to You can be a source of blessing to other people—as You enable me to *reflect Your Glory* in this dark world.

In Your bright, shining Name, Jesus, amen.

As the deer pants for streams of water, so my soul pants for you, O God. My soul thirsts for God, for the living God. When can I go and meet with God? —PSALM 42:1–2

Seek the LORD and His strength; seek His face continually. —1 CHRONICLES 16:11 NASB 1995

Those who look to him are radiant; their faces are never covered with shame. —PSALM 34:5

And we, who with unveiled faces all reflect the Lord's glory, are being transformed into his likeness with ever-increasing glory, which comes from the Lord, who is the Spirit. —2 CORINTHIANS 3:18

July

Therefore, there is now no condemnation for those who are in Christ Jesus. —ROMANS 8:1

Infinitely wise God,

I know that You are good, but Your ways are often mysterious. When I look at world events—with so much rampant evil—it's easy for me to feel fearful and discouraged. I find it impossible to fathom why You allow such cruelty and suffering. Of course, I recognize that You are infinite and I am not. There are so many things that are simply beyond my ability to comprehend.

Thankfully, every time I reach the limits of my understanding, I can keep moving onward by relying on my trust in You. Help me to stay in communication with You through silent and spoken prayers—*trusting in You with all my heart* instead of *leaning on my understanding.*

I don't want to be stuck in a presumptuous posture of demanding to know why things happen as they do. I realize it's much better to ask: "How do You want me to view this situation?" and "What do You want me to do right now?" Though I can't change the past, I can start with the present moment and seek to find Your way forward.

Lord, teach me to trust You one day at a time. Let me hear You whispering this precious assurance, *"Do not fear; I will help You."*

In Your trustworthy Name, Jesus, amen.

Trust in the LORD with all your heart, and do not lean on your own understanding. —PROVERBS 3:5 ESV

The wicked plot against the righteous and gnash their teeth at them; but the Lord laughs at the wicked, for he knows their day is coming. —PSALM 37:12–13

"For I am the LORD, your God, who takes hold of your right hand and says to you, Do not fear; I will help you." —ISAIAH 41:13

Glorious Savior,

I'm grateful that You are *in my midst* and You are mighty. Just as the sun is at the center of the solar system, *You* are at the center of my entire being—physical, emotional, and spiritual. You, *the Mighty One* who created the universe, *live in me*! I want to take time to absorb this amazing truth—letting it reverberate in my mind and soak into my innermost being.

I delight in pondering what it means to have so much Power dwelling within me. As I think about Your powerful Presence, I realize I don't need to worry about my lack of strength. Moreover, I'm comforted to know that *Your Power is completed and shows itself most effectively in my weakness.*

Jesus, please remind me frequently that You live in me and You are mighty! I ask that my awareness of Your indwelling Presence may drive out discouragement and fill me with Joy. I'm so thankful that Your Life flows into me continually, strengthening me with Your divine might.

In Your mighty Name, Jesus, amen.

"The LORD your God in your midst, the Mighty One, will save; He will rejoice over you with gladness, He will quiet you with His love." —ZEPHANIAH 3:17 NKJV

I have been crucified with Christ and I no longer live, but Christ lives in me. —GALATIANS 2:20

Now to him who is able to do immeasurably more than all we ask or imagine, according to his power that is at work within us. —EPHESIANS 3:20

But He has said to me, "My grace is sufficient for you . . . for [My] power is being perfected [and is completed and shows itself most effectively] in [your] weakness." Therefore, I will all the more gladly boast in my weaknesses, so that the power of Christ [may completely enfold me and] may dwell in me. —2 CORINTHIANS 12:9 AMP

Precious Jesus,

Help me to look for You—and find You—in the hard places of my life. It's easy for me to find You in answered prayer, in beauty and heartfelt Joy. But I know You are also tenderly present in my difficulties. Teach me to view my problems as opportunities to grow in grace, experiencing Your loving Presence in greater depth and breadth. I must search for *You* in my dark times—both past and present. When I'm troubled by thoughts of hurtful experiences in my past, I'll look for You in those painful memories. You know all about them, and You are ready to meet me there. I can invite You into those broken places and collaborate with You in putting the fragments back together in *new* ways.

When I'm walking through tough times in the present, please remind me to keep clinging to Your hand. Against the dark backdrop of adversity, the Light of Your Presence shines in transcendent radiance. This Light blesses me abundantly. It provides both comfort and guidance—illuminating the way forward step by step. As I seek to walk close to You, please draw me into deeper, richer intimacy with You.

In Your compassionate Name, amen.

If I say, "Surely the darkness will overwhelm me, and the light around me will be night," even the darkness is not dark to You, and the night is as bright as the day. Darkness and light are alike to You. —Psalm 139:11–12 nasb 1995

His life is the light that shines through the darkness —and the darkness can never extinguish it. —John 1:5 tlb

Yet I am always with you; you hold me by my right hand. You guide me with your counsel, and afterward you will take me into glory. —Psalm 73:23–24

Invincible Jesus,

Your Love has conquered me and *set me free*! The Power of Your Love is so great that it has enslaved me to You. *I am not my own; I was bought with a price*—Your holy blood. Because of Your amazing sacrifice for me, I want to serve You with every fiber of my being. I know that my service is woefully inadequate. Nonetheless, when I yield myself to Your will, You bless me with Joy.

Because You are perfect in all Your ways, I can give myself whole-heartedly to You without fear that You might take advantage of me. Actually, being conquered by You protects me and makes me truly free. You have invaded the innermost core of my being, and Your Spirit is taking over more and more territory within me. As Your Word teaches, *where the Spirit of the Lord is, there is freedom*. I rejoice in the freedom I have found in You, Jesus. And I surrender gladly to Your conquering Love!

In Your powerful, loving Name, amen.

But thanks be to God that, though you used to be slaves to sin, you wholeheartedly obeyed the form of teaching to which you were entrusted. You have been set free from sin and have become slaves to righteousness. —ROMANS 6:17–18

Or do you not know that your body is a temple of the Holy Spirit within you, whom you have from God? You are not your own, for you were bought with a price. So glorify God in your body. —1 CORINTHIANS 6:19–20 ESV

Now the Lord is the Spirit, and where the Spirit of the Lord is, there is freedom. —2 CORINTHIANS 3:17

Gracious God,

You are so great, glorious, and compassionate that it's impossible to praise or thank You too much! *You inhabit the praises of Your people,* and I delight in drawing near You through worship. Sometimes my adoration is a spontaneous overflow of Joy—in response to rich blessings or radiant beauty. At other times my praise is more disciplined and measured—an act of my will. I'm grateful that You dwell in both types of praise.

I've discovered that thankfulness is a wonderful way to enjoy Your Presence. A grateful heart has plenty of room for You. When I thank You for the many good gifts You bestow, I affirm that You are the One from whom all blessings flow. Help me to thank You also in the midst of adversity—trusting in Your goodness *and* Your sovereignty.

Please teach me how to fill up the spare moments of my life with praise and thanksgiving. This joyous discipline will enable me to live in the intimacy of Your loving Presence.

In Your praiseworthy Name, Jesus, amen.

But thou art holy, O thou that inhabitest the praises of Israel. —PSALM 22:3 KJV

Praise the LORD. Praise the LORD, O my soul. I will praise the LORD all my life; I will sing praise to my God as long as I live. —PSALM 146:1–2

Give thanks in all circumstances, for this is God's will for you in Christ Jesus. —1 THESSALONIANS 5:18

Enter His gates with thanksgiving and His courts with praise. Give thanks to Him and praise His name. —PSALM 100:4 HCSB

Majestic Jesus,

I come joyfully into Your Presence, my *Prince of Peace*. I love to hear You whispering the words You spoke to Your fearful disciples: *"Peace be with you!"* I rejoice that Your Peace is always with me because You are my constant Companion. When I keep my focus on You, I can experience both Your Presence and Your Peace. You are worthy of all my worship—for You are King of kings, Lord of lords, and Prince of Peace.

I need Your Peace each moment in order to accomplish Your purposes in my life. I confess that sometimes I'm tempted to take shortcuts—to reach my goals as quickly as possible. But I'm learning that if the shortcuts involve turning away from Your peaceful Presence, I must choose the longer route.

Lord, please help me to keep walking with You along *the path of Peace*—enjoying the journey in Your Presence.

In Your worthy Name, amen.

For to us a child is born, to us a son is given, and the government will be on his shoulders. And he will be called Wonderful Counselor, Mighty God, Everlasting Father, Prince of Peace. —Isaiah 9:6

On the evening of that first day of the week, when the disciples were together, with the doors locked for fear of the Jews, Jesus came and stood among them and said, "Peace be with you!" —John 20:19

Show me Your ways, O Lord; teach me Your paths. —Psalm 25:4 nkjv

"To shine on those living in darkness and in the shadow of death, to guide our feet into the path of peace." —Luke 1:79

Everlasting God,

You, the Creator of the universe, are *with me* and *for me*. You are all I need! When I feel as if something is lacking, it's because I'm not connecting with You at a deep level. You offer me abundant Life. Help me respond to Your abundance by receiving Your blessings gratefully—trusting in Your provision and refusing to worry about anything.

I'm learning that it's not primarily the adverse events in my world that make me anxious; the main culprit is my thoughts about those events. When something troubles me, my mind starts working strenuously to take control of the situation—striving to bring about the result I desire. My thoughts close in on the problem like ravenous wolves. Determined to make things go my way, I forget that *You* are in charge of my life. At such times, I desperately need to switch my focus from the problem to Your Presence. Teach me how to stop my anxious striving and *wait for You—watching in hope* to see what You will do. You are *God my Savior*!

In Your redeeming Name, Jesus, amen.

*"Don't be afraid, for I am with you. Don't be discouraged, for I am your God. I will strengthen you and help you. I will hold you up with my victorious right hand." —*ISAIAH 41:10 NLT

*What, then, shall we say in response to this? If God is for us, who can be against us? He who did not spare his own Son, but gave him up for us all —how will he not also, along with him, graciously give us all things? —*ROMANS 8:31–32

*"The thief comes only to steal and kill and destroy. I came that they may have life and have it abundantly." —*JOHN 10:10 ESV

But as for me, I watch in hope for the LORD, *I wait for God my Savior; my God will hear me. —*MICAH 7:7

My loving Lord,

You are good and Your Love endures forever! The best response to this promise is *giving thanks to You and praising Your Name*. Please help me to do this more consistently.

Lord, I'm so grateful for Your goodness! If there were even a speck of badness in You, I would be in uttermost peril. But Your absolute goodness guarantees that You always do what is best. I say this as a statement of faith because I live in such a fractured, fallen world. So it's essential that I *walk by faith, not by sight*, as I journey through the wilderness of this world.

Giving You thanks and praising Your Name are ways I find strength for my journey. Thanksgiving and worship lift my perspective from my worries and woes to the glorious Treasure I have in You, Jesus. Thankfulness puts me in proper alignment with You—my Creator and Savior. Worship deepens and enriches my intimacy with You. I rejoice that the more I praise You, the closer to You I grow. As I spend time worshiping You, I delight in remembering that *Your steadfast Love endures forever*!

In Your faithful Name, Jesus, amen.

Enter his gates with thanksgiving and his courts with praise; give thanks to him and praise his name. For the LORD is good and his love endures forever; his faithfulness continues through all generations. —PSALM 100:4–5

For we walk by faith, not by sight. —2 CORINTHIANS 5:7 NKJV

Give thanks to the LORD, for he is good, for his steadfast love endures forever. —PSALM 136:1 ESV

Beloved Jesus,

I come to You feeling *weary and burdened.* Please *give me rest,* and refresh me in the Peace of Your Presence. I'm thankful that *Your Peace,* which *transcends all understanding,* is available at all times and in all circumstances.

Teach me to *hide in the secret place of Your Presence* even as I carry out my duties in the world. Because You are unlimited by time and space, You're able to walk beside me step by step, while going before me to open up the way ahead. There could never be another companion as faithful and wonderful as You!

Since You are my constant Companion, I long for there to be a lightness to my steps that's observable to others. Help me not to be weighed down with problems and unresolved issues. Instead, I want to bring my burdens to You—asking You to carry them. You tell me in Your Word that *I will have trials and distress in the world,* but I don't have to let trouble drag me down. *You have conquered the world and deprived it of power to harm me. In You I may have perfect Peace and confidence.*

In Your conquering Name, amen.

*"Come to Me, all of you who are weary and burdened, and I will give you rest." —*Matthew 11:28 hcsb

*The peace of God, which transcends all understanding, will guard your hearts and your minds in Christ Jesus. —*Philippians 4:7

*You hide [those who fear you] in the secret place of Your presence from the conspiracies of man. —*Psalm 31:20 nasb 1995

*"I have told you these things, so that in Me you may have [perfect] peace and confidence. In the world you have tribulation and trials . . . but be of good cheer . . . ! For I have overcome the world. [I have deprived it of power to harm you and have conquered it for you.]" —*John 16:33 ampc

Delightful Lord,

Your comforts delight my soul. This world presents me with a *multitude of anxieties*—too numerous for me to count. Everywhere I look, I see problems and trouble. In the midst of all this mess, I need to look to You over and over again. When I whisper Your Name, "Jesus," my awareness of Your Presence is renewed. My perspective changes dramatically as Your Presence lights up my mind—brightening my worldview. Your comforts delight my soul and soothe my troubled heart.

I realize I would never experience the pleasure of receiving comfort from You if the world were perfect. So instead of letting problems discourage me, I can choose to view them as reminders to seek *You*—Your Presence, Your Peace, Your Love. These invisible realities are always available to me, and they provide *Joy that no one will take away from me.*

I am blessed and encouraged by Your comforting invitation: *"Come to Me, all you who are weary and burdened, and I will give you rest."* Lord Jesus, I come to You.

In Your wonderful Name, Jesus, amen.

In the multitude of my anxieties within me, Your comforts delight my soul. —PSALM 94:19 NKJV

"A woman giving birth to a child has pain because her time has come; but when her baby is born she forgets the anguish because of her joy that a child is born into the world. So with you: Now is your time of grief, but I will see you again and you will rejoice, and no one will take away your joy." —JOHN 16:21–22

"Come to me, all you who are weary and burdened, and I will give you rest." —MATTHEW 11:28

Mighty God,

I'm thankful that *You are able to do immeasurably more than all I ask or imagine.* I like to think big when I pray, but I know that You always think much bigger! You are continually at work in my life, even when I can see nothing happening.

I tend to feel stuck in situations I'd like to change because I can see only the present moment. But *You* look at the big picture—all the moments of my life—and You are doing far more than I can comprehend.

Please help me stay in communication with You as I go through this day. I want to begin the day in joyful awareness of Your Presence—bringing You my praises and requests. This time of focusing my attention on You makes it easier to continue talking with You as I go about my activities.

I've learned that the longer I wait to start communicating with You, the more effort it takes. So I like to come to You early, while the day is young and distractions are few. Sometimes I think I can't spare the time for this, but then I remember that I don't do my tasks alone. I work alongside the One *who can do more than I ask or imagine*!

In Your glorious Name, Jesus, amen.

Now to him who is able to do immeasurably more than all we ask or imagine, according to his power that is at work within us. —EPHESIANS 3:20

Jesus looked at them and said, "With man this is impossible, but with God all things are possible." —MATTHEW 19:26

Your eyes saw me when I was formless; all my days were written in Your book and planned before a single one of them began. —PSALM 139:16 HCSB

In the morning, O LORD, you hear my voice; in the morning I lay my requests before you and wait in expectation. —PSALM 5:3

My Jesus,

Help me to *be joyful always and pray continually*. I've learned that the only way I can keep rejoicing is to find moment-by-moment pleasure in my relationship with You—the One who is always with me. This relationship is so full of comfort and encouragement that it's possible for me to *be joyful in hope* even when I'm struggling with adversity.

Your Word instructs me to *give thanks in all circumstances*. I've found it immensely beneficial to pray, "Thank You, Jesus." This three-word prayer is appropriate for all times and circumstances because of Your supreme sacrifice for me—for all who know You as Savior. You've been teaching me to praise You for every good thing as soon as I become aware of it. And I've seen how this practice adds sparkle to my blessings.

When I'm feeling sad or discouraged, it is still a good time to thank You. This brightens my perspective and demonstrates my trust in You. Thanking You in every situation strengthens my relationship with You and increases my Joy.

In Your joyous Name, amen.

Be joyful always; pray continually; give thanks in all circumstances, for this is God's will for you in Christ Jesus. —1 Thessalonians 5:16–18

Be joyful in hope, patient in affliction, faithful in prayer. —Romans 12:12

In him we have redemption through his blood, the forgiveness of sins, in accordance with the riches of God's grace that he lavished on us with all wisdom and understanding. —Ephesians 1:7–8

Let us come before His presence with thanksgiving; let us make a joyful noise to Him with songs of praise! —Psalm 95:2 AMPC

My perfect Guide,

You are my Shepherd who guides and shields me. You're the perfect Shepherd, and Your care for me is wonderfully complete: You love me with endless, *unfailing Love.* You know *everything* about me—my weaknesses and limitations, my struggles and sins, my strengths and abilities. So You are able to shepherd me like no other!

Help me walk through this perilous world in trusting dependence on You. I know that You go before me and open up the way, carefully preparing the path I will follow. I'm counting on You to remove many dangers and obstacles from the road ahead—and to provide all I need for coping with the difficulties that remain.

Even when I walk through the darkest valley, I will not be afraid, for You are close beside me. Your nearness comforts and delights me. As I stay in communication with You, I trust You to guide me faithfully through this day—and all my days. *For You are my God forever and ever; You will be my Guide even to the end.*

In Your comforting Name, Jesus, amen.

The Lord is my Shepherd [to feed, guide, and shield me], I shall not lack. —PSALM 23:1 AMPC

"In your unfailing love you will lead the people you have redeemed. In your strength you will guide them to your holy dwelling." —EXODUS 15:13

Even when I walk through the darkest valley, I will not be afraid, for you are close beside me. Your rod and your staff protect and comfort me. —PSALM 23:4 NLT

For this God is our God for ever and ever; he will be our guide even to the end. —PSALM 48:14

Blessed Jesus,

I invite You to permeate my moments with Your Presence so I can see things from Your perspective. When I'm around someone who irritates me, I'm prone to focus on that person's flaws. Instead of this negative focus, I need to gaze at *You* through the eyes of my heart and let those irritants wash over me without sinking in. I know that judging other people is a sinful snare—and it draws me away from You. How much better it is to simply *be joyful in You, my Savior!*

Strength and Joy are in Your dwelling place. The more I *fix my eyes on You*, the more You strengthen me and fill me with Joy. Please train my mind to stay aware of You even when other things are demanding my attention. Thank You for creating me with an amazing brain that can be conscious of several things at once. I want to keep my eyes on You, Lord, enjoying the Light of Your Presence continually.

In Your strong Name, amen.

"Do not judge, so that you won't be judged." —MATTHEW 7:1 HCSB

Yet I will rejoice in the LORD, I will be joyful in God my Savior. —HABAKKUK 3:18

Splendor and majesty are before him; strength and joy in his dwelling place. —1 CHRONICLES 16:27

Let us fix our eyes on Jesus, the author and perfecter of our faith, who for the joy set before him endured the cross, scorning its shame, and sat down at the right hand of the throne of God. —HEBREWS 12:2

Holy Lord,

Help me to *worship You in the beauty of holiness.* There is magnificent beauty in the world around me, but none of it is perfectly holy. So *the beauty of holiness* is something I know only in part—for now. But someday *I will know fully, just as I am fully known.*

Even now, awareness of Your holiness draws me into worship. Pondering Your perfections—untainted by even a speck of sin— delights me and fills me with awe. I want to join with the angels in proclaiming: *"Holy, holy, holy is the Lord Almighty; the whole earth is full of Your Glory."*

I'm finding that worshiping You well is transformational; it changes me more and more into the one You designed me to be. I realize that knowing You correctly is vital for genuine worship. Although I can't comprehend You perfectly or completely, I *can* endeavor to know You accurately—as You are revealed in the Bible. Through studying Your Word and deepening my understanding of You, I am transformed and You are glorified—in beautiful worship!

In Your spectacular Name, Jesus, amen.

*Give unto the L*ORD *the glory due to His name; worship the* L*ORD in the beauty of holiness.* —PSALM 29:2 NKJV

Now we see but a poor reflection as in a mirror; then we shall see face to face. Now I know in part; then I shall know fully, even as I am fully known. —1 CORINTHIANS 13:12

*And they were calling to one another: "Holy, holy, holy is the L*ORD *Almighty; the whole earth is full of his glory."* —ISAIAH 6:3

Cherished Jesus,

Help me to rest in Your Presence, trusting that *nothing will be able to separate me from Your Love.* This promise assures me that the worst thing imaginable in my life—that You might stop loving me—is not even in the realm of possibility. I'm grateful that I don't have to perform at a certain standard in order to earn Your Love, *or* to keep it. Instead, I can receive this Love as pure gift—flowing out of Your own perfect righteousness. This means that my connection to You is secure for all eternity!

Since losing Your Love is not possible, I can relax and live *more abundantly.* When things are going well, I want to enjoy those good times freely—without worrying about what is on the road ahead. When I'm facing tough times, I know I can count on You to strengthen me with Your Love. I live in a world where trouble is inescapable, but I'm learning that *in You I may have Peace.* You've been teaching me to *be of good cheer* in the midst of difficulties—finding hope in Your powerful words of assurance: *"I have overcome the world."*

In Your victorious Name, amen.

For I am convinced that neither death nor life, neither angels nor demons, neither the present nor the future, nor any powers, neither height nor depth, nor anything else in all creation, will be able to separate us from the love of God that is in Christ Jesus our Lord. —ROMANS 8:38–39

"The thief does not come except to steal, and to kill, and to destroy. I have come that they may have life, and that they may have it more abundantly." —JOHN 10:10 NKJV

"These things I have spoken to you, that in Me you may have peace. In the world you will have tribulation; but be of good cheer, I have overcome the world." —JOHN 16:33 NKJV

My great God,

Sometimes I hesitate to receive Joy from You, even though I know You have limitless supplies of it. Please help me to receive Your Joy in full measure—opening wide my arms in Your Presence. I've found that the more I rest with You, the more freely Your blessings flow into me. In the Light of Your Love, I am gradually *being transformed from one degree of Glory to another.* Through spending time with You, I begin *to grasp how wide and long and high and deep is Your Love* for me.

Sometimes the relationship You offer me seems too good to be true. You pour Your very Life into me, and all I have to do is receive You. In a world characterized by working and taking, Your directive to rest and receive seems too easy. However, I've discovered that there's a close connection between believing and receiving. As I grow to trust You more fully, I am able to receive You and Your blessings abundantly.

O Lord, I long to *be still* in Your Presence—*and know that You are God.*

In Your blessed Name, Jesus, amen.

We all, with unveiled face, beholding the glory of the Lord, are being transformed into the same image from one degree of glory to another. —2 Corinthians 3:18 esv

I pray that you, being rooted and established in love, may have power, together with all the saints, to grasp how wide and long and high and deep is the love of Christ. —Ephesians 3:17–18

To all who received him, to those who believed in his name, he gave the right to become children of God. —John 1:12

"Be still, and know that I am God; I will be exalted among the nations, I will be exalted in the earth." —Psalm 46:10

My Shepherd,

Please help me to relax and enjoy this day. It's easy for me to get so focused on my goals that I push myself too hard—and neglect my need for rest. I tend to judge myself on the basis of how much I'm accomplishing. I know it's important for me to use the opportunities and abilities You provide, but I want to learn to accept myself as much when I'm relaxing as when I'm achieving.

Teach me how to rest deeply in the truth that I'm a beloved child of God, *saved by grace through faith* in You. I know *this* is my ultimate—and foundational—identity. I rejoice that I've been adopted into Your royal family forever! Instead of striving and straining, I need to stay mindful of who I really am.

I've found that I'm more effective in Your kingdom when I'm comfortable enough in my true identity to balance work and rest. With a refreshed mind, I'm able to think more clearly and biblically. And a *restored soul* enables me to be more loving with other people.

Lord, I long to spend time relaxing in Your Presence today—enjoying the *fresh green pastures* and *still, restful waters* You provide.

In Your refreshing Name, Jesus, amen.

For it is by grace you have been saved, through faith —and this not from yourselves, it is the gift of God —not by works, so that no one can boast. —EPHESIANS 2:8–9

Rest in God alone, my soul, for my hope comes from Him. —PSALM 62:5 HCSB

He restores my soul; He leads me in the paths of righteousness for His name's sake. —PSALM 23:3 NKJV

He makes me lie down in [fresh, tender] green pastures; He leads me beside the still and restful waters. —PSALM 23:2 AMPC

Ever-present God,

This is a time in my life when I must learn to let go—of loved ones, of possessions, of control. To let go of things that are precious to me, I need to rest in Your Presence, where I am complete. As I take time to bask in the Light of Your Love, I'm able to relax more fully. Then my grasping hand gradually opens up—releasing my prized possession into Your care.

You have been teaching me that it's possible to feel secure even in the midst of the most difficult, painful circumstances—through staying aware of Your continual Presence with me. I rejoice that You are always with me *and* You never change. *You are the same yesterday, today, and forever!* As I release more and more things into Your care, I'm blessed by Your assurance that You never let go of my hand. I love to hear You speaking to me through Your Word, *"I am the Lord your God who takes hold of your right hand and says to you, Do not fear; I will help you."* Thank You for being my firm, secure foundation that no one and no circumstance can take away from me.

In Your steadfast, loving Name, Jesus, amen.

*Blessed are those who have learned to acclaim you, who walk
in the light of your presence, O Lord.* —Psalm 89:15

Jesus Christ is the same yesterday, today, and forever. —Hebrews 13:8 nkjv

*"For I am the Lord, your God, who takes hold of your right hand
and says to you, Do not fear; I will help you."* —Isaiah 41:13

Gentle Jesus,

I come to You with my gaping emptiness—knowing that in You I am complete. As I rest quietly in Your Presence, Your glorious Light shines within me. You've been teaching me that facing the emptiness inside me is the prelude to being filled with Your fullness. So I can rejoice on the days when I have to drag myself out of bed, feeling sluggish and inadequate. I'm learning that this sort of day is a perfect opportunity to depend on You in childlike trust.

Please help me persevere in this dependent stance as I go through the day. If I continue walking in trusting reliance on You, at bedtime I discover that Joy and Peace have become my companions. Usually I can't pinpoint the time that these delightful friends joined me on my journey. Still, I can feel the beneficial effects of their companionship.

The perfect end to such a day is a doxology of gratitude—praising You for Your bountiful blessings! *Let everything that has breath praise You, Lord.*

In Your exalted Name, amen.

For God, who said, "Let light shine out of darkness," has shone in our hearts to give the light of the knowledge of the glory of God in the face of Jesus Christ. —2 CORINTHIANS 4:6 ESV

For in Christ all the fullness of the Deity lives in bodily form, and you have been given fullness in Christ, who is the head over every power and authority. —COLOSSIANS 2:9–10

Perseverance must finish its work so that you may be mature and complete, not lacking anything. —JAMES 1:4

Let everything that has breath praise the LORD. Praise the LORD. —PSALM 150:6

My living Lord,

Help me not to be so hard on myself! I know that You can bring good out of everything—even my mistakes. My finite mind tends to look backward, longing to undo decisions I have come to regret. This is such a waste of time and energy, leading only to frustration! Instead of floundering in the past, I want to release my mistakes to You. As I look to You in trust, I'm confident that Your infinite creativity can weave my good choices *and* my bad ones into a lovely design.

I know I'll continue to make mistakes in this life—because I'm only human. You've shown me that thinking I should live an error-free life is a symptom of pride. My failures can actually be a source of blessing—humbling me and giving me empathy for other people in their weaknesses. Also, failure vividly highlights my dependence on You.

I'm grateful that You are able to bring beauty out of the morass of my mistakes. My part is to trust You and watch to see what You will do.

In Your marvelous Name, Jesus, amen.

And we know that for those who love God all things work together for good, for those who are called according to his purpose. —ROMANS 8:28 ESV

Trust in the LORD with all your heart, and do not lean on your own understanding. —PROVERBS 3:5 ESV

When pride comes, then comes disgrace, but with humility comes wisdom. —PROVERBS 11:2

But as for me, I watch in hope for the LORD, I wait for God my Savior; my God will hear me. —MICAH 7:7

Dear Jesus,

Help me to keep climbing this high mountain with You. Sometimes I look back nostalgically at a long-ago stage of my journey—yearning for that easier, less complicated time. But I've come to recognize it for what it was: a base camp. It was a time and place of preparation for the arduous adventure that was ahead of me.

This mountain that I'm climbing is exceedingly tall; the top of it is hidden in clouds. So it's impossible for me to know how far up the heights I've already come—and how far I have yet to go. However, the higher I go, the better view I have.

Although each day is a challenge and I often feel weary, I can still enjoy the magnificent scenery. This journey with You is training me to see from a heavenly perspective that transcends my circumstances. The higher up this mountain I climb, the steeper and more challenging the trail becomes—but the greater my adventure as well. Please keep reminding me that the higher I go with You, the closer I get to my *ultimate* goal: the heights of heaven—an eternity with You!

In Your breathtaking Name, amen.

Now after six days Jesus took Peter, James, and John his brother, led them up on a high mountain by themselves; and He was transfigured before them. His face shone like the sun, and His clothes became as white as the light. —MATTHEW 17:1–2 NKJV

The LORD GOD is my strength . . . He has made my feet [steady and sure] like hinds' feet and makes me walk [forward with spiritual confidence] on my high places [of challenge and responsibility]. —HABAKKUK 3:19 AMP

Our citizenship is in heaven. And we eagerly await a Savior from there, the Lord Jesus Christ. —PHILIPPIANS 3:20

My King,

Your thoughts are not my thoughts; neither are Your ways my ways. As the heavens are higher than the earth, so are Your ways and thoughts higher than mine.

Help me to rejoice as I ponder how great You are. I marvel at the wonder of being able to commune with You—the King of the universe—any time, any place! Please don't ever let me take this amazing prayer-privilege for granted.

Even though You are infinitely higher and greater than I am, You're training me to think Your thoughts. As I spend time in Your Presence—reading Your Word and praying—Your thoughts gradually form in my mind. I realize that Your Spirit is the Director of this process. He guides my mind while I'm waiting in Your Presence, making plans or mulling over problems. Sometimes He brings specific Bible verses to mind just when I need them.

These communications strengthen me and prepare me for whatever is before me on my life-path. Lord, spending time with You has blessed me far more than I dared to ask—or even imagine!

In Your majestic Name, Jesus, amen.

"For my thoughts are not your thoughts, neither are your ways my ways," declares the Lord. *"As the heavens are higher than the earth, so are my ways higher than your ways and my thoughts than your thoughts." —*Isaiah 55:8–9

*Devote yourselves to prayer, being watchful and thankful. —*Colossians 4:2

*"But the Helper, the Holy Spirit, whom the Father will send in My name, He will teach you all things, and bring to your remembrance all things that I said to you." —*John 14:26 nkjv

My guiding God,

Thank You for this day of life; I receive it as a precious, one-of-a-kind gift. And I trust that You are with me each moment, whether I can sense Your Presence or not. Having a thankful, trusting attitude enables me to see events in my life from Your perspective. Please increase my thankfulness and trust in You more and more.

Help me to view today as an adventure, carefully planned out by You—my Guide. Instead of staring into this day that is before me, attempting to make it go according to my will, I want to be attentive to You and to all You've prepared for me.

I'm thankful that a life lived close to You is never dull or predictable. I can expect to encounter some surprises each day. Instead of following my natural tendency—to search for the easiest route through the day—I want to follow *You*, wherever You lead. No matter how steep or treacherous the path that lies before me, I don't need to be afraid. You are always near.

In Your protecting Name, Jesus, amen.

This is the day the LORD has made; we will rejoice and be glad in it. —PSALM 118:24 NKJV

"So do not fear, for I am with you; do not be dismayed, for I am your God. I will strengthen you and help you; I will uphold you with my righteous right hand." —ISAIAH 41:10

Whenever I am afraid, I will trust in You. —PSALM 56:3 NKJV

The LORD is near to all who call on him, to all who call on him in truth. —PSALM 145:18

Eternal God,

I come to You, yearning to rest in *Your everlasting arms.* I'm trying to view my weakness as an opportunity to grow strong in awareness of Your Almighty Presence. When my energy fails me, I tend to look inward and lament the lack I find there. Help me instead to look to You and Your sufficiency—rejoicing in Your radiant riches that are abundantly available to me.

I need to go gently through this day, leaning on You and enjoying Your Presence. I'm learning to thank You for my neediness, realizing that acceptance of my insufficiency is building trust-bonds between us. As I look back on my life-journey thus far, I'm encouraged to see that days of extreme weakness have been some of my most precious times. My memories of those days are richly interwoven with golden strands of Your intimate Presence.

In Your glorious Name, Jesus, amen.

"The eternal God is your refuge, and underneath are the everlasting arms. He will drive out your enemy before you, saying, 'Destroy him!'" —DEUTERONOMY 33:27

In the same way, the Spirit helps us in our weakness. We do not know what we ought to pray for, but the Spirit himself intercedes for us with groans that words cannot express. —ROMANS 8:26

And my God will supply all your needs according to His riches in glory in Christ Jesus. —PHILIPPIANS 4:19 NASB 1995

I am still confident of this: I will see the goodness of the LORD in the land of the living. Wait for the LORD; be strong and take heart and wait for the LORD. —PSALM 27:13–14

Righteous Jesus,

Your Word tells me that *the path of the righteous is like the first gleam of dawn, shining ever brighter till the full light of day.* This beautiful verse applies to *me* because You have clothed me in Your perfect righteousness. *The clothing of salvation* You have provided is not something that could ever be removed, nor will it ever wear out. This *robe of righteousness* is mine forever—just as I am *Yours* forever!

As I journey along this pathway, I long to stay aware of Your loving Presence with me. It's tough going at times, and I am weak. Help me to walk close to You and keep my eyes on the goal: my heavenly home. Right now, my glimpse of Glory is dim—like the first gleam of dawn. But as I persevere along this trail with You, I trust that I'm getting closer and closer to the glorious goal.

I rejoice in knowing that Your Light will gradually shine brighter and brighter during this arduous journey. And eventually—in Your perfect timing—I will experience *the full Light of day*!

In Your bright, shining Name, amen.

The path of the righteous is like the first gleam of dawn, shining ever brighter till the full light of day. —PROVERBS 4:18

I am overwhelmed with joy in the LORD my God! For he has dressed me with the clothing of salvation and draped me in a robe of righteousness. I am like a bridegroom dressed for his wedding or a bride with her jewels. —ISAIAH 61:10 NLT

He restores my soul; He leads me in the paths of righteousness for His name's sake. —PSALM 23:3 NKJV

I press on toward the goal to win the prize for which God has called me heavenward in Christ Jesus. —PHILIPPIANS 3:14

Wonderful Savior,

How thankful I am to be *a child of God*! Someday *I will see You as You are*: I'll be face to Face with You in Glory! Now, however, I am in training—*putting on the new self and being made new in the attitude of my mind.* Although my new self is being conformed to Your image, I'm thankful that this process doesn't erase the essence of who I am. On the contrary, the more I become *like You*, the more I develop into the unique person You created me to be.

Ever since I trusted in You as my Savior, I've been a member of Your royal family. Moreover, I'm a *fellow heir with You*—sharing Your magnificent inheritance. Yet Your Word tells me I must *suffer with You so that I may be glorified with You.* When I go through hard times, help me turn to You and find You lovingly present with Me in my trouble. Please enable me to suffer well, in a manner worthy of Your royal household. I realize that everything I endure can train me to become more like You.

The psalmist describes my ultimate goal superbly: *I will see Your Face in righteousness—and be satisfied!*

In Your regal Name, Jesus, amen.

Now we are children of God; and it has not yet been revealed what we shall be, but we know that when He is revealed, we shall be like Him, for we shall see Him as He is. —1 JOHN 3:2 NKJV

You were taught . . . to put off your old self, which is being corrupted by its deceitful desires; to be made new in the attitude of your minds; and to put on the new self, created to be like God in true righteousness and holiness. —EPHESIANS 4:22–24

If children, heirs also, heirs of God and fellow heirs with Christ, if indeed we suffer with Him so that we may also be glorified with Him. —ROMANS 8:17 NASB 1995

As for me, I will see Your face in righteousness; I shall be satisfied when I awake in Your likeness. —PSALM 17:15 NKJV

Compassionate Jesus,

I come to You, feeling weak and weary, seeking to rest in Your refreshing Presence. I know that You are always by my side, but sometimes I'm forgetful of Your nearness. I confess that I'm easily distracted by the expectations of other people. If their demands on me are too numerous and weighty, eventually I feel as if I'm carrying a crushing load.

Today I find myself sinking under *heavy burdens,* so I'm coming to You for help. I ask You to lift the weights from my shoulders and carry them for me. As I talk with You about the matters that concern me, please shine the Light of Your Presence on each one—showing me the way forward. May this same Light that illuminates my path soak into the depths of my being, soothing and strengthening me.

Lord, I open my heart to Your healing, holy Presence. *I lift up my hands* in joyful adoration, eager for Your abundance to flow freely into me.

I desire You above all else, for *My soul finds rest in You alone.* I'm grateful that *You give strength to Your people and bless Your people with Peace.*

In Your peaceful, holy Name, amen.

Then Jesus said, "Come to me, all of you who are weary and carry heavy burdens, and I will give you rest." —MATTHEW 11:28 NLT

Lift up your hands in the sanctuary and praise the LORD. —PSALM 134:2

My soul finds rest in God alone; my salvation comes from him. —PSALM 62:1

The LORD gives strength to his people; the LORD blesses his people with peace. —PSALM 29:11

Ever-near Jesus,

Your Word assures me that even in the most desperate circumstances, I don't need to *be afraid, for You are close beside me—guarding, guiding all the way.* Yet I confess that I'm often unaware of Your Presence, even though You are always with me.

Whenever I start to feel afraid, help me to use this emotion as a wake-up call to my heart, alerting me to reconnect with You. Instead of giving in to rising anxiety, I can turn to You and let the Light of Your Presence shine upon me—and within me. As I rest in the warmth of Your Love-Light, the cold, hard fear gradually melts away. Experiencing this wondrous Love increases my love for You and my trust in You.

I'm grateful that You are *guarding and guiding me all the way.* You protect me from harm more often than I can imagine—and You guard my soul. Because I'm Your follower, my soul is eternally secure in You; *no one can snatch me out of Your hand!* Moreover, as I go along the path toward heaven, I rejoice in the assurance that *You will be my Guide even to the end.*

In Your guarding, guiding Name, amen.

Even when walking through the dark valley of death I will not be afraid, for you are close beside me, guarding, guiding all the way. —Psalm 23:4 TLB

"I give them eternal life, and they shall never perish; no one can snatch them out of my hand." —John 10:28

For this God is our God for ever and ever; he will be our guide even to the end. —Psalm 48:14

All-powerful God,

You are *the Rock that is higher than I.* You are *my* Rock in whom I can *take refuge*—any time, any place. O Lord, I come to You, seeking to rest in the Peace of Your Presence. I long to take a break from trying to figure everything out.

I realize that many things are completely beyond my understanding—and my control. This should not surprise me because Your Word teaches that *Your ways and thoughts are higher than mine, as the heavens are higher than the earth.*

When the world around me looks confusing and evil appears to be winning, help me find hope in You—the Light that keeps on shining in all situations. Since I am Your follower, I want to shine brightly in this troubled world—telling others the *good tidings of great Joy*: that You are our *Savior, Christ the Lord.*

Whispering Your Name and singing songs of praise are ways I like to draw near You. As I keep looking to You, Your Presence illuminates my path.

In Your luminous Name, Jesus, amen.

From the ends of the earth I call to you, I call as my heart grows faint; lead me to the rock that is higher than I. —PSALM 61:2

The LORD is my rock, my fortress and my deliverer; my God is my rock, in whom I take refuge. He is my shield and the horn of my salvation, my stronghold. —PSALM 18:2

"As the heavens are higher than the earth, so are my ways higher than your ways and my thoughts than your thoughts." —ISAIAH 55:9

Then the angel said to them, "Do not be afraid, for behold, I bring you good tidings of great joy which will be to all people. For there is born to you this day in the city of David a Savior, who is Christ the Lord." —LUKE 2:10–11 NKJV

My Savior-God,

My soul clings to You; Your right hand upholds me. I know that You use difficult times to strengthen me spiritually. Just as gold is refined by fire, so *my faith* is refined by trials—to prove that it is genuine. As I cling to You in the midst of adversity, my faith grows stronger and I find comfort in You. When I endure trials in dependence on You, I gain confidence that I can cope with future hardships. More and more, I'm able to trust that You will always help me in my time of need.

In the middle of the night or in the midst of tough times, I remember that Your right hand is supporting me. This hand that holds me up is super-strong; there's no limit to how much support You can provide. So when I'm feeling overwhelmed, I won't give up. Instead, I'll *look to You and Your strength.*

Your hand is not only powerful but *righteous.* I love the assurance You give me in Your Word: *"Do not fear, for I am with you; do not be dismayed, for I am your God. I will strengthen you and help you; I will uphold you with My righteous right hand."*

In Your powerful Name, Jesus, amen.

On my bed I remember you; I think of you through the watches of the night. . . . My soul clings to you; your right hand upholds me. —PSALM 63:6, 8

These have come so that your faith —of greater worth than gold, which perishes even though refined by fire —may be proved genuine and may result in praise, glory and honor when Jesus Christ is revealed. —1 PETER 1:7

Look to the LORD and his strength; seek his face always. —PSALM 105:4

"So do not fear, for I am with you; do not be dismayed, for I am your God. I will strengthen you and help you; I will uphold you with my righteous right hand." —ISAIAH 41:10

August

*"You will seek Me and find Me,
when you search for Me with all your
heart."* —Jeremiah 29:13 nkjv

Light of the world,

I yearn to *walk in the Light of Your Presence—rejoicing in Your Name all day long, exulting in Your righteousness.* This world is increasingly dark, but the Light of Your Presence is as bright as ever. Against the dark backdrop of evil, Your Glory shines brilliantly! When Your goodness collides with worldly vileness, this collision of spiritual opposites creates conditions that are favorable for Your mighty interventions. So I'll be on the lookout for miracles, watching for what You will do.

Whenever I'm in the midst of difficult circumstances, it's crucial for me to keep *rejoicing in Your Name.* The essence of all that You are is distilled into this beautiful word: *Jesus.* I love to use Your Name as a whispered prayer, a praise, a protection; and it never loses its power.

I can *exult in Your righteousness* even in the darkest situations. Nothing can tarnish Your glorious righteousness, which You have woven into shining *garments of salvation* for me to wear forever. This is how I walk in Your Light—by making good use of Your holy Name and by wearing Your *robe of righteousness* joyfully!

In Your righteous Name, Jesus, amen.

*"I am the light of the world. Whoever follows me will not walk in darkness, but will have the light of life." —*JOHN 8:12 ESV

Blessed are those who have learned to acclaim you, who walk in the light of your presence, O LORD. *They rejoice in your name all day long; they exult in your righteousness. —*PSALM 89:15–16

*"There is salvation in no one else! God has given no other name under heaven by which we must be saved." —*ACTS 4:12 NLT

I will greatly rejoice in the LORD *. . . for He has clothed me with the garments of salvation, He has covered me with the robe of righteousness. —*ISAIAH 61:10 NKJV

Gracious Jesus,

Thank You for the gift of this new day! I want to nurture well my thankfulness—it's the royal road to Joy. In fact, I've discovered that no pleasure is really complete without expressing gratitude for it. I know it's good to thank the people through whom I receive blessings, but I need to remember that You are the One from whom all blessings flow. Please remind me to praise and thank You frequently throughout the day. This delightful discipline nurtures my soul and enhances my relationship with You—providing an easy way for me to draw near You.

You have blessed me with the glorious gift of grace—undeserved, unearned favor. I rejoice that no one and no set of circumstances can strip me of this lavish gift. I belong to You forever! *Nothing in all creation will be able to separate me from Your loving Presence.*

Please keep me aware of Your Presence as I walk with You through this day. Help me to stay alert so I can find the blessings and pleasures You scatter along my path. The greatest treasure is *You*, Jesus, for You are the *indescribable Gift!*

In Your treasured Name, amen.

Let us come before His presence with thanksgiving; let us make a joyful noise to Him with songs of praise! —PSALM 95:2 AMPC

For it is by grace you have been saved, through faith —and this not from yourselves, it is the gift of God —not by works, so that no one can boast. —EPHESIANS 2:8–9

For I am convinced that neither death nor life, neither angels nor demons, neither the present nor the future, nor any powers, neither height nor depth, nor anything else in all creation, will be able to separate us from the love of God that is in Christ Jesus our Lord. —ROMANS 8:38–39

Thanks be to God for His indescribable gift! —2 CORINTHIANS 9:15 NKJV

Precious Savior,

You've been helping me understand that Joy is a choice. I don't have much control over my circumstances, but I can still choose to be joyful.

You created me *a little lower than the heavenly beings*, and You gave me an amazing mind—with the ability to think things through and make decisions. I've learned that my thoughts are extremely important because they strongly influence my emotions and behavior. So endeavoring to make good thought-choices is well worth my efforts.

Whenever I'm feeling joyless, I need to pause and remember that *You are with me—watching over me* continuously. Thank You, Lord, for loving me with *unfailing Love* and for giving me Your Spirit. This Holy One within me helps me line up my thinking with the glorious truths of Scripture. Your continual Presence is a biblical promise, and I long to find *You* in the midst of my circumstances. As I'm seeking You, at first I can see only my problems. But if I keep on looking, eventually I'll see the Light of Your Presence shining upon my difficulties—reflecting sparkles of Joy back to me!

In Your brilliant, joyful Name, Jesus, amen.

Yet you have made him a little lower than the heavenly beings and crowned him with glory and honor. —PSALM 8:5 ESV

"I am with you and will watch over you wherever you go, and I will bring you back to this land. I will not leave you until I have done what I have promised you." —GENESIS 28:15

Let them give thanks to the LORD for his unfailing love and his wonderful deeds for men. —PSALM 107:8

May the God of hope fill you with all joy and peace as you trust in him, so that you may overflow with hope by the power of the Holy Spirit. —ROMANS 15:13

Jesus, my good Shepherd,

I want You to be my primary Focus. You are all around me—constantly aware of me—taking note of every thought and prayer. Many, many things vie for my attention, but I must not let them crowd You out. Directing my mind toward You requires very little energy, yet it blesses me immensely. The more I focus on You, the more fully You live in me and work through me.

Help me remember that You are with me each moment of my life, watching over me with perfect Love. Your Word teaches that *Your unfailing Love surrounds the one who trusts in You*. You've been training me to be increasingly aware of Your loving Presence, even when other things demand my attention.

Lord, *You* are the constant in my life that provides stability and direction in an unpredictable environment. *You are the same yesterday, today, and forever.* So You're the perfect fixed point for me to focus on while making my way through this ever-changing world. As I keep redirecting my thoughts to You, please show me the way forward—and *give me Your Peace.*

In Your steadfast Name, amen.

"I am the good shepherd. The good shepherd lays down his life for the sheep." —JOHN 10:11

Many are the woes of the wicked, but the LORD'S *unfailing love surrounds the man who trusts in him.* —PSALM 32:10

Jesus Christ is the same yesterday, today, and forever. —HEBREWS 13:8 NKJV

"Peace I leave with you, My peace I give to you; not as the world gives do I give to you. Let not your heart be troubled, neither let it be afraid." —JOHN 14:27 NKJV

My great, loving God,

You are my living Lord, *my Rock*, my Savior-God! Help me to spend ample time with You—pondering Your greatness and Your endless commitment to me. I live in a culture where so many people are leery of making commitments. Even those who say "I do" often change their minds later and leave. You, however, are my forever-Friend and the eternal Lover of my soul. I am utterly secure in Your Love!

Instead of focusing on troubles in my life and in the world, I want to think more about who You are. Not only are You my living Lord and unchanging Rock; You are *God my Savior.* Your death on the cross for my sins *saves me to the uttermost* because You are *eternal God.* I don't need to worry that You will stop loving me if my performance isn't good enough—it's *Your* goodness and *Your* righteousness that keep me secure in Your Love. Your unending commitment to me strengthens and comforts me as I journey through this trouble-filled world. And I eagerly await the time when I will live with You in Glory!

In Your breathtaking Name, Jesus, amen.

The Lord lives! Praise be to my Rock! Exalted be God my Savior! —Psalm 18:46

Therefore He is also able to save to the uttermost those who come to God through Him, since He always lives to make intercession for them. —Hebrews 7:25 nkjv

"The eternal God is your refuge, and underneath are the everlasting arms. He will drive out your enemy before you, saying, 'Destroy him!'" —Deuteronomy 33:27

For He made Him who knew no sin to be sin for us, that we might become the righteousness of God in Him. —2 Corinthians 5:21 nkjv

Dearest Jesus,

Thank You that I am safe, secure, and complete in You. Help me to stop my anxious striving and just come to You with the matters that are on my heart. I need to trust You enough to be open and honest as I tell You about the concerns weighing me down. I can *give all my worries and cares to You, for You care about me*—You are taking care of me! I find rest *in the shelter of Your Presence.*

Whenever I wander away and leave You out of my life, I no longer feel complete. The restlessness I experience in these times is actually a gift from You, reminding me to return to *my First Love.* I need to make You central in my thoughts and feelings, my plans and actions. When You are the Center of my life, I'm able to live meaningfully, according to Your will.

You have set my feet on a pathway to heaven, and You are my constant Companion. When I encounter trouble as I journey with You, I love to hear Your words of reassurance: *"Take heart! I have overcome the world."*

O Lord, in Your Presence I am indeed safe, secure, and complete!

In Your victorious Name, amen.

Give all your worries and cares to God, for he cares about you. —1 PETER 5:7 NLT

In the shelter of your presence you hide them from the intrigues of men; in your dwelling you keep them safe from accusing tongues. —PSALM 31:20

"Yet I hold this against you: You have forsaken your first love." —REVELATION 2:4

"I have told you these things, so that in me you may have peace. In this world you will have trouble. But take heart! I have overcome the world." —JOHN 16:33

Glorious God,

Your Word assures me that *all those who wait for You are blessed.* Waiting patiently does not come easily to me, but I know it is worth the effort. I like to plan ahead, make definitive decisions, and make things *happen.* There is a time for that, but this seems to be a time for waiting—sitting in Your Presence, seeking to trust You with my whole being. Though this discipline is certainly challenging for me, it is also quite delightful. Moreover, it brings a wealth of blessings.

Many of the good things You offer me reside in the future. While I spend time resting in Your Presence, You're preparing me for those not-yet blessings. Because they're veiled in the mystery of the future, I cannot see them clearly. Other blessings are for the present. I've found that the very process of waiting for You is highly beneficial. It keeps my soul on tiptoe as I look up to You in hope—acknowledging that You're in control and You are good. When I'm struggling to understand why I have to wait so long, please help me change my focus from *relying on my understanding* to *trusting You with all my heart.*

In Your hope-filled Name, Jesus, amen.

Yet the LORD longs to be gracious to you; he rises to show you compassion. For the LORD is a God of justice. Blessed are all who wait for him! —ISAIAH 30:18

I waited patiently for the LORD; he turned to me and heard my cry. —PSALM 40:1

Let the morning bring me word of your unfailing love, for I have put my trust in you. Show me the way I should go, for to you I lift up my soul. —PSALM 143:8

Trust in the LORD with all your heart, and do not rely on your own understanding. —PROVERBS 3:5 HCSB

Mighty Lord,

You are my Help and my Shield. I'm thankful for the possessive pronoun *my*; You're not just *a* Help and *a* Shield. You are *mine*—for all time and throughout eternity. Your forever-commitment to me strengthens and encourages me as I walk with You through this day. You have promised that *You will never leave me.* I can depend on You!

Because You are *my Help*, I don't need to fear my inadequacy. When the task I'm facing looks daunting, I find hope through turning to You—openly admitting my insufficiency and trusting in Your infinite sufficiency. *I can do all things through You*, the One *who strengthens me.*

I definitely need You as *my Shield.* I know You protect me from many dangers—physical, emotional, and spiritual. Sometimes I'm aware of Your protective work on my behalf, yet I'm sure You also shield me from perils I never even suspect. I find great comfort in knowing that Your powerful Presence is watching over me. *I will fear no evil, for You are with me.*

In Your shielding Name, Jesus, amen.

We wait in hope for the LORD; he is our help and our shield. —PSALM 33:20

"The LORD himself goes before you and will be with you; he will never leave you nor forsake you. Do not be afraid; do not be discouraged." —DEUTERONOMY 31:8

I can do all things through Christ who strengthens me. —PHILIPPIANS 4:13 NKJV

Even though I walk through the valley of the shadow of death, I will fear no evil, for you are with me; your rod and your staff, they comfort me. —PSALM 23:4

Loving Jesus,

I rejoice that You understand me completely and love me with perfect, unending Love! I've struggled with the fear that anyone who comes to know me fully might look down on me and judge me. So my natural tendency is to keep others at a safe distance, disclosing only the parts of myself that I think are acceptable. This way of interacting with others feels safer, but it leads to loneliness.

I'm grateful that You see straight through my defenses and pretenses. There is no hiding from You! You know absolutely everything about me. Please help me to rest in the wonder of being *fully known*—yet delighted in!

Instead of striving to earn Your Love, I can relax in the truth that nothing could ever stop You from loving me. Because I am Yours—bought with Your precious blood—I am *accepted* forever. I need to keep telling myself this truth over and over, until it seeps into my inner being and changes the way I view myself. You've been showing me that living in awareness of Your acceptance is the path to self-forgetfulness, which is the highway to Joy!

In Your jubilant Name, amen.

Oh give thanks to the LORD, for he is good, for his steadfast love endures forever! . . . Whoever is wise, let him attend to these things; let them consider the steadfast love of the LORD. —PSALM 107:1, 43 ESV

Now we see but a poor reflection as in a mirror; then we shall see face to face. Now I know in part; then I shall know fully, even as I am fully known. —1 CORINTHIANS 13:12

For the LORD takes delight in his people. —PSALM 149:4

Having predestined us to adoption as sons by Jesus Christ to Himself, according to the good pleasure of His will, to the praise of the glory of His grace, by which He made us accepted in the Beloved. —EPHESIANS 1:5–6 NKJV

Cherished Jesus,

This world abounds with negative things for me to think about. Sometimes problems—mine and others'—seem to shout for my attention. The difficulties can occupy more and more of my thinking, causing me to *grow weary and lose heart*. When this happens, please remind me that I can *choose* the subject of my thoughts. Instead of wallowing in the darkness of discouragement, I can turn toward You and let Your Light shine upon me.

Help me not to be defeated by wrong choices I have made in the past. And don't let me define who I am *now* on the basis of past decisions that were hurtful. Each moment provides a fresh opportunity to draw near You and enjoy Your Presence. Even when I'm struggling, I can choose to seek *You* in the midst of my problems instead of just focusing on the difficulties.

I love hearing Your words of encouragement: *"In Me you may have Peace. In this world you will have trouble. But take heart! I have overcome the world."*

In Your triumphant Name, amen.

For consider Him who has endured such hostility by sinners against Himself, so that you will not grow weary and lose heart. —HEBREWS 12:3 NASB 1995

This poor man cried out, and the LORD heard him, and saved him out of all his troubles. The angel of the LORD encamps all around those who fear Him, and delivers them. —PSALM 34:6–7 NKJV

"I have told you these things, so that in me you may have peace. In this world you will have trouble. But take heart! I have overcome the world." —JOHN 16:33

My vigilant God,

I delight in these reassuring words from You: *"I am with you and will watch over you wherever you go."* An adventurous journey awaits me, yet I'm anticipating it with mixed feelings. In some ways I'm eager to step into this new adventure—I'm hoping to find bountiful blessings along the way. However, part of me fears leaving my comfortable, predictable routine. When fearful thoughts assail me, please remind me that You will be watching over me constantly—wherever I am. I'm grateful that the comfort of Your Presence is a forever-promise!

You've been teaching me that essential preparation for the journey ahead is practicing Your Presence each day. I need to keep calling to mind that You are with me and You're taking care of me. As I walk with You along my life-path, I like to imagine Your strong hand holding on to mine. Help me to trust You, *my Guide*, to show me the way forward step by step. Because Your sense of direction is perfect, I don't need to worry about getting lost. I can relax in Your Presence—rejoicing in the wonder of sharing my whole life with You!

In Your comforting Name, Jesus, amen.

"I am with you and will watch over you wherever you go, and I will bring you back to this land. I will not leave you until I have done what I have promised you." —GENESIS 28:15

"Have I not commanded you? Be strong and courageous. Do not be frightened, and do not be dismayed, for the LORD your God is with you wherever you go." —JOSHUA 1:9 ESV

I will instruct you and teach you in the way you should go; I will counsel you and watch over you. —PSALM 32:8

For this God is our God for ever and ever; he will be our guide even to the end. —PSALM 48:14

King Jesus,

When I begin a day—or a task—feeling inadequate, I need to pause and hear You saying: *"My grace is sufficient for you, for My Power is made perfect in weakness."* The present tense of the verb *is* highlights the continual availability of Your wondrous grace. I don't want to waste energy regretting how weak I feel. Instead, I can embrace my insufficiency—rejoicing that it helps me realize how much I need You. As I come to You in weakness, I delight in Your infinite sufficiency!

When I go about a task in joyful dependence on You, I'm often surprised by how much I can accomplish. Moreover, the quality of my work is greatly enhanced by collaborating with You. It is such an astonishing privilege to live and work alongside You—the *King of kings and Lord of lords.*

As I seek to align myself with Your will, I want to be *a living sacrifice, pleasing to You.* Your Word says this is a form of worship—and it makes my life both meaningful and joyful. I know this is only a tiny foretaste of the indescribably glorious Joy awaiting me in heaven!

In Your joyous Name, amen.

But he said to me, "My grace is sufficient for you, for my power is made perfect in weakness." —2 CORINTHIANS 12:9

And He has on His robe and on His thigh a name written: KING OF KINGS AND LORD OF LORDS. —REVELATION 19:16 NKJV

Therefore, I urge you, brothers, in view of God's mercy, to offer your bodies as living sacrifices, holy and pleasing to God —this is your spiritual act of worship. —ROMANS 12:1

You have not seen him, but you love him. You do not see him now but you believe in him, and so you rejoice with an indescribable and glorious joy. —1 PETER 1:8 NET

Magnificent Jesus,

Living in dependence on You is a glorious adventure! Most people scurry around busily, trying to accomplish things through their own strength and ability. Some succeed magnificently; others fail miserably. But both groups miss what life is meant to be: living and working in collaboration with You. Please train me to depend on You more and more, Lord.

When I depend on You, my whole perspective changes. I'm able to see Your miraculous works, though others see only natural occurrences and "coincidences." I begin each day with joyful expectation, eager to see what You will do. I accept weakness as a gift from You, knowing that *Your Power is fulfilled and completed—shows itself most effective—in my weakness.* I keep my plans tentative, trusting that Your plans are far superior. I consciously *live, move, and have my being in You,* rejoicing that You live in me.

How marvelous it is to know that *I am in You, and You are in me!* Thank You for this intimate adventure of sharing my life with You.

In Your exhilarating Name, amen.

> *But He said to me, My grace (My favor and loving-kindness and mercy) is enough for you [sufficient against any danger and enables you to bear the trouble manfully]; for My strength and power are made perfect (fulfilled and completed) and show themselves most effective in [your] weakness. Therefore, I will all the more gladly glory in my weaknesses and infirmities, that the strength and power of Christ (the Messiah) may rest (yes, may pitch a tent over and dwell) upon me!* —2 Corinthians 12:9 AMPC

> *"For in him we live and move and have our being." As some of your own poets have said, "We are his offspring."* —Acts 17:28

> *"On that day you will realize that I am in my Father, and you are in me, and I am in you."* —John 14:20

Compassionate Jesus,

Help me to *remember You on my bed, thinking of You through the watches of the night*. When I'm wakeful at night, thoughts can fly at me from all directions. Unless I take charge of them, I start to feel anxious. I've found that my best strategy during these night watches is to think about *You*—communicating with You about whatever is on my mind. Your Word tells me to *cast all my anxiety on You because You care for me*. Knowing that You're taking care of me makes it possible for me to relax in Your Presence.

As I remember You during the night, I try to think about who You really are. I ponder Your perfections: Your Love, Joy, and Peace. I find comfort in Your names: Shepherd, Savior, Immanuel, Prince of Peace. I rejoice in Your majesty, wisdom, mercy, and grace. I delight in Your Power and Glory, for You are *King of kings and Lord of lords*! Thus I worship You and enjoy Your Presence. These thoughts of You refresh my entire being and clear my mind—enabling me to see things from Your perspective.

In Your refreshing Name, amen.

*On my bed I remember you; I think of you through
the watches of the night.* —PSALM 63:6

Cast all your anxiety on him because he cares for you. —1 PETER 5:7

*On his robe and on his thigh he has a name written, King of
kings and Lord of lords.* —REVELATION 19:16 ESV

Sovereign God,

Help me to *lead the life that You have assigned to me*—and to be content. I need to beware of comparing my situation with someone else's, feeling dissatisfied because of the comparison. I realize it's also hurtful to compare my current circumstances with how things used to be or with fantasies that bear little resemblance to reality. Instead, I must make every effort to accept as my *calling* the life You have assigned to me. This perspective takes the sting out of painful, difficult circumstances. If You have called me to a situation, I know You'll give me everything I need to endure it—and even to find some Joy in the midst of it.

Please train my mind to trust Your sovereign ways with me—bowing before Your mysterious, infinite intelligence. I need to search for You in the details of my day, all the while looking expectantly for good to emerge from trouble. I'm learning to accept things the way they are, without losing hope for a better future. And I rejoice in the hope of heaven, knowing that indescribably joyful Life is my *ultimate* calling!

In Your supremely wise Name, Jesus, amen.

Only let each person lead the life that the Lord has assigned to him, and to which God has called him. This is my rule in all the churches. —1 CORINTHIANS 7:17 ESV

I know what it is to be in need, and I know what it is to have plenty. I have learned the secret of being content in any and every situation, whether well fed or hungry, whether living in plenty or in want. —PHILIPPIANS 4:12

Oh, the depth of the riches of the wisdom and knowledge of God! How unsearchable his judgments, and his paths beyond tracing out! "Who has known the mind of the Lord? Or who has been his counselor?" —ROMANS 11:33–34

Marvelous Savior,

Help me to find Joy in You—for You are *my Strength*. I know that keeping Joy alive is crucial, especially when I'm in the throes of adversity. Whenever I'm struggling with difficulties, I need to guard my thoughts and words very carefully. If I focus too much on all the things that are wrong, I become increasingly discouraged—and my strength is sapped. As soon as I realize what's happening, I must stop this hurtful process immediately. You've been training me to turn to You quickly and ask You to *show me the way I should go.*

When I'm struggling, I need to take time to praise You—speaking or singing words of worship, reading promises and praises in Scripture. *O my Strength, I sing praise to You. I sing the Glory of Your Name!*

It's essential for me to remember that my problems are temporary but *You* are eternal—and so is my relationship with You. As I find Joy in You, delighting in Your *unfailing Love*, my strength invariably increases.

In Your glorious Name, Jesus, amen.

O my Strength, I sing praise to you; you, O God, are my fortress, my loving God. —Psalm 59:17

Let the morning bring me word of your unfailing love, for I have put my trust in you. Show me the way I should go, for to you I lift up my soul. —Psalm 143:8

Shout with joy to God, all the earth! Sing the glory of his name; make his praise glorious! —Psalm 66:1–2

Dear brothers and sisters, when troubles of any kind come your way, consider it an opportunity for great joy. —James 1:2 NLT

Gentle Jesus,

When I'm feeling overwhelmed by my circumstances, please remind me to spend time focusing on You and listening to You. I love to hear You saying to me, *"Take courage! It is I. Don't be afraid."*

Listening to You while I'm feeling stressed requires a lot of discipline and trust. My racing thoughts make it hard to hear Your *gentle whisper*. So I'm thankful for the help of Your Spirit, who calms my mind when I ask.

I rejoice that You—the *Prince of Peace*—are with me at all times. Not only are You with me, but You are also in my circumstances. You're in control of everything that happens to me! I know that You are never the author of evil, yet You're able to take bad things and use them for good. This doesn't always remove my suffering, but it *does* redeem it—infusing it with meaning. So whenever I'm in a storm of difficulties, I'll listen for Your voice saying, "Take courage! It is I." And I'll search for signs of Your abiding Presence in the storm. Your Word assures me that *I will seek You and find You when I search for You with all my heart.*

In Your calming Name, amen.

*But Jesus immediately said to them: "Take courage! It is I. Don't be afraid." —*MATTHEW 14:27

After the earthquake came a fire, but the LORD *was not in the fire. And after the fire came a gentle whisper. —*1 KINGS 19:12

*For a child will be born to us, a son will be given to us; and the government will rest on His shoulders; and His name will be called Wonderful Counselor, Mighty God, Eternal Father, Prince of Peace. —*ISAIAH 9:6 NASB 1995

*"And you will seek Me and find Me, when you search for Me with all your heart." —*JEREMIAH 29:13 NKJV

Awesome God,

Help me to *trust You and not be afraid*. Sometimes I am frightened by world events and news reports. But I realize that these reports are biased—presented as if You do not exist. News clips show tiny bits of current events from which the most important factor has been carefully removed: Your Presence in the world! As journalists sift through massive amounts of information, they tend to strain out everything about *You* and what You're accomplishing on this planet.

Whenever my world is feeling like a scary place, I need to turn to You and find encouragement in Your Presence. I'm inspired by the example of David, who *strengthened himself in the Lord* when his men were threatening to stone him. Like David, I can find courage through remembering who You are—pondering Your awesome Power and Glory, delighting in *Your unfailing Love.* I rejoice in knowing I'm on an adventurous journey with You and my ultimate destination is heaven!

As I keep focusing on You and enjoying the rich relationship You offer, my fear gradually subsides. *I will trust and not be afraid, for You are my Strength and my Song.*

In Your matchless Name, Jesus, amen.

"Behold, God is my salvation, I will trust and not be afraid; for the LORD GOD is my strength and song, and He has become my salvation." —ISAIAH 12:2 NASB 1995

The LORD loves righteousness and justice; the earth is full of his unfailing love. —PSALM 33:5

Now David was greatly distressed, for the people spoke of stoning him, because the soul of all the people was grieved, every man for his sons and his daughters. But David strengthened himself in the LORD his God. —1 SAMUEL 30:6 NKJV

Jesus, my Redeemer,

I love to hear You speaking these words to me through Scripture: *"I give eternal Life to you, and you will never perish; no one will snatch you out of My hand."* This is astonishingly good news! You have promised me *a heavenly inheritance that can never perish, spoil, or fade.*

Your gift of eternal Life provides a Light that keeps on shining—even during my darkest days. This brightness beckons me onward and protects me from discouragement. So I can refuse to let hard circumstances or the wickedness of the world drag me down. Instead, I'll look ahead to the Glory that awaits me—sparkling in the distance, just beyond the horizon.

I know I'll have to go through some deep waters on my journey toward heaven. But You have assured me: *"When you pass through the waters, I will be with you. They will not sweep over you."* Help me to keep holding on to Your hand in trusting dependence—confident that You love me and that *nothing will be able to separate me from You.* Rather than dreading the challenging times ahead, I want to enjoy the adventure of journeying with You through every day of my life.

In Your strong, dependable Name, amen.

*"I give eternal life to [My sheep], and they will never perish; and no one will snatch them out of My hand." —*John 10:28 nasb 1995

*He has given us new birth into a living hope through the resurrection of Jesus Christ from the dead, and into an inheritance that can never perish, spoil or fade. —*1 Peter 1:3–4

*"When you pass through the waters, I will be with you; and when you pass through the rivers, they will not sweep over you. When you walk through the fire, you will not be burned; the flames will not set you ablaze." —*Isaiah 43:2

*Neither height nor depth, nor anything else in all creation, will be able to separate us from the love of God that is in Christ Jesus our Lord. —*Romans 8:39

Beloved Jesus,

Help me to think Your thoughts more and more. When the worries of this world are pressing down on me, I need to take time to think things out in Your Presence. As I relax with You, Your *everlasting arms* enfold me in Peace. It's such a blessing to take a break from obsessing about my concerns—and just enjoy this time of *looking to You.*

I like to intersperse quietness with reading Scripture and speaking or singing praises to You. Thank You for guiding me to use Bible verses in my prayers and petitions. When my prayers are permeated with Scripture, I'm able to pray with more confidence.

I long to *be transformed by the renewal of my mind.* The world exerts massive amounts of pressure on me through ever-present electronic communications. Instead of letting the world press me into its mold, I ask You to transform the way I think. As You gradually renew my mind, I yearn for my thoughts and attitudes to reflect *You* in ever-increasing measure.

In Your transforming Name, amen.

"The eternal God is your refuge, and underneath are the everlasting arms; He will thrust out the enemy from before you, and will say, 'Destroy!'" —DEUTERONOMY 33:27 NKJV

Those who look to Him are radiant with joy; their faces will never be ashamed. —PSALM 34:5 HCSB

For the word of God is living and active. Sharper than any double-edged sword, it penetrates even to dividing soul and spirit, joints and marrow; it judges the thoughts and attitudes of the heart. —HEBREWS 4:12

Do not be conformed to this world, but be transformed by the renewal of your mind, that by testing you may discern what is the will of God, what is good and acceptable and perfect. —ROMANS 12:2 ESV

Immanuel,

Stillness is increasingly hard to come by in this restless, agitated world. I really have to fight to carve out time for You. Distractions come at me from all sides when I try to sit quietly with You. But having an intimate connection with You is worth fighting for, so I won't give up!

Please help me in my quest to set aside uninterrupted time to spend with You—focusing on You and Your Word. I'm so grateful that You are *Immanuel—God with us.* As I relax in Your peaceful Presence, letting my concerns slip away, I can hear You whispering to me: *"Be still, and know that I am God."*

The longer I gaze at You, the more I can rejoice in Your majestic splendors—and trust in Your sovereign control. *You are my Refuge, though the earth give way and the mountains fall into the heart of the sea.* There is transcendent stability in Your Presence, Lord. As I ponder the vastness of Your Power and Glory, my perspective changes and my problems look smaller. I know *I will have trouble in this world*, but I'm encouraged by Your assurance that *You have overcome the world.*

In Your conquering Name, Jesus, amen.

"Behold, the virgin shall be with child, and bear a Son, and they shall call His name Immanuel," which is translated, "God with us." —MATTHEW 1:23 NKJV

"Be still, and know that I am God; I will be exalted among the nations, I will be exalted in the earth!" —PSALM 46:10 NKJV

God is our refuge and strength, an ever-present help in trouble. Therefore we will not fear, though the earth give way and the mountains fall into the heart of the sea. —PSALM 46:1–2

"I have told you these things, so that in me you may have peace. In this world you will have trouble. But take heart! I have overcome the world." —JOHN 16:33

Precious Jesus,

Help me to trust You in the midst of a messy day. I don't want my inner calm—my Peace in Your Presence—to be shaken by what's going on around me. Even though I live in a temporal world, I know that my innermost being is rooted and grounded in eternity. When I start to feel stressed, I need to detach myself from the disturbances around me. As I stop striving to maintain control, You enable me to relax in Your sovereign control—and receive *Your Peace that transcends understanding.*

Your Word instructs me to *seek Your Presence continually!* Please share Your mind with me and open my eyes to see things from Your perspective more and more. I love to hear You telling me: *"Do not let your heart be troubled and do not be afraid. Take heart! I have overcome the world."* Lord, I rejoice that the Peace You give me is sufficient for all my circumstances!

In Your all-powerful Name, amen.

Do not be anxious about anything, but in everything, by prayer and petition, with thanksgiving, present your requests to God. And the peace of God, which transcends all understanding, will guard your hearts and your minds in Christ Jesus. —Philippians 4:6–7

Seek the Lord and his strength; seek his presence continually! —Psalm 105:4 esv

"Peace I leave with you; my peace I give you. I do not give to you as the world gives. Do not let your hearts be troubled and do not be afraid." —John 14:27

"I have told you these things, so that in me you may have peace. In this world you will have trouble. But take heart! I have overcome the world." —John 16:33

Merciful Jesus,

I ask You to smooth out the tangled-up places in my life, including those in my mind and heart. I come to You just as I am—with all my knotty problems and loose ends. Many of my difficulties are complicated by other people's problems. So it's hard to sort out how much of the mess is mine and how much is theirs. I want to take responsibility for my mistakes and sins without feeling responsible for the sinful failures of others. Please help me untangle my complex circumstances and find the best way forward.

I'm realizing that Christian growth is all about transformation—a lifelong process. Some of the knots from my past are very hard to untie, especially those that involve people who continue to hurt me. Instead of obsessing about how to fix things, I need to keep turning toward You—*seeking Your Face* and Your will. As I wait with You, help me to relax and trust in Your timing for smoothing out my tangled-up places. Show me how to live with unresolved problems without letting them distract me from You. I rejoice that Your abiding Presence is *my portion*—and my boundless blessing!

In Your magnificent Name, amen.

And we all, with unveiled face, beholding the glory of the Lord, are being transformed into the same image from one degree of glory to another. For this comes from the Lord who is the Spirit. —2 CORINTHIANS 3:18 ESV

Seek the LORD and His strength; seek His face continually.
—1 CHRONICLES 16:11 NASB 1995

"The LORD is my portion and my inheritance," says my soul; "Therefore I have hope in Him and wait expectantly for Him." —LAMENTATIONS 3:24 AMP

Triumphant God,

If You are for me, who can be against me? Please help me to grasp—in the depths of my being—that You really *are* for me. When things don't go my way or someone I trusted turns against me, it's easy for me to feel abandoned. So it's essential at such times to remind myself of the truth: You are not only *with* me always, You are *for* me all the time. This is true on days when I perform well and on days when I don't, when people treat me well and when they don't.

I can face adversity more calmly and courageously by trusting whole-heartedly that You are *for me*. Knowing that You will never turn against me gives me confidence to persevere during tough times. Because I belong to You forever, I am continually in Your *approving* Presence. I'm thankful that it's ultimately *Your* opinion of me that matters—and will continue to matter throughout all eternity. And I rejoice that *nothing in all creation will be able to separate me from Your Love*!

In Your invincible Name, Jesus, amen.

What, then, shall we say in response to this? If God is for us, who can be against us? —ROMANS 8:31

"Teach these new disciples to obey all the commands I have given you. And be sure of this: I am with you always, even to the end of the age." —MATTHEW 28:20 NLT

"The Lord lift up His [approving] countenance upon you and give you peace (tranquility of heart and life continually)." —NUMBERS 6:26 AMPC

Neither height nor depth, nor anything else in all creation, will be able to separate us from the love of God that is in Christ Jesus our Lord. —ROMANS 8:39

Delightful Jesus,

Thank You for showing me that heaven is both present and future. As I walk along my life-path holding Your hand, I am already in touch with the essence of heaven—nearness to You! While journeying with You, I perceive lovely hints of heaven. The earth is radiantly alive with Your Presence. Shimmering sunshine awakens my heart, gently reminding me of Your brilliant Light. Birds and flowers, trees and skies evoke praises to Your holy Name. Help me to be fully open to the splendors of Your creation as I walk in the Light of Your Love.

I rejoice that there's an entrance to heaven at the end of my journey. Only *You* know when I'll reach that destination, but I trust that You're preparing me for it each step of the way. The absolute assurance of my forever-home *fills me with Joy and Peace*. I know I'll arrive at this glorious haven in Your perfect timing—not one moment too soon or too late. While I walk with You down *the path of life*, the sure hope of heaven strengthens and encourages me!

In Your heavenly Name, amen.

But Christ has indeed been raised from the dead, the firstfruits of those who have fallen asleep. . . . In Christ all will be made alive. But each in his own turn: Christ, the firstfruits; then, when he comes, those who belong to him. —1 CORINTHIANS 15:20–22

We have this hope as an anchor for the soul, firm and secure. It enters the inner sanctuary behind the curtain. —HEBREWS 6:19

May the God of hope fill you with all joy and peace as you trust in him, so that you may overflow with hope by the power of the Holy Spirit. —ROMANS 15:13

You will show me the path of life; in Your presence is fullness of joy; at Your right hand are pleasures forevermore. —PSALM 16:11 NKJV

Wonderful Lord,

This is a time of abundance in my life—*my cup overflows* with blessings. After plodding uphill for many weeks, now I feel as if I'm traipsing through lush meadows drenched in sunshine. Help me enjoy this time of ease and refreshment to the max. Thank You for providing it for me!

I admit that sometimes I hesitate to receive Your good gifts with open hands. Feelings of false guilt creep in, telling me I shouldn't accept these gifts since I don't deserve to be so richly blessed. But I realize this is fuzzy thinking, because no one *deserves* anything good from You. How I rejoice that Your kingdom is *not* about earning and deserving! It's about believing and receiving.

Instead of balking at accepting Your gracious gifts, I want to receive all Your blessings with a grateful heart. Then Your pleasure in giving and my pleasure in receiving can flow together joyously.

In Your generous Name, Jesus, amen.

You prepare a table before me in the presence of my enemies; You anoint my head with oil; my cup overflows. —PSALM 23:5 HCSB

"For God so loved the world that he gave his one and only Son, that whoever believes in him shall not perish but have eternal life." —JOHN 3:16

"So I say to you: Ask and it will be given to you; seek and you will find; knock and the door will be opened to you. For everyone who asks receives; he who seeks finds; and to him who knocks, the door will be opened." —LUKE 11:9–10

He who did not spare his own Son, but gave him up for us all —how will he not also, along with him, graciously give us all things? —ROMANS 8:32

My Strength,

You've been showing me that living in dependence on You is the way to enjoy abundant life. I'm learning to appreciate tough times because they amplify my awareness of Your Presence. Tasks that I used to dread are becoming rich opportunities for me to enjoy Your closeness. I delight in remembering that You are *my Strength*—especially when I'm feeling weary. Leaning on You is becoming increasingly natural and pleasurable.

Please help me to focus on You more consistently. This is much easier for me to do when I am alone. I confess that when I'm with other people I often lose sight of Your Presence. My people-pleasing tendency puts me in bondage to others, and they become my primary focus. Thankfully, I can turn back to You quickly by whispering Your Name, "Jesus." This tiny act of trust brings You to the forefront of my mind, where You belong. As I relax in the blessing of Your nearness, Your life can flow through me to bless other people. You came into the world *so that we may have life—and have it more abundantly*!

In Your bountiful Name, Jesus, amen.

I love you, O Lord, my strength. The Lord is my rock, my fortress and my deliverer; my God is my rock, in whom I take refuge. He is my shield and the horn of my salvation, my stronghold. —Psalm 18:1–2

Fear of man will prove to be a snare, but whoever trusts in the Lord is kept safe. —Proverbs 29:25

"The thief does not come except to steal, and to kill, and to destroy. I have come that they may have life, and that they may have it more abundantly." —John 10:10 nkjv

Faithful God,

My times are in Your hands, so my best response to the circumstances I face is *trusting in You*. You're training me to feel secure in the midst of change and uncertainty. I've found it can actually be a relief to realize I'm not in control of my life. When I accept this human condition while resting in Your sovereignty, I become increasingly free.

I know it's important not to be passive or fatalistic but to use the energy and abilities You have given me—*prayerfully*. You've been teaching me to pray about everything and to search for You in my moments. I'm learning to look for You in unexpected places because You are a God of surprises!

Help me to *rejoice in this day that You have made*; please orchestrate its details and events according to Your will. Since You are in control of *my times*, I don't need to be anxious about trying to make things happen faster. Rushing and anxiety go hand in hand, and You have instructed me to *not be anxious*. So I invite You to set the pace—blessing me with *Peace that transcends all understanding*.

In Your trustworthy Name, Jesus, amen.

But I trust in you, O LORD; I say, "You are my God." My times are in your hands; deliver me from my enemies and from those who pursue me. —PSALM 31:14–15

This is the day that the LORD has made; let us rejoice and be glad in it. —PSALM 118:24 ESV

Do not be anxious about anything, but in everything, by prayer and petition, with thanksgiving, present your requests to God. And the peace of God, which transcends all understanding, will guard your hearts and your minds in Christ Jesus. —PHILIPPIANS 4:6–7

Blessed Jesus,

Please help me not to be afraid of being happy. Sometimes anxiety intrudes upon my carefree moments. I start wondering whether there are things I should be doing or plans I should be making. My underlying feeling is that it really isn't safe to let down my guard and simply savor the moment. But I know this kind of thinking is all wrong. Because I belong to You, I can expect to experience a measure of happiness—even in this deeply broken world.

The Bible teaches me to *cease striving*—let go, relax—*and know that You are God.* I used to think I needed to have all my ducks in a row before I could relax and enjoy Your Presence. But then I considered the overall context of this command: *though the earth give way and the mountains fall into the heart of the sea.* The psalmist who penned these words was describing a terrifying catastrophe! So I don't have to wait until all my problems are solved before daring to be happy. This very moment is the perfect time to *delight myself in You.*

Lord Jesus, I choose to enjoy You here and now!

In Your joyful Name, amen.

Happy are the people who are in such a state; happy are the people whose God is the LORD! —PSALM 144:15 NKJV

"Cease striving and know that I am God; I will be exalted among the nations, I will be exalted in the earth." —PSALM 46:10 NASB 1995

God is our refuge and strength, an ever-present help in trouble. Therefore we will not fear, though the earth give way and the mountains fall into the heart of the sea. —PSALM 46:1–2

Delight yourself in the LORD; and He will give you the desires of your heart. —PSALM 37:4 NASB 1995

Lovely Lord Jesus,

Help me to look in the right direction as I go through this day. In the world around me, there are vistas of bright beauty as well as dark, ugly wastelands. When I look the right way—toward what is *true, noble, lovely*—I'm encouraged and strengthened. You created me with a wonderful capacity to enjoy beauty and goodness. My soul resonates with these blessings and draws strength from them.

Every day I encounter some things that make me cringe—things that are wrong and ugly. Help me deal with these things without letting them become my focus. I need to bring these matters to You and seek Your perspective. Then I can go on my way lightheartedly. I'm blessed by hearing You say time after time, "Beloved, look the *right* way."

This world in its fallen condition can never satisfy me fully. I yearn for perfection, and only *You* are the fulfillment of that deep longing. You are perfect and holy, yet You choose to stay close to me as I walk through this sin-stained world. When I look the right way—toward blessings, toward You—*the Joy of Your Presence* shines brightly upon me.

In Your perfect, holy Name, amen.

Finally, brothers, whatever is true, whatever is noble, whatever is right, whatever is pure, whatever is lovely, whatever is admirable —if anything is excellent or praiseworthy —think about such things. —PHILIPPIANS 4:8

"The LORD bless you and keep you; the LORD make His face shine upon you, and be gracious to you." —NUMBERS 6:24–25 NKJV

You have shown me the way of life, and you will fill me with the joy of your presence. —ACTS 2:28 NLT

Jesus, my splendid Companion,

I desire to walk with You in close, trusting Love-bonds of joyful dependence. The companionship You offer me sparkles with precious promises from the Bible: You love me with perfect, *everlasting Love*. You are always with me, each moment of my life. You know everything about me, and You have already paid the penalty for all my sins. My inheritance—*kept in heaven for me—can never perish, spoil, or fade*. You guide me through my life, and *afterward You will take me into Glory*!

You've shown me that dependence is an inescapable part of being human—You designed me to rely on You continually. Help me to view my constant need of You as a blessing. When I accept my dependent condition and stop striving to be self-sufficient, my awareness of Your loving Presence increases. Draw me closer to You, Lord, so I can enjoy Your marvelous Companionship.

I delight in Your invitation to walk with You in joyful dependence along the pathway of my life. And I love hearing You whisper: "Beloved, I am with you."

In Your marvelous Name, amen.

The LORD has appeared of old to me, saying: "Yes, I have loved you with an everlasting love; therefore with lovingkindness I have drawn you." —JEREMIAH 31:3 NKJV

In him we have redemption through his blood, the forgiveness of sins. —EPHESIANS 1:7

In his great mercy he has given us new birth into a living hope through the resurrection of Jesus Christ from the dead, and into an inheritance that can never perish, spoil or fade —kept in heaven for you. —1 PETER 1:3–4

You guide me with your counsel, and afterward you will take me into glory. —PSALM 73:24

September

"I am the LORD, your God,
who takes hold of your right hand
and says to you, Do not fear;
I will help you." —ISAIAH 41:13

Glorious Savior,

Please fill me with Your Love, Joy, and Peace in ever-increasing measure! These are Glory-gifts that flow from Your living Presence. I know I'm just an *earthen vessel*, but I rejoice that You designed me to overflow with Your heavenly contents. I've learned that my weakness is not a deterrent to being filled with Your Spirit. On the contrary, my inadequacy provides the perfect setting for Your Power to shine brighter.

As I walk with You through this day, help me to keep trusting You to provide the strength I need, moment by moment. I don't want to waste my precious energy wondering whether I have enough stamina for today's journey. Instead, I can rest in the knowledge that Your Spirit within me is more than sufficient to handle whatever comes my way.

Lord, You provide everything I need. *In quietness* (spending time alone with You) *and confident trust* (relying on Your adequacy) *is my strength.*

In Your powerful Name, Jesus, amen.

But we have this treasure in earthen vessels, so that the surpassing greatness of the power will be of God and not from ourselves. —2 CORINTHIANS 4:7 NASB 1995

May He grant you out of the riches of His glory, to be strengthened and spiritually energized with power through His Spirit in your inner self, [indwelling your innermost being and personality]. —EPHESIANS 3:16 AMP

For the LORD GOD, the Holy One of Israel has said this, "In returning [to Me] and rest you shall be saved, in quietness and confident trust is your strength." But you were not willing. —ISAIAH 30:15 AMP

Dear Jesus,

My natural inclination is to regret or run from the difficulties in my life. But You've been showing me that these problems are not random mistakes; they are hand-tailored blessings designed for my benefit and growth. Please help me embrace all the circumstances You allow in my life—trusting You to bring good out of them. Rather than dreading problems, I want to be able to view them as opportunities to rely more fully on You.

Whenever I start to feel stressed, I can let those feelings alert me to my need for You. Thus my struggles become doorways to deeper dependence on You—increasing my intimacy with You. Although self-sufficiency is acclaimed in the world, I realize that it's actually a form of idolatry. Instead of trying to be self-reliant, I desire to grow increasingly dependent on You.

Lord, I thank You for the difficulties I encounter in this fallen world. And I look forward to spending eternity with You—enjoying endless problem-free living in Your glorious Presence!

In Your holy, awesome Name, amen.

"I am the Vine; you are the branches. Whoever lives in Me and I in him bears much (abundant) fruit. However, apart from Me [cut off from vital union with Me] you can do nothing." —JOHN 15:5 AMPC

But we have this treasure in jars of clay to show that this all-surpassing power is from God and not from us. We are hard pressed on every side, but not crushed; perplexed, but not in despair. —2 CORINTHIANS 4:7–8

Always giving thanks to God the Father for everything, in the name of our Lord Jesus Christ. —EPHESIANS 5:20

My loving God,

You are *my Strength*! This promise is a lifeline full of encouragement and hope—and it's always available to me. On days when I'm feeling strong, I appreciate this truth but it doesn't speak as powerfully to me. It's when I'm feeling weak that I grab on to this secure lifeline with gratitude. I know I can call out to You at any time, *"Lord, save me!"*

I'm grateful that You *save me in Your unfailing Love.* If I feel as if I'm sinking in my struggles, it's crucial to hold on to something that will not fail me—something I can trust with my very life. Your powerful Presence not only strengthens me, it holds me close and doesn't let go. Help me remember that You have a firm grip on me at all times.

Because You are always near, I don't need to fear being weak. In fact, Your Word tells me that *Your Strength is made perfect in my weakness*—the two fit together like a hand in a glove. Please enable me to be thankful for my weaknesses, trusting in Your ever-present Strength.

In Your strong Name, Jesus, amen.

O my Strength, I sing praise to you; you, O God, are my fortress, my loving God. —PSALM 59:17

But when he saw the wind, he was afraid and, beginning to sink, cried out, "Lord, save me!" —MATTHEW 14:30

Let your face shine on your servant; save me in your unfailing love. —PSALM 31:16

And He said to me, "My grace is sufficient for you, for My strength is made perfect in weakness." Therefore most gladly I will rather boast in my infirmities, that the power of Christ may rest upon me. —2 CORINTHIANS 12:9 NKJV

Almighty God,

My world is looking bleak and threatening, so I draw nearer to You. I *pour out my heart to You*, trusting that You're listening—and You care. I find so much comfort in Your sovereignty, knowing that You're in control even when things in this fallen world look terribly out of control.

When I'm struggling with the brokenness of this world, I find strength and encouragement in Scripture. I'm especially comforted by the words the prophet Habakkuk wrote as he awaited the brutal Babylonian invasion of Judah. After describing utterly desperate circumstances, he concluded: *"Yet I will rejoice in the Lord, I will be joyful in God my Savior."*

Thank You, Lord, for allowing me to wrestle with You about my deep concerns. Please bring me to a place of confident trust and transcendent Joy, just as You did with Habakkuk. I cannot understand Your mysterious ways, but I can find *hope in You* and *praise You for the help of Your Presence. You are my Strength!*

In Your hopeful Name, Jesus, amen.

Trust in him at all times, O people; pour out your hearts to him, for God is our refuge. —PSALM 62:8

Though the fig tree does not bud and there are no grapes on the vines, though the olive crop fails and the fields produce no food, though there are no sheep in the pen and no cattle in the stalls, yet I will rejoice in the LORD, I will be joyful in God my Savior. The Sovereign LORD is my strength; he makes my feet like the feet of a deer, he enables me to go on the heights. —HABAKKUK 3:17–19

Why are you in despair, O my soul? And why have you become disturbed within me? Hope in God, for I shall again praise Him for the help of His presence. —PSALM 42:5 NASB 1995

Cherished Jesus,

My life is a precious gift from You. So I open my hands and heart to receive this day of life gratefully. I love relating to You as my Friend and Savior, but I need to remember that You are also my Creator-God. The Bible proclaims that *all things were created by You and for You.* As I go through this day that You've gifted to me, help me to find signs of Your abiding Presence along the way. And please attune my heart to hear You whisper: "*I am with you and will watch over you wherever you go.*"

On bright, joyful days, I can speak to You about the pleasures You provide. Thanking You for them makes my Joy expand exponentially! On dark, difficult days, I can grasp Your hand in trusting dependence—clinging to Your promise that *You will help me.*

My physical life is an amazing gift, but my spiritual life is a treasure of *infinite* value. Because I belong to You, I will live with You forever—enjoying a glorified body that will never get sick or grow tired. Thank You for the priceless gift of salvation *by grace through faith*!

In Your saving Name, amen.

For by him all things were created: things in heaven and on earth, visible and invisible, whether thrones or powers or rulers or authorities; all things were created by him and for him. —COLOSSIANS 1:16

"I am with you and will watch over you wherever you go, and I will bring you back to this land. I will not leave you until I have done what I have promised you." —GENESIS 28:15

"For I am the LORD, your God, who takes hold of your right hand and says to you, Do not fear; I will help you." —ISAIAH 41:13

For by grace you have been saved through faith, and that not of yourselves; it is the gift of God. —EPHESIANS 2:8 NKJV

Trustworthy Jesus,

Help me overcome my unbelief! I'm trying to learn a new habit— saying, "I trust You, Jesus," in response to whatever happens to me. This is not an easy habit for me to form, but I'm finding that it's well worth the effort. The practice of affirming my faith in You helps me see *You* in every situation.

I like to spend time thinking about how truly trustworthy You are— delighting in *Your steadfast Love* and pondering *Your Power and Your Glory.* As I acknowledge Your sovereign control over everything, I can view events through the Light of Your abiding Presence. Then fear loses its grip on me. Adverse circumstances become growth opportunities when I assert my trust in You no matter what. And I grow more grateful for blessings, realizing that all of them flow from Your hand of grace.

This practice of voicing my trust in You keeps me close to You and strengthens our relationship. I trust You, Jesus. Help me trust You more and more!

In Your steadfast Name, amen.

Immediately the boy's father exclaimed, "I do believe; help me overcome my unbelief!" —MARK 9:24

Let me hear in the morning of your steadfast love, for in you I trust. Make me know the way I should go, for to you I lift up my soul. —PSALM 143:8 ESV

I have seen you in the sanctuary and beheld your power and your glory. —PSALM 63:2

See, the Sovereign LORD comes with power, and his arm rules for him. See, his reward is with him, and his recompense accompanies him. He tends his flock like a shepherd: He gathers the lambs in his arms and carries them close to his heart; he gently leads those that have young. —ISAIAH 40:10–11

O Lord,

You are my lamp; You turn my darkness into Light. You are both with me and within me, and *You are the Light of the world.* Every day, I encounter darkness in the world—and in my own heart—but I *take courage*, knowing that *You have overcome the world.* So instead of focusing on hurtful, wrong things, I choose to focus on *You*—the brilliant Overcomer.

You have called me to walk with You along *the way of Peace.* Yet so many distractions tug at my consciousness, and I have very real responsibilities in my life. Please help me turn my thoughts to You more and more—enjoying the Peace of Your Presence in tough times as well as good times. I certainly cannot do this perfectly, but I *can* make progress little by little. As I direct my attention to You, Jesus, You push back the darkness with Your invincible Light! This is how You *turn my darkness into Light.*

In Your brilliant Name, Jesus, amen.

*"You are my lamp, O LORD; the LORD turns my
darkness into light."* —2 SAMUEL 22:29

*Then Jesus spoke to them again, saying, "I am the light of the world. He who
follows Me shall not walk in darkness, but have the light of life."* —JOHN 8:12 NKJV

*"These things I have spoken to you, so that in Me you may have
peace. In the world you have tribulation, but take courage; I
have overcome the world."* —JOHN 16:33 NASB 1995

*"And you, child, will be called the prophet of the Highest; for you will go before the
face of the Lord to prepare His ways . . . to give light to those who sit in darkness and
the shadow of death, to guide our feet into the way of peace."* —LUKE 1:76, 79 NKJV

Beloved Jesus,

You taught Your disciples that *each day has enough trouble of its own*. So I can expect to encounter *some* trouble every day. Please help me to handle calmly and confidently the difficulties that come my way. It's comforting to remember that You are *not* surprised by events that surprise me. You are *the Beginning and the End*; You know everything! Moreover, You're continually with me—to guide and comfort me as I go through turbulent times.

Having *enough* trouble in each day can even be a blessing—keeping me focused on the present. My active mind seeks challenges to chew on. If I don't have enough to occupy my mind today, I'm more likely to worry about the future.

I've learned that difficulties can draw me closer to You when I collaborate with You in handling them. As You and I deal with my problems *together*, I gain confidence in my ability to cope—and I enjoy Your nearness. The pleasure of Your Company blesses me immensely!

In Your delightful Name, amen.

"Therefore do not worry about tomorrow, for tomorrow will worry about itself. Each day has enough trouble of its own." —MATTHEW 6:34

And He said to me, "It is done! I am the Alpha and the Omega, the Beginning and the End. I will give of the fountain of the water of life freely to him who thirsts." —REVELATION 21:6 NKJV

Rejoice and exult in hope; be steadfast and patient in suffering and tribulation; be constant in prayer. —ROMANS 12:12 AMPC

Compassionate God,

How comforting it is to know that *You broaden the path beneath me so that my ankles do not turn.* Because You are in control, I don't need to worry about what will happen or wonder if I'll be able to cope. I realize that only *You* know what my future really holds—and You're the only One who fully understands what I'm capable of. Moreover, You can alter my circumstances at any time—gradually or dramatically. In fact, You can even widen the path I'm walking on right now.

Help me to really grasp how intricately involved You are in every aspect of my life. You're always taking care of me—tweaking my circumstances to protect me from unnecessary hardship. Your Word says *You are a shield for all who take refuge in You.* I'm learning that my role in our adventurous journey is to trust You, stay in communication with You, and walk with You in steps of joyful dependence.

I know You don't remove all adversity from my life, but I'm thankful that You go before me and widen my pathway. This is one of the many ways You *bless me and keep me* safe.

In Your blessed Name, Jesus, amen.

You broaden the path beneath me, so that my ankles do not turn. —Psalm 18:36

As for God, his way is perfect; the word of the Lord is flawless. He is a shield for all who take refuge in him. —Psalm 18:30

"The Lord bless you and keep you; the Lord make His face shine upon you, and be gracious to you; the Lord lift up His countenance upon you, and give you peace." —Numbers 6:24–26 nkjv

Precious Jesus,

Help me to keep my eyes on You and think great thoughts of You. It's easy for me to grow discouraged when I focus on less important things—the news, the economy, loved ones' problems, my own problems, and so on. This world is full of trouble, but I don't want difficulties to be my primary focus. Please keep reminding me that You are with me and *You have overcome the world*. You are nearer than the air I breathe, yet You are infinite God—*King of kings and Lord of lords*. You are also my loving Savior and faithful Friend. In You I have everything I need!

One of my favorite ways to increase my awareness of Your greatness is to praise You. This connects me with You—Father, Son, and Spirit—in a glorious way! Worshiping You pushes back the darkness, expanding Your kingdom of Light in the world. I'm blessed when I praise You through reading or singing the Psalms. Filling my mind with biblical truth strengthens me and equips me to resist discouragement. As troubles come my way, it's crucial for me to draw near You and spend time thinking about who You are—my Savior and Friend who is *Almighty* God!

In Your exalted Name, amen.

*"I have told you these things, so that in me you may have peace. In this world you will have trouble. But take heart! I have overcome the world." —*JOHN 16:33

*And on His robe and on His thigh He has a name written, "KING OF KINGS, AND LORD OF LORDS." —*REVELATION 19:16 NASB 1995

*"I am the Alpha and the Omega, the Beginning and the End," says the Lord, "who is and who was and who is to come, the Almighty." —*REVELATION 1:8 NKJV

My Savior-God,

As the world seems increasingly unsafe, I need to turn my attention to You more and more. Help me to remember that You are with me at *all* times and You have already won the ultimate victory. Because *I am in You and You are in me*, I have an eternity of stress-free life awaiting me in heaven—where there will be not even a trace of fear or worry. Instead, I will experience perfect Peace and limitless Love in Your Presence. Even now, thinking about this glorious future with You, *the King of Glory*, floods me with Joy!

Pondering this *future hope* strengthens and encourages me while I continue to live in this deeply fallen world. Whenever I start to feel anxious about something I've seen, heard, or thought, please prompt me to bring this concern straight to You. I know that *You* are the One who makes me secure—no matter what is happening. When my mind turns toward an idolatrous way of trying to feel safe, remind me to speak truth to myself: "*That's* not what makes me safe." This frees me to turn toward You and think about who You are—the victorious Savior who is also my forever-Friend. In You I am absolutely secure!

In Your triumphant Name, Jesus, amen.

*"On that day you will realize that I am in my Father, and you are in me, and I am in you." —*JOHN 14:20

*Lift up your heads, O you gates! And be lifted up, you everlasting doors! And the King of glory shall come in. —*PSALM 24:7 NKJV

*There is surely a future hope for you, and your hope will not be cut off. —*PROVERBS 23:18

*"Greater love has no one than this, that he lay down his life for his friends." —*JOHN 15:13

My living Lord,

As I focus my attention on You, I yearn for the dew of Your Presence to refresh my mind and heart. So many, many things vie for my attention in these complex times of instant communication. The world has changed enormously since You first gave the command: *"Be still, and know that I am God."* Nonetheless, I realize this timeless truth is essential for the well-being of my soul. Just as dew refreshes grass and flowers during the stillness of the night, so Your Presence revitalizes me as I spend time sitting quietly with You.

When my mind is refreshed and revitalized, I'm able to sort out what is important and what is not. In its natural condition, my mind easily gets stuck on trivial matters. Like the spinning wheels of a car stuck in mud, the cogs of my brain spin impotently when I focus on something insignificant. But as soon as I start communicating with You about the matter, my thoughts gain traction and I can move on to more important concerns.

Please put Your thoughts into my mind more and more. Help me stay in communication with You, Lord.

In Your refreshing Name, Jesus, amen.

Therefore, holy brothers, who share in the heavenly calling, fix your thoughts on Jesus, the apostle and high priest whom we confess. —HEBREWS 3:1

"Be still, and know that I am God. I will be exalted among the nations, I will be exalted in the earth!" —PSALM 46:10 ESV

She had a sister called Mary, who sat at the Lord's feet listening to what he said. But Martha was distracted by all the preparations that had to be made. She came to him and asked, "Lord, don't you care that my sister has left me to do the work by myself? Tell her to help me!" "Martha, Martha," the Lord answered, "you are worried and upset about many things, but only one thing is needed. Mary has chosen what is better, and it will not be taken away from her." —LUKE 10:39–42

Jesus, my Refuge,

Your Word says that *You are a Shield for all who take refuge in You*. Help me to remember this precious promise when my world feels threatening and unsafe. How comforting it is to know that You personally protect *all* who make You a refuge. You're a safe place in the midst of trouble.

Taking refuge in You involves *trusting in You* and *pouring out my heart to You*. I'm learning that no matter what is happening in my life, it's always the right time to voice my trust in You. Of course, sometimes I have to attend to the demands of my circumstances before I pause to pour out my heart. But I can just whisper my trust—and wait till I find the right time and place for expressing my emotions to You. Then, when circumstances permit, I can speak freely in the safety of Your Presence. This rich communication with You brings me real relief. It also strengthens my relationship with You and helps me find the way forward.

I rejoice that Your shielding Presence is always available to me. Whenever I'm feeling fearful, I like to turn to You and say: "Jesus, I take refuge in You."

In Your protecting Name, amen.

"As for God, his way is perfect; the word of the LORD is flawless. He is a shield for all who take refuge in him." —2 SAMUEL 22:31

God is our refuge and strength, always ready to help in times of trouble. —PSALM 46:1 NLT

Trust in him at all times, O people; pour out your hearts to him, for God is our refuge. —PSALM 62:8

Dearest Jesus,

You are worthy of all my confidence, all my trust! So instead of letting world events spook me, I'll pour my energy into trusting You and looking for evidence of Your Presence in the world. I love to whisper Your Name—to reconnect my heart and mind to You. *You are near to all who call upon You.* Please wrap me in Your abiding Presence and comfort me with Your Peace.

Help me remember that You are both loving and faithful. *Your Love reaches to the heavens, Your faithfulness to the skies.* This means that I can never come to the end of Your Love; it is limitless and everlasting! Moreover, I can stand on the Rock of Your faithfulness, no matter what circumstances I'm facing.

I realize that putting my confidence in my abilities, education, or success is futile and displeasing to You. Teach me to place my confidence fully in *You*—the Savior whose sacrificial death and miraculous resurrection opened the way for me into *eternal Glory*!

In Your breathtaking Name, amen.

The LORD is near to all who call upon Him, to all who call upon Him in truth. —PSALM 145:18 NKJV

Your love, O LORD, reaches to the heavens, your faithfulness to the skies. —PSALM 36:5

For our light and momentary troubles are achieving for us an eternal glory that far outweighs them all. —2 CORINTHIANS 4:17

Faithful God,

I need to stop trying to work things out before their times have come. Help me to accept the limitations of living one day at a time. When something comes to my attention, I can pause and ask You whether it's part of today's agenda for me. If it is not, I can just release it into Your care and keeping—and move on to today's responsibilities. I've found that when I follow this practice, there's a beautiful simplicity about my life: *a time for everything*, and everything in its time.

You have promised many blessings to *those who wait for You: new strength*, resurgence of hope, awareness of Your continual Presence. Waiting for You enables me to glorify You by living in deep dependence on You, ready to do Your will.

I've discovered that living close to You makes my life less complicated and cluttered. Though the world around me is messy and confusing, I rejoice that *You have overcome the world*. Thank You for *telling me these things, so that in You I may have Peace*.

In Your wonderful Name, Jesus, amen.

There is a time for everything, and a season for every activity under heaven: a time to be born and a time to die, a time to plant and a time to uproot. —ECCLESIASTES 3:1–2

Though youths grow weary and tired, and vigorous young men stumble badly, yet those who wait for the LORD will gain new strength; they will mount up with wings like eagles, they will run and not get tired, they will walk and not become weary. —ISAIAH 40:30–31 NASB 1995

"I have told you these things, so that in me you may have peace. In this world you will have trouble. But take heart! I have overcome the world." —JOHN 16:33

Merciful Jesus,

When I'm going through a dark time—an especially hard time—it's easy for me to project that darkness into the future. The longer I struggle with adverse circumstances, the darker the way ahead looks—and the harder it is for me to imagine myself walking along bright paths again. It's so tempting to just give up and let misery become my companion. But I know that *You* are my constant Companion, Jesus. So help me cling to You, Lord, trusting that You are able to *turn my darkness into Light.*

Instead of focusing on the circumstances that are weighing me down, I need to look to You—remembering that *You are continually with me. You hold me by my right hand*, encouraging me to *walk by faith* through the darkness. Through eyes of faith, I can anticipate brighter times ahead and praise You for them. As I walk worshipfully with You through the darkness, You enable me to see *the first gleam of dawn* on the path before me. Please help me persevere along this path, trusting that the dim light will gradually *shine brighter and brighter—till the full light of day.*

In Your spectacular Name, amen.

*You, Lord, keep my lamp burning; my God turns
my darkness into light.* —Psalm 18:28

*Nevertheless I am continually with You; You hold me
by my right hand.* —Psalm 73:23 nkjv

For we walk by faith, not by sight. —2 Corinthians 5:7 nkjv

*The path of the righteous is like the first gleam of dawn, shining
ever brighter till the full light of day.* —Proverbs 4:18

Gracious God,

Your Word says I can *cast my cares on You, and You will sustain me.* I've been carrying my own burdens, and it's wearing me out! My shoulders aren't strong enough to bear these heavy loads, so please help me to cast my burdens on You, Lord.

When I realize that something is weighing me down, I need to examine the problem to figure out whether it's mine or someone else's. If it isn't mine, I can simply let go of it and leave it behind. If it *is* my problem, I'll talk about it with You and ask You to show me how You want me to deal with it.

My usual tendency is to let worries weigh me down—becoming my focus. Please keep reminding me to bring my cares to You and leave them there. I know You can carry them on Your strong shoulders with ease. Handing my burdens over to You lightens my load and frees me to live in joyful dependence on You.

Lord, I'm encouraged by Your commitment to *sustain me*—to hold me up and provide what I need. I rejoice in Your promise to *supply every need of mine according to Your riches in Glory*!

In Your magnificent Name, Jesus, amen.

Cast your cares on the LORD and he will sustain you; he will never let the righteous fall. —PSALM 55:22

For a child will be born to us, a son will be given to us; and the government will rest on His shoulders; and His name will be called Wonderful Counselor, Mighty God, Eternal Father, Prince of Peace. —ISAIAH 9:6 NASB 1995

And my God will supply every need of yours according to his riches in glory in Christ Jesus. —PHILIPPIANS 4:19 ESV

Powerful Lord,

Help me to *trust You and not be afraid*, remembering that *You are my Strength and my Song*. It blesses me to ponder what it means to have You as my Strength. You spoke the universe into existence—Your Power is absolutely unlimited! When I face my weakness and entrust it to You, Your Power can flow freely into me. However, I've found that my fears can hinder the flow of Your Strength. I've learned that trying to fight my fears is counterproductive—this keeps me focused on fear rather than on You. Instead, I need to concentrate on *Your great faithfulness*. When I relate to You in confident trust, there's no limit to how much You can strengthen me.

I'm thankful that You are *my Song*, and You share Your Joy with me. I yearn to be increasingly aware of Your Presence, where *there is fullness of Joy*. O Lord, I rejoice as I journey with You toward my heavenly home—and I join You in singing Your Song!

In Your joyful Name, Jesus, amen.

"Surely God is my salvation; I will trust and not be afraid. The LORD, the LORD, is my strength and my song; he has become my salvation." With joy you will draw water from the wells of salvation. —ISAIAH 12:2–3

Whenever I am afraid, I will trust in You. —PSALM 56:3 NKJV

The steadfast love of the LORD never ceases; his mercies never come to an end; they are new every morning; great is your faithfulness. —LAMENTATIONS 3:22–23 ESV

You make known to me the path of life; in your presence there is fullness of joy; at your right hand are pleasures forevermore. —PSALM 16:11 ESV

Sovereign God,

Your Word tells me that *You guide me in the way of wisdom and lead me along straight paths.* Yet I sometimes feel so confused—struggling to find the right way forward. I've tried so many things, and I've been so hopeful at times. But my hope-filled paths have led to disappointment. I'm thankful that You fully understand how hard my journey has been. Even though I wish for easier circumstances, I believe that You can bring good out of every bit of my struggle.

Help me to walk in the way of wisdom—trusting You no matter what happens in my life. I know that steadfast trust in You is essential for finding and following the right path. As I go along my journey, I encounter many things that seem random or wrong. Yet I believe that You are fitting all of them into a comprehensive *plan for good*—Your Master Plan.

I realize that I can see only a very small piece of a massively big picture. From my limited vantage point, my journey looks confusing, with puzzling twists and turns. But I'm learning to *walk by faith, not by sight*—trusting that You are indeed *leading me along straight paths.*

In Your great, wise Name, Jesus, amen.

I guide you in the way of wisdom and lead you
along straight paths. —PROVERBS 4:11

We are assured and know that [God being a partner in their labor] all things
work together and are [fitting into a plan] for good to and for those who love God
and are called according to [His] design and purpose. —ROMANS 8:28 AMPC

A man's steps are directed by the LORD. How then can anyone
understand his own way? —PROVERBS 20:24

For we walk by faith, not by sight. —2 CORINTHIANS 5:7 NKJV

Splendid Savior,

I come into Your Presence seeking rest. My mind needs a break from its habitual judging. I form judgments about this situation, that situation, this person, that person, even the weather—as if judging were my job description. But the Bible tells me that You created me first and foremost to *know You* and live in rich communion with You. When I become preoccupied with passing judgment, I usurp Your role. Help me turn away from this sinful attitude and keep turning toward You—living in joyful awareness of Your loving Presence.

Teach me to relate to You as creature to Creator, sheep to Shepherd, subject to King, and clay to Potter. I want You to have Your way in my life more and more. Rather than evaluating Your ways with me, I need to accept them with trust and thankfulness. I realize that the intimacy You offer me is not an invitation to act as if I were Your equal. My heart's desire is to worship You as *King of kings* while walking hand in hand with You along my life-path.

In Your glorious Name, Jesus, amen.

*"Do not judge, so that you won't be judged." —*Matthew 7:1 hcsb

*"And this is eternal life, that they may know You, the only true God, and Jesus Christ whom You have sent." —*John 17:3 nkjv

*But who are you, O man, to talk back to God? "Shall what is formed say to him who formed it, 'Why did you make me like this?'" Does not the potter have the right to make out of the same lump of clay some pottery for noble purposes and some for common use? —*Romans 9:20–21

*And on His robe and on His thigh He has a name written, "KING OF KINGS, AND LORD OF LORDS." —*Revelation 19:16 nasb 1995

Precious Lord Jesus,

You are *Immanuel, God with us*—and You are enough! When things in my life are flowing smoothly, it's easy for me to trust in Your sufficiency. But when I encounter rough patches—one after another after another—I sometimes feel as if Your provision is inadequate. At times like this, my mind tends to go into high gear, obsessing about ways to make things better. I've come to realize that problem solving can turn into an addiction. There are times when my mind spins with so many plans and possibilities that I become confused and exhausted.

Instead of being overly focused on problems, I need to remember that *You are with me always*, taking care of me. Help me to *rejoice in You* and proclaim Your sufficiency even during my most difficult times. This is a supernatural response, and I must rely on Your Spirit to empower me. I also have to discipline myself to make wise choices—day by day and moment by moment. Lord, I choose to *be joyful in You, my Savior*, for You are indeed enough!

In Your all-sufficient Name, amen.

*"She will give birth to a son, and you are to give him the name Jesus, because he will save his people from their sins." All this took place to fulfill what the Lord had said through the prophet: "The virgin will be with child and will give birth to a son, and they will call him Immanuel" —which means, "God with us." —*MATTHEW 1:21–23

*"Teaching them to observe all that I have commanded you. And behold, I am with you always, to the end of the age." —*MATTHEW 28:20 ESV

Though the fig tree does not bud and there are no grapes on the vines, though the olive crop fails and the fields produce no food, though there are no sheep in the pen and no cattle in the stalls, yet I will rejoice in the LORD, *I will be joyful in God my Savior. —*HABAKKUK 3:17–18

My ardent Lord,

Your Love chases after me every day of my life! So I'll look for signs of Your loving Presence as I go through this day. You disclose Yourself to me in a variety of ways—words of Scripture just when I need them, helpful words spoken through other people, "coincidences" orchestrated by Your Spirit, nature's beauty, and so on. Your Love for me is not passive. It actively chases after me and leaps into my life! Please open the eyes of my heart so I can "see" You blessing me in myriad ways—both small and great.

I want to not only receive Your bountiful blessings but also take careful note of them—treasuring them and *pondering them in my heart.* I'm thankful for the countless ways You show up in my life. I like to write down some of these blessings so I can enjoy them again and again. These signs of Your Presence strengthen me and prepare me for whatever difficulties I'll encounter on the road ahead. Help me to remember that *nothing in all creation can separate me from Your Love!*

In Your conquering Name, Jesus, amen.

Your beauty and love chase after me every day of my life. I'm back home in the house of God for the rest of my life. —PSALM 23:6 THE MESSAGE

Your word I have hidden in my heart, that I might not sin against You. —PSALM 119:11 NKJV

But Mary treasured up all these things and pondered them in her heart. —LUKE 2:19

Neither height nor depth, nor anything else in all creation, will be able to separate us from the love of God that is in Christ Jesus our Lord. —ROMANS 8:39

My great God,

I'm grateful that *Your compassions never fail; they are new every morning.* So I can begin each day confidently, knowing that Your vast reservoir of blessings is full to the brim! This knowledge helps me wait for You, entrusting my long-unanswered prayers into Your care and keeping. I trust that not even one of my petitions has slipped past You unnoticed. As I wait in Your Presence, help me to drink deeply from Your fountain of limitless Love and unfailing compassion. These divine provisions are freely available to me—and essential for my spiritual health.

Although many of my prayers are not yet answered, I find hope in *Your great faithfulness.* You keep *all* Your promises—in Your perfect way and Your perfect timing. You have promised to give me Peace that can displace the trouble and fear in my heart. If I become weary of waiting, please remind me that You also wait—*so that You may be gracious to me and have mercy on me.* You hold back until I am ready to receive the things You have lovingly prepared for me. As I spend time in Your Presence, I rejoice in the promise that *all those who wait for You are blessed.*

In Your gracious Name, Jesus, amen.

Because of the Lord's great love we are not consumed, for his compassions never fail. They are new every morning; great is your faithfulness. I say to myself, "The Lord is my portion; therefore I will wait for him." —Lamentations 3:22–24

"Peace I leave with you; my peace I give you. I do not give to you as the world gives. Do not let your hearts be troubled and do not be afraid." —John 14:27

Therefore the Lord will wait, that He may be gracious to you; and therefore He will be exalted, that He may have mercy on you. For the Lord is a God of justice; blessed are all those who wait for Him. —Isaiah 30:18 NKJV

Beloved Lord Jesus,

Please infuse Your Peace into my innermost being. As I sit quietly in the Light of Your Presence, I long to sense Your Peace growing within me. This isn't something I can accomplish through self-discipline and willpower; it's a matter of opening up myself to receive Your blessing.

In this age of independence, it's countercultural as well as counterintuitive to acknowledge my neediness. However, You have taken me along a path that has highlighted my need for You—placing me in situations where my strengths were irrelevant and my weaknesses were glaringly evident. Through the aridity of those desert marches, You drew me closer and closer to Yourself. Moreover, You provided lovely surprises in that *sun-scorched land*. I discovered plants of Peace blossoming in the most desolate places!

You've been teaching me to thank You for hard times and difficult journeys—trusting that, through them, You accomplish Your best work. And I'm learning that needing You is the key to knowing You intimately, which is the gift above all gifts!

In Your incomparable Name, amen.

*"Peace I leave with you, My peace I give to you; not as the world gives do I give to you. Let not your heart be troubled, neither let it be afraid." —*JOHN 14:27 NKJV

"The LORD *will guide you always; he will satisfy your needs in a sun-scorched land and will strengthen your frame. You will be like a well-watered garden, like a spring whose waters never fail." —*ISAIAH 58:11

*Always give thanks for all things to God the Father in the name of our Lord Jesus Christ. —*EPHESIANS 5:20 NLV

Gentle Jesus,

I come wearily into Your Presence—feeling weighed down by yesterday's failures. I wish I could undo my decisions that I now regret. However, I know that the past is beyond the realm of change and cannot be undone. Even *You*, though You live in timelessness, respect the boundaries of time that exist in this world. So I don't want to waste energy bemoaning bad choices I have made. Instead, I ask You to forgive me and help me learn from my mistakes.

When I'm feeling weighed down by things I regret, it's as if I'm dragging my failures around like heavy chains clamped to my ankles. At such times, I find it beneficial to picture You coming to my rescue and cutting off those chains. You came to set Your followers free, and I want to walk in the truth that *I am free indeed*!

Lord, I rejoice that You redeem my failures—forgiving me and leading me along paths of newness. As I talk with You about my mistakes, I need to *learn from You*. Please show me the changes You want me to make and *guide me along right paths*.

In Your redeeming Name, amen.

*"Come to me, all you who are weary and burdened, and I will give you rest. Take my yoke upon you and learn from me, for I am gentle and humble in heart, and you will find rest for your souls." —*MATTHEW 11:28–29

*"So if the Son sets you free, you will be free indeed." —*JOHN 8:36

*He renews my strength. He guides me along right paths, bringing honor to his name. —*PSALM 23:3 NLT

Victorious Jesus,

Help me to welcome problems as perspective lifters. When things are going smoothly in my life, it's easy for me to sleepwalk through my days—just following my routines. But if I bump into an obstacle that blocks my way, I suddenly wake up and become more attentive.

I've discovered that when I encounter a problem with no immediate solution, my response to that situation takes me either up or down. I can lash out at the difficulty—resenting it and feeling sorry for myself. But experience has taught me that this negative attitude will take me down into a pit of self-pity. Instead of this hurtful response, I can view the problem as a ladder—enabling me to climb up and see my life from Your perspective. Looking down at the problem from this elevation, I'm able to see that the obstacle that stymied me is only a *light and momentary trouble.*

Once my perspective has been heightened, I'm free to look away from the difficulty and turn wholeheartedly to You. As I focus my attention on You, *the Light of Your Presence* shines upon me—blessing and refreshing me.

In Your radiant, refreshing Name, amen.

For our light and momentary troubles are achieving for us an eternal glory that far outweighs them all. So we fix our eyes not on what is seen, but on what is unseen. For what is seen is temporary, but what is unseen is eternal. —2 Corinthians 4:17–18

Blessed are those who have learned to acclaim you, who walk in the light of your presence, O Lord. —Psalm 89:15

"The Lord bless you and keep you; the Lord make His face shine upon you, and be gracious to you." —Numbers 6:24–25 nkjv

Loving Savior,

Help me to stop overthinking things—obsessing about unimportant matters. When my mind is idle, I tend to go into planning mode, attempting to figure things out and make decisions before I really need to. I realize this is an ineffective way of trying to be in control; it's also a waste of precious time. I often end up changing my mind anyway, or even forgetting what I decided. I know there is a time for planning, but it's definitely not *all* the time—or even most of it.

I really want to live in the present, where Your beautiful Presence awaits me continually. As I refresh myself in Your nearness, Your Love soaks into my innermost being. I delight in relaxing with You—putting aside problems so I can be attentive to You and receptive to Your Love. *My soul thirsts for You*, but so often I don't realize what I'm really longing for: awareness of Your Presence with me.

Lord, please *lead me beside quiet waters and restore my soul*. Just as lovers can communicate deeply with very few words, so it is in my relationship with You—the Lover of my soul.

In Your tender Name, Jesus, amen.

I pray that out of his glorious riches he may strengthen you with power through his Spirit in your inner being, so that Christ may dwell in your hearts through faith. And I pray that you, being rooted and established in love, may have power, together with all the saints, to grasp how wide and long and high and deep is the love of Christ. —EPHESIANS 3:16–18

O God, You are my God; early will I seek You; my soul thirsts for You; my flesh longs for You in a dry and thirsty land where there is no water. —PSALM 63:1 NKJV

He makes me lie down in green pastures, he leads me beside quiet waters, he restores my soul. He guides me in paths of righteousness for his name's sake. —PSALM 23:2–3

Mighty God,

Your sovereign hand—Your control over my life—has placed me in humbling circumstances. I feel held down, held back, and powerless to change things. Because this feels so uncomfortable, part of me longs to break free and regain some control. Yet I know that this humbling position is actually a good place for me to be. My discomfort awakens me from the slumber of routine and reminds me that *You* are in charge of my life.

The difficulties I face present me with a crucial choice. I can grumble about my troubles—resenting Your ways with me—or I can come closer to You. When I'm suffering, my need for closeness with You is greater than ever. The more I choose to draw near You, affirming my trust in You, the more I can find hope in *Your unfailing Love*. You are teaching me to *be joyful in hope* while waiting in Your Presence—where Joy abounds!

Help me to persevere in trusting You, Lord, believing that *You will lift me up in due time.* Meanwhile, I'll keep *casting all my anxiety on You,* knowing that *You care for me* affectionately and are watching over me continually.

In Your powerful Name, Jesus, amen.

May your unfailing love rest upon us, O LORD, even
as we put our hope in you. —PSALM 33:22

Be joyful in hope, patient in affliction, faithful in prayer. —ROMANS 12:12

You will show me the path of life; in Your presence is fullness of joy; at
Your right hand are pleasures forevermore. —PSALM 16:11 NKJV

Humble yourselves, therefore, under God's mighty hand, that he may lift you up in
due time. Cast all your anxiety on him because he cares for you. —1 PETER 5:6–7

Generous Lord Jesus,

I come to You with a thankful heart, aware that my cup is overflowing with blessings. Gratitude enables me to perceive You more clearly and to rejoice in our Love-relationship. I'm so grateful that *nothing can separate me from Your loving Presence*! This assurance of Your continual Presence with me is the basis of my security. Whenever I start to feel anxious, please remind me that my security rests in You alone—and You are totally trustworthy.

I realize I will never be in control of my life circumstances, but I'm learning to relax and trust in *Your* control. You are teaching me to seek You and know You in greater depth and breadth—rather than striving for a predictable, safe lifestyle. Help me, Lord, to cling to *You* instead of clinging to my old ways. I want to live my life as a glorious adventure shared with You, my forever-Friend and constant Companion. You are always doing something new in me, and You're at work in all my circumstances. So I need to stay alert and be on the lookout for everything You have prepared for me.

In Your marvelous Name, amen.

For I am convinced that neither death nor life, neither angels nor demons, neither the present nor the future, nor any powers, neither height nor depth, nor anything else in all creation, will be able to separate us from the love of God that is in Christ Jesus our Lord. —ROMANS 8:38–39

When I am afraid, I will trust in you. In God, whose word I praise, in God I trust; I will not be afraid. What can mortal man do to me? —PSALM 56:3–4

"See, I am doing a new thing! Now it springs up; do you not perceive it? I am making a way in the desert and streams in the wasteland." —ISAIAH 43:19

My Refuge,

You are worthy of all my confidence, all my trust! There are people and things that deserve *some* of my confidence and trust, but only You deserve *all* of it. In a world that seems increasingly unsafe and unpredictable, You are the Rock that provides a firm foundation for my life—*my Rock in whom I take refuge.*

Because You are my Refuge, my sense of security doesn't rest in my circumstances. My natural inclination is to strive to be in control of my life, but You're training me to relax in *Your* sovereign control. You are *a well-proved help in trouble,* and You're always present with me. Please help me to face unwelcome changes and unnerving circumstances without fear.

Instead of letting anxious thoughts roam freely in my mind, I need to lasso them—voicing my trust in You. When I bring those captive thoughts into Your Presence, You subdue them and give me Your Peace. As Your Word assures me, *whoever trusts in You is kept safe.*

In Your strong Name, Jesus, amen.

The LORD is my rock, my fortress and my deliverer; my God is my rock, in whom I take refuge. He is my shield and the horn of my salvation, my stronghold. —PSALM 18:2

God is our Refuge and Strength [mighty and impenetrable to temptation], a very present and well-proved help in trouble. Therefore we will not fear, though the earth should change and though the mountains be shaken into the midst of the seas. —PSALM 46:1–2 AMPC

We demolish arguments and every pretension that sets itself up against the knowledge of God, and we take captive every thought to make it obedient to Christ. —2 CORINTHIANS 10:5

Fear of man will prove to be a snare, but whoever trusts in the LORD is kept safe. —PROVERBS 29:25

October

*May the God of hope fill you with all joy
and peace as you trust in him, so that
you may overflow with hope by the power
of the Holy Spirit.* —ROMANS 15:13

Cherished Jesus,

You are my Joy! These four words light up my life when I think them, whisper them, or speak them out loud. Since You are always with me, *the Joy of Your Presence* is continually available to me. I can open my heart to Your Presence by affirming my trust in You, my love for You. Your Light shines upon me and within me as I *rejoice in You, my Savior*. I delight in thinking about all that You are to me and all You have done for me.

When I became Your follower, You empowered me to rise above the circumstances in my life. You filled me with Your Spirit, and this Holy Helper has limitless Power. Moreover, You promised that *You will come back and take me to be with You so that I may be where You are*—forever!

Whenever my world looks dark, focusing on You—*the Light of the world*—brightens my perspective. As I relax in Your Presence, I can almost hear You whispering, "Beloved, I am Your Joy."

In Your beautiful Name, amen.

Surely you have granted him eternal blessings and made him glad with the joy of your presence. —PSALM 21:6

Rejoice in the Lord always. Again I will say, rejoice! —PHILIPPIANS 4:4 NKJV

"And if I go and prepare a place for you, I will come back and take you to be with me that you also may be where I am." —JOHN 14:3

When Jesus spoke again to the people, he said, "I am the light of the world. Whoever follows me will never walk in darkness, but will have the light of life." —JOHN 8:12

Glorious God,

I delight in the stunning truth that *You will be my Guide even to the end*! How comforting it is to know that the One who leads me through each day will never abandon me. You are the Constant I can always count on—the One who goes before me, opening up the way, yet remains close beside me. *You hold me by my right hand. You guide me with Your counsel, and afterward You will take me into Glory.*

I have a hard time making decisions, so sometimes I'm tempted to be overly dependent on other people. But You have been showing me a much better way. Because You're my Lord and Savior, I have a completely trustworthy, infinitely wise Leader who is *always with me. You guide me in Your truth and teach me*, equipping me to make good decisions.

As I journey with You, I'm thankful for the magnificent map You have provided: the Bible. *Your Word is a lamp to my feet and a light for my path.* Help me to follow this Light and follow *You*—for You are the One who knows the best way for me to go.

In Your trustworthy Name, Jesus, amen.

For this God is our God for ever and ever; he will be our guide even to the end. —PSALM 48:14

Yet I am always with you; you hold me by my right hand. You guide me with your counsel, and afterward you will take me into glory. —PSALM 73:23–24

Guide me in Your truth and teach me, for You are the God of my salvation; I wait for You all day long. —PSALM 25:5 HCSB

Your word is a lamp to my feet and a light for my path. —PSALM 119:105

Dear Jesus,

Help me remember that I am *not* on trial. Your Word assures me *there is no condemnation for those who belong to You*—those who know You as Savior. I have already been judged "Not guilty!" in the courts of heaven through Your finished work on the cross. Your sacrificial death and miraculous resurrection have set me free from bondage to sin. I want to live joyfully in this freedom—learning to relax and savor my guilt-free position in Your kingdom. Yet I struggle to live in this amazing freedom You won for me, Lord.

I'm so thankful for the grace You have *lavished on me*. Please work in my heart so that gratitude for Your grace fuels my desire to live according to Your will. The closer I live to You, the better I can discern Your will—and the more fully I can experience Your Joy and Peace. Knowing You intimately helps me trust You enough to receive Your Peace even in the midst of trouble. And *overflowing with thankfulness* has the delightful "side effect" of increasing my Joy!

In Your gracious Name, amen.

So now there is no condemnation for those who belong to Christ Jesus. —ROMANS 8:1 NLT

"So if the Son sets you free, you will be free indeed." —JOHN 8:36 ESV

In him we have redemption through his blood, the forgiveness of sins, in accordance with the riches of God's grace that he lavished on us with all wisdom and understanding. —EPHESIANS 1:7–8

So then, just as you received Christ Jesus as Lord, continue to live in him, rooted and built up in him, strengthened in the faith as you were taught, and overflowing with thankfulness. —COLOSSIANS 2:6–7

Invincible Lord Jesus,

You are the Foundation and Focus of my life. I'm grateful that You're such a firm Foundation: *my Rock* that is not shaken by even the fiercest storms. I praise You, mighty Lord!

Before I knew You as my Savior-God, I had nothing to build my life upon. Every time I tried to create something meaningful, it would eventually collapse like a house of cards. Without You, everything was ultimately *"Meaningless! Meaningless!"* But ever since You became my Savior, I've been building on the solid Rock of Your Presence. Some of the things I've worked on have flourished, and others have not, but I always have *a firm place to stand*—the foundation You provided for me.

I've found that the key to steadiness in my life is to *set You continually before me*. When I make You my Focus, I can walk more steadily along my life-path. Many distractions still vie for my attention, but *You* are the Guide who is always before me. As I keep looking ahead to You, I can see You beckoning me on—step by step by step—all the way to heaven!

In Your majestic Name, amen.

"The Lord lives! Praise be to my Rock! Exalted be God, the Rock, my Savior!" —2 Samuel 22:47

"Meaningless! Meaningless!" says the Teacher. "Utterly meaningless! Everything is meaningless." —Ecclesiastes 1:2

He lifted me out of the slimy pit, out of the mud and mire; he set my feet on a rock and gave me a firm place to stand. —Psalm 40:2

I have set the Lord continually before me; because He is at my right hand, I will not be shaken. —Psalm 16:8 NASB 1995

Compassionate Savior,

Your Word teaches that *You care for me*—You are taking care of me! But when conditions that are troubling me get worse instead of better, it's easy for me to feel as if You're letting me down—as if You don't really care about all that I'm going through. I know You could easily change my circumstances, yet You don't.

Please help me calm down and stop striving to control things. I really want to give up my futile efforts to think my way through my problems. I long to *be still* in Your Presence and just fall back into Your strong arms with a sigh of trust. Even though there are so many things I don't understand, I can enjoy Your Presence and rest in Your unfailing Love.

Lord, Your ways are mysterious and unfathomable; Your Love is wonderful and never-ending. *I will watch in hope for You*, because You are *God my Savior*—the God who *hears me*.

In Your saving Name, Jesus, amen.

Therefore humble yourselves under the mighty hand of God, that He may exalt you at the proper time, casting all your anxiety on Him, because He cares for you. —1 PETER 5:6–7 NASB 1995

"Be still, and know that I am God; I will be exalted among the nations, I will be exalted in the earth." —PSALM 46:10

And He said, "My Presence will go with you, and I will give you rest." —EXODUS 33:14 NKJV

But as for me, I watch in hope for the LORD, I wait for God my Savior; my God will hear me. —MICAH 7:7

Precious Jesus,

Please help me to *be joyful in hope*. Sometimes the circumstances of my life and the condition of this world make it difficult for me to be joyful. You have been showing me that *hope* is one of the best places to find true Joy. I want to know more and more fully *the hope to which You have called me* and *the riches of Your glorious inheritance*. How amazing it is that You have shared Your inheritance with me: making me a co-heir with You!

When circumstances are weighing me down, I must grasp on to hope for dear life! This empowers me not only to survive but to thrive—living joyously.

I've discovered that hope is like a hot-air balloon. Because it's very buoyant, it can lift me up above my troubles. This enables me to soar in the heavens with You—where I can see things from a heightened, big-picture perspective. However, to embark on this heavenly journey, I must climb into the basket beneath the balloon—trusting fully that my hope in You will not let me down.

I trust You, Jesus; *help my unbelief!*

In Your exalted Name, amen.

Be joyful in hope, patient in affliction, faithful in prayer. —ROMANS 12:12

I pray also that the eyes of your heart may be enlightened in order that you may know the hope to which he has called you, the riches of his glorious inheritance in the saints. —EPHESIANS 1:18

There is surely a future hope for you, and your hope will not be cut off. —PROVERBS 23:18

Immediately the father of the child cried out and said, "I believe; help my unbelief!" —MARK 9:24 ESV

Ever-present Jesus,

I long to give myself fully to the adventure of today! I want to walk boldly along the path of Life—relying on You, my ever-present Companion. I have every reason to be confident because Your Presence accompanies me all the days of my life—and onward into eternity.

Help me not to give in to fear or worry, those robbers of abundant living. Teach me to trust You enough to face problems as they come. My natural tendency is to anticipate and prepare for trouble—in a vain attempt to stay in control. But You've been showing me that if I *fix my eyes on You, the Author and Perfecter of my faith*, many obstacles on the road ahead will vanish before I reach them.

Whenever I start to feel afraid, please *take hold of my right hand* and remind me that You are continually with me. Your Word assures me that *neither height nor depth, nor anything else in all creation, will be able to separate me from Your loving Presence.*

In Your triumphant Name, amen.

For this God is our God for ever and ever; he will be our guide even to the end. —PSALM 48:14

Let us fix our eyes on Jesus, the author and perfecter of our faith, who for the joy set before him endured the cross, scorning its shame, and sat down at the right hand of the throne of God. —HEBREWS 12:2

"For I am the LORD, your God, who takes hold of your right hand and says to you, Do not fear; I will help you." —ISAIAH 41:13

For I am convinced that neither death nor life, neither angels nor demons, neither the present nor the future, nor any powers, neither height nor depth, nor anything else in all creation, will be able to separate us from the love of God that is in Christ Jesus our Lord. —ROMANS 8:38–39

Delightful Lord,

Help me not to think of prayer as a chore. Instead, I want to view it as communicating with the One I adore—*You*! *Delighting myself in You* draws me into sweet communion with You. I like to spend time thinking about all You are to me and all You do for me. The Bible gives me amazing assurances: *You take great delight in me*, and You love me with perfect, everlasting Love. As I rest in Your Presence, may Your tenderness embrace me—convincing me that I am indeed Your beloved. I rejoice in knowing that You will never let me go!

An easy way for me to start talking with You is to thank You for being my Savior-God and beloved Friend. I can also give You thanks for things that are happening in my life, in my family, and beyond. These prayers of thanksgiving connect me with You and ease my way into other types of prayers.

I can talk with You freely because You understand everything about me and my circumstances. Since You paid the full penalty for all my sins, I know You never reject me. So I am free to *pour out my heart to You—trusting in You, my Refuge.*

In Your redeeming Name, Jesus, amen.

Delight yourself in the LORD and he will give you the desires of your heart. —PSALM 37:4

"The LORD your God is with you, he is mighty to save. He will take great delight in you, he will quiet you with his love, he will rejoice over you with singing." —ZEPHANIAH 3:17

You are my God, and I will give You thanks. You are my God; I will exalt You. —PSALM 118:28 HCSB

Trust in him at all times, O people; pour out your hearts to him, for God is our refuge. —PSALM 62:8

Wonderful Counselor,

I know that You understand me far, far better than I understand myself. So I come to You with my problems and insecurities, seeking Your counsel. In the Light of Your loving Presence, I can see myself as I truly am: beautifully clothed in Your flawless righteousness. Even though Your righteousness is perfect, I realize I will continue to struggle with imperfections—mine and others'—as long as I live in this world. But Your Word assures me that my standing with You is secure. *Nothing in all creation will be able to separate me from Your Love!*

Because You're such a great Counselor, You help me recognize truth and live according to it. So I can be honest and open when I bring You my concerns. The Bible tells me that *knowing the truth will set me free*, and Your wonderful counseling is freeing me from sin and shame.

Lord Jesus, You are teaching me to *delight myself in You* above all else. I rejoice that You really *are* the deepest Desire of my heart. Please keep me close to You—joyously aware of Your loving Presence.

In Your joyful Name, Jesus, amen.

For a child will be born to us, a son will be given to us; and the government will rest on His shoulders; and His name will be called Wonderful Counselor, Mighty God, Eternal Father, Prince of Peace. —ISAIAH 9:6 NASB 1995

Neither height nor depth, nor anything else in all creation, will be able to separate us from the love of God that is in Christ Jesus our Lord. —ROMANS 8:39

"And you will know the truth, and the truth will set you free." —JOHN 8:32 NLT

Delight yourself in the LORD; and He will give you the desires of your heart. —PSALM 37:4 NASB 1995

My Jesus,

You know about every one of my troubles; *You have collected all my tears and preserved them in Your bottle.* So please help me not to be afraid of tears—or of the hardships that cause them. I know that my problems are not random or meaningless. You've been teaching me to trust You and find comfort in Your sovereignty. I'm confident that You know what You are doing!

Because Your perspective is infinite—unlimited by time or space— Your ways of working in the world are far beyond my comprehension. If it were possible for me to see things from Your God-perspective, I would marvel at the perfection of Your will—and revel in Your Glory. But *now I see only a poor reflection*, so I must live with mystery.

Your assurance that You preserve my tears in Your bottle shows me how precious I am to You. And the Bible promises that someday *You will wipe every tear from my eyes. There will be no more death or mourning or crying or pain.* How I rejoice in that glorious, heavenly future awaiting me!

In Your victorious Name, amen.

You have seen me tossing and turning through the night. You have collected all my tears and preserved them in your bottle! You have recorded every one in your book. —Psalm 56:8 tlb

Now we see but a poor reflection as in a mirror; then we shall see face to face. Now I know in part; then I shall know fully, even as I am fully known. —1 Corinthians 13:12

"He will wipe every tear from their eyes. There will be no more death or mourning or crying or pain, for the old order of things has passed away." —Revelation 21:4

Beloved Jesus,

When the task before me looks daunting, help me to view the challenge as a privilege rather than a burdensome duty. You've been training me to replace my "I have to" mentality with an "I get to" approach. I've found that this makes all the difference in my perspective—transforming drudgery into delight. I realize this is not a magic trick; the work still has to be done. But this change in my viewpoint enables me to face the challenging chore joyfully and confidently.

I'm learning that perseverance is essential as I go about my work. If I start to grow weary or discouraged, I need to remind myself: "I *get* to do this!" I can thank You for giving me the strength and ability to do what needs to be done. Thankfulness clears my mind and draws me closer to You.

Please guide my mind as I'm thinking things out in Your Presence—pondering problems and seeking solutions. *Whatever I do*, I want to *work at it with all my heart, as working for You.*

In Your transforming Name, amen.

Devote yourselves to prayer with an alert mind and a thankful heart. —COLOSSIANS 4:2 NLT

I can do all things through Christ who strengthens me. —PHILIPPIANS 4:13 NKJV

Whatever you do, work at it with all your heart, as working for the Lord, not for men. —COLOSSIANS 3:23

Jesus, my Treasure,

Teach me how to live more fully in the present—refusing to *worry about tomorrow.* I really do want to live present tense in Your Presence, making *You* the main pursuit of my life. This is quite a struggle for me because planning and worrying come so naturally to me.

Please help me resist the temptation to worry. I live in such a fallen world—full of sin and struggles. I'm continually faced with things that can make me anxious if I let them. But Your Word tells me that *each day has enough trouble of its own.* You carefully calibrate the amount of difficulty I'll encounter on a given day, and You know exactly how much I can handle. Moreover, You are always near—ready to strengthen, encourage, and comfort me.

I've found that pursuing a close walk with You is the most effective way to live abundantly. I need to keep bringing my thoughts back to You whenever they wander. I can return to You joyfully, knowing that *You take great delight in me and rejoice over me with singing.*

In Your delightful Name, amen.

*"Therefore do not worry about tomorrow, for tomorrow will worry about itself. Each day has enough trouble of its own." —*Matthew 6:34

*"Do not fear, for I am with you; do not be afraid, for I am your God. I will strengthen you; I will help you; I will hold on to you with My righteous right hand." —*Isaiah 41:10 hcsb

*"The thief comes only to steal and kill and destroy. I came that they may have life and have it abundantly." —*John 10:10 esv

"The Lord *your God is with you, he is mighty to save. He will take great delight in you, he will quiet you with his love, he will rejoice over you with singing." —*Zephaniah 3:17

My living God,

I come into Your gracious Presence, asking You to lead me step by step through this day. I know You provide Light for only one day at a time. Whenever I try to look into the future, I find myself peering into darkness. *Your Face shines upon me* only in the present! *This* is where I find Your unfailing, unquenchable Love—stronger than the bond between a mother and her nursing baby. *Though she may forget the baby at her breast, You will not forget me!* Your Word assures me that *You have engraved me on the palms of Your hands.*

I want to *really come to know—practically, through experience— Your Love that far surpasses mere knowledge.* This is a lofty goal, Lord. I need the help of Your indwelling Spirit, who empowers me to experience Your boundless Love. I long to *be filled through all my being with Your fullness—having the richest measure of Your divine Presence, becoming a body wholly filled and flooded with You!*

In Your sacred Name, Jesus, amen.

"The Lord make His face shine upon you, and be gracious to you." —Numbers 6:25 nkjv

"Can a mother forget the baby at her breast and have no compassion on the child she has borne? Though she may forget, I will not forget you! See, I have engraved you on the palms of my hands; your walls are ever before me." —Isaiah 49:15–16

[That you may really come] to know [practically, through experience for yourselves] the love of Christ, which far surpasses mere knowledge [without experience]; that you may be filled [through all your being] unto all the fullness of God [may have the richest measure of the divine Presence, and become a body wholly filled and flooded with God Himself]! —Ephesians 3:19 ampc

Lord Jesus,

There's a mighty battle going on for control of my mind. Heaven and earth intersect in my brain; I can feel the influence of both realms tugging at my thoughts. Thank You, Lord, for creating me with the capacity to experience tiny foretastes of heaven. When I shut out distractions and focus on Your Presence, I can enjoy sitting with You *in the heavenly realms.* This is an incredible privilege reserved for those who belong to You and seek Your Face. You have instilled in me a strong desire to spend time communing with You. As I concentrate on You and Your Word, Your Spirit fills my mind with *Life and Peace.*

The world exerts a downward pull on my thoughts. Media bombard me with cynicism, lies, greed, and lust. Please give me discernment and protection when I'm facing these things. I need to stay in communication with You whenever I walk through the wastelands of this world. Help me resist the temptation to worry—a form of worldliness that weighs me down and blocks awareness of Your Presence. And keep me alert to the battle that is continually being waged against my mind.

O Lord, how I look forward to an eternity of strife-free living in heaven!

In Your powerful Name, amen.

And God raised us up with Christ and seated us with him in the heavenly realms in Christ Jesus. —EPHESIANS 2:6

For the mind set on the flesh is death, but the mind set on the Spirit is life and peace. —ROMANS 8:6 NASB 1995

Be self-controlled and alert. Your enemy the devil prowls around like a roaring lion looking for someone to devour. —1 PETER 5:8

Majestic Jesus,

I come into Your Presence seeking rest and refreshment. Spending focused time with You strengthens and encourages me. Lord, I marvel at the wonder of communing with You—the Creator of the universe—while sitting in the comfort of my home.

Kings who reign on earth tend to make themselves inaccessible. Ordinary people almost never gain an audience with them. Even dignitaries must plow through red tape and protocol in order to speak with royalty. I rejoice that *You* are totally accessible to me—even though You are King of this vast, awesome universe.

Please help me remember that You are with me at all times and in all circumstances. *Nothing* can separate me from Your loving Presence! When You cried out from the cross, *"It is finished!" the curtain of the temple was torn in two from top to bottom.* This opened the way for me to meet You face to Face, with no need of protocol or priests. How breathtaking it is that You, *the King of kings*, are my constant Companion!

In Your kingly Name, amen.

For by Him all things were created, both in the heavens and on earth, visible and invisible, whether thrones or dominions or rulers or authorities —all things have been created through Him and for Him. —Colossians 1:16 nasb 1995

So when Jesus had received the sour wine, He said, "It is finished!" And bowing His head, He gave up His spirit. —John 19:30 nkjv

And when Jesus had cried out again in a loud voice, he gave up his spirit. At that moment the curtain of the temple was torn in two from top to bottom. The earth shook and the rocks split. —Matthew 27:50–51

God will bring this about in His own time. He is the blessed and only Sovereign, the King of kings, and the Lord of lords. —1 Timothy 6:15 hcsb

My Creator,

As I grow increasingly aware of Your Presence, I find it easier to discern the way I should go. This is one of the practical benefits of living close to You, Lord. Instead of wondering what's on the road ahead or worrying about what I should do if—or when—I can concentrate on staying in communication with You. Once I actually arrive at a choice-point, I can trust You to show me which direction I should go.

I confess that sometimes I get so preoccupied with future plans and decisions that I fail to see the choices I need to make now. Without really thinking, I just go through the day on autopilot. When I live this way for a while, dullness starts to creep into my life. I sleepwalk through my days, following well-worn paths of routine.

You, the Creator of the universe, are the most creative Being imaginable! I'm thankful that You don't leave me circling in deeply rutted paths. Instead, You lead me along fresh trails of adventure, revealing to me things I did not know.

Help me stay in communication with You—following Your guiding Presence.

In Your breathtaking Name, Jesus, amen.

I will instruct you and teach you in the way you should go;
I will counsel you and watch over you. —PSALM 32:8

In the beginning God created the heavens and the earth. —GENESIS 1:1 NKJV

"The LORD will guide you always; he will satisfy your needs in a sun-
scorched land and will strengthen your frame. You will be like a well-
watered garden, like a spring whose waters never fail." —ISAIAH 58:11

Loving Savior,

I confess that I tend to search for security in the wrong place: this broken world. I make mental and written checklists of things I need to do in order to gain control of my life. My goal is to check everything off my lists so that I can finally relax and be at peace. But I've discovered that the more I work to achieve this goal, the more things crop up on my lists. The harder I try, the more frustrated I become!

You've been showing me a far better way to find security in this life. Instead of scrutinizing my checklists, I need to *fix my thoughts on You*—rejoicing in Your Presence with me. The Bible tells me *You will keep me in perfect Peace* as I stay attentive to You. Moreover, being in communication with You helps me sort out what is important and what is not, what needs to be done now and what does not.

Lord, please train me to *fix my eyes not on what is seen*—my circumstances—*but on what is unseen*: Your loving Presence.

In Your matchless Name, Jesus, amen.

Therefore, holy brothers, who share in the heavenly calling, fix your thoughts on Jesus, the apostle and high priest whom we confess. —HEBREWS 3:1

You will keep him in perfect peace, whose mind is stayed on You, because he trusts in You. —ISAIAH 26:3 NKJV

So we fix our eyes not on what is seen, but on what is unseen. For what is seen is temporary, but what is unseen is eternal. —2 CORINTHIANS 4:18

Magnificent Savior,

The Joy I have in You is independent of my circumstances. I am never separated from You, and *in Your Presence there is fullness of Joy*! As I go along today's pathway, I'll search for signs of Your unseen yet ever-so-real Presence. Sometimes You communicate with me in grand, unmistakable ways—"coincidences" that are clearly the work of Your hands. At other times I get more subtle glimpses of You. These are often so personal and intimate that other people wouldn't even notice them. Yet these subtle signs bring me profound Joy.

The more attentive I am, the more I can find You in the details of my day. So please help me stay alert—being on the lookout for delightful displays of Your Presence.

I want to fill my mind and heart with Scripture, where You reveal Yourself most clearly. As Your promises permeate my thinking, they keep me close to You. I love to hear You speaking to me through Your Word: *"Listen to My voice. I know you, and you follow Me. I give you eternal Life, and no one can snatch you out of My hand."*

In Your invincible Name, Jesus, amen.

You make known to me the path of life; in your presence there is fullness of joy; at your right hand are pleasures forevermore. —PSALM 16:11 ESV

"And you will seek Me and find Me, when you search for Me with all your heart." —JEREMIAH 29:13 NKJV

"My sheep listen to my voice; I know them, and they follow me. I give them eternal life, and they shall never perish; no one can snatch them out of my hand." —JOHN 10:27–28

Sovereign Lord,

You are my Strength! You enable me to go on the heights—to wander with You in the Glory of Your Presence. I admit, though, that sometimes I feel as if I can barely take the next step on this long journey upward. As I look ahead, I see steep mountains that seem insurmountable. *Yet I am always with You; You hold me by my right hand. You guide me with Your counsel*, helping me find the best way to scale those heights.

Although my journey with You is challenging—even grueling at times—it is much more than an endurance contest. The fact that You are with me can infuse Joy into the most arduous climb! So I'll be on the lookout for all the pleasures You have prepared for me. Yet no matter what delights I discover, the greatest treasure is *You*, my beloved Companion.

I used to think that "the heights" referred to the very top of the mountain I'm climbing. But when I stop and look back at where my journey began, I can see how far up I've already come. As I take time to relax and gaze lovingly at You, I sense the Glory of Your Presence all around me!

In Your glorious Name, Jesus, amen.

The Sovereign LORD *is my strength; he makes my feet like the feet of a deer, he enables me to go on the heights.* —HABAKKUK 3:19

Yet I am always with you; you hold me by my right hand. You guide me with your counsel, and afterward you will take me into glory. —PSALM 73:23–24

And He is the radiance of His glory and the exact representation of His nature, and upholds all things by the word of His power. When He had made purification of sins, He sat down at the right hand of the Majesty on high. —HEBREWS 1:3 NASB 1995

Merciful Jesus,

I want to make *You* the focal point of my search for security. In my private thoughts, I've been trying to order my world so that it's predictable and feels safe. However, I realize this is an impossible goal; it's also counterproductive to my spiritual growth.

Help me learn to rely on You more and more, especially when my private world feels unsteady. Instead of striving to regain control, I need to grip Your hand for support—living in conscious dependence on You.

I've been yearning for a problem-free life, but You've been showing me that trouble can highlight my awareness of Your Presence. In the darkness of adversity, the radiance of Your Face shines brightly— beaming out encouragement and comfort.

Please enable me to view the problems in my life as beneficial, *considering it pure joy whenever I face trials of many kinds.* No matter what is happening, I can always rejoice that I have an eternity of trouble-free living awaiting me in heaven!

In Your amazing Name, amen.

If I take the wings of the morning, and dwell in the uttermost parts of the sea, even there Your hand shall lead me, and Your right hand shall hold me. —PSALM 139:9–10 NKJV

Consider it pure joy, my brothers, whenever you face trials of many kinds. —JAMES 1:2

Rejoice in the Lord always. I will say it again: Rejoice! —PHILIPPIANS 4:4

My faithful God,

I look to You this day for help, comfort, and companionship. I know You are always by my side, so even a glance can connect me with You. When I look to You for help, it flows freely from Your Presence. You are teaching me to recognize my constant need for You—in small matters as well as large ones.

When I need comfort, You lovingly enfold me in Your arms. You enable me not only to feel comforted but to be a channel through whom You comfort others. As a result, I am doubly blessed. While Your comfort is flowing through me to others, some of that blessing absorbs into me.

Your continual Companionship is an amazing gift! As I look to You, I find You faithful, true, and lovingly present with me. No matter what losses I may experience in my life, I know that *nothing can separate me from Your Loving Presence*!

In Your comforting Name, Jesus, amen.

Look to the LORD and his strength; seek his face always. —PSALM 105:4

Those who look to him are radiant; their faces are never covered with shame. —PSALM 34:5

Praise be to the God and Father of our Lord Jesus Christ, the Father of compassion and the God of all comfort, who comforts us in all our troubles, so that we can comfort those in any trouble with the comfort we ourselves have received from God. —2 CORINTHIANS 1:3–4

For I am convinced that neither death nor life, neither angels nor demons, neither the present nor the future, nor any powers, neither height nor depth, nor anything else in all creation, will be able to separate us from the love of God that is in Christ Jesus our Lord. —ROMANS 8:38–39

Glorious Jesus,

You are the firm foundation on which I can dance and sing and celebrate Your glorious Presence! I receive this precious gift as Your high and holy calling for me. You've shown me that glorifying and enjoying You is vastly more important than maintaining a tidy, structured life. Still, my natural tendency is to pour my energy into trying to keep everything under control. Help me relinquish this striving to be in control—recognizing that it's both an impossible task and an affront to *Your faithfulness.*

I realize that You guide each of Your children individually. That's why listening to You—through Scripture and prayer—is essential for me to find the way forward. Please prepare me for the day that awaits me and point me in the right direction. Because You are with me continually, I don't have to be intimidated by fear. Though it stalks me, I know it can't harm me as long as I cling to Your hand. Instead of being fearful, I want to walk trustingly with You along my pathway— enjoying Peace in Your Presence.

In Your high and holy Name, amen.

But let all who take refuge in You be glad, let them ever sing for joy; and may You shelter them, that those who love Your name may exult in You. —PSALM 5:11 NASB 1995

Because of the LORD's faithful love we do not perish, for His mercies never end. They are new every morning; great is Your faithfulness! —LAMENTATIONS 3:22–23 HCSB

To him who is able to keep you from falling and to present you before his glorious presence without fault and with great joy —to the only God our Savior be glory, majesty, power and authority, through Jesus Christ our Lord, before all ages, now and forevermore! Amen. —JUDE 24–25

Gracious Jesus,

From Your fullness I have received grace upon grace. I worship You as I ponder Your astonishing gift of salvation—*by grace through faith* in You. Because it's entirely a gift, *not a result of works*, my salvation is absolutely secure! My part was just to receive this precious gift—believing with the faith that You provided. I rejoice in this infinitely costly treasure, bought with the price of Your blood.

I've found that multiple blessings flow out of Your wondrous grace. My guilt feelings melt away in the warm Light of Your forgiveness. My identity as a *child of God* gives my life meaning and purpose. My relationships with other people improve as I relate to them with the love and forgiveness You've given me.

O Lord, fill my heart with overflowing gratitude as I ponder Your glorious grace. Please remind me to spend time thinking about and thanking You for the bountiful blessings in my life. This protects my heart from the weeds of ingratitude that spring up so easily. Teach me to *be thankful*!

In Your merciful Name, amen.

For from his fullness we have all received, grace upon grace. —JOHN 1:16 ESV

For by grace you have been saved through faith. And this is not your own doing; it is the gift of God, not a result of works, so that no one may boast. —EPHESIANS 2:8–9 ESV

But to all who did receive Him, He gave them the right to be children of God, to those who believe in His name. —JOHN 1:12 HCSB

Therefore, since we are receiving a kingdom that cannot be shaken, let us be thankful, and so worship God acceptably with reverence and awe. —HEBREWS 12:28

Strong Savior,

Your Word assures me that You are both with me and *for me*. When I decide on a course of action that conforms to Your will, nothing can stop me. So I won't give up, even if I encounter multiple obstacles as I move toward my goal. I know there will be many ups and downs as I journey with You, but *with Your help* I can overcome any obstacle. I'm encouraged by the glorious truth that You, my *ever-present Help*, are omnipotent!

I've found that much of the stress in my life results from trying to make things happen before their time has come. You assert Your sovereignty in various ways—including the timing of events. Even though I sometimes get impatient, I really do want to stay close to You on my life-path and do things *Your* way. Please lead me each moment along the way You want me to go. Instead of dashing headlong toward my goal, I invite You to set the pace. As I slow down, I can enjoy the journey in Your Presence.

In Your splendid Name, Jesus, amen.

What, then, shall we say in response to this? If God is for us, who can be against us? —ROMANS 8:31

With your help I can advance against a troop; with my God I can scale a wall. —PSALM 18:29

God is our refuge and strength, an ever-present help in trouble. —PSALM 46:1

"For nothing will be impossible with God." —LUKE 1:37 ESV

Steadfast Lord,

I long to walk more steadily along paths of trust—staying in communication with You. You've shown me that the most direct route between point A and point B on my life-journey is the path of unwavering trust in You. When my faith falters, I invariably choose a trail that meanders and takes me well out of my way. Because You are sovereign, I eventually get to point B, but I lose precious time and energy as a result of my unbelief. So as soon as I realize I've wandered away from my trust-path, I need to whisper, "I trust You, Jesus." This simple affirmation helps me get back on track.

I've found that the farther I roam along paths of unbelief, the harder it is for me to remember You are with me. Anxious thoughts branch off in all directions, taking me farther and farther from awareness of Your Presence. To stay on course, I need to voice my trust in You frequently! This small act of faith keeps me walking in step with You. Help me to *trust in You with all my heart; please make my paths straight.*

In Your dependable Name, Jesus, amen.

Trust in the LORD forever, for the LORD GOD is an everlasting rock. —ISAIAH 26:4 ESV

And those who know Your name will put their trust in You; for You, LORD, have not forsaken those who seek You. —PSALM 9:10 NKJV

Show me your ways, O LORD, teach me your paths. —PSALM 25:4

Trust in the LORD with all your heart and do not lean on your own understanding. In all your ways acknowledge Him, and He will make your paths straight. —PROVERBS 3:5–6 NASB 1995

Gentle Jesus,

When things are not going my way, my natural tendency is to get flustered. Help me, instead, to stop what I'm doing and *seek Your Face*—spending a few moments enjoying Your Presence. As I talk with You about the matters that are frustrating me, You enable me to see things from Your perspective and sort out what is really important. Then You open up the way before me as I go forward in trusting dependence, staying in communication with You.

I confess that the culprit behind my frustration is my strong desire to be in control. I plan my day and expect others to behave in ways that don't interfere with those plans. But I need to remember that *You* are in control and *Your ways are higher than mine, as the heavens are higher than the earth.* Rather than letting setbacks and interruptions upset me, I want to use them as reminders—that You are the sovereign God and I am Your beloved follower. Help me to *trust in Your unfailing Love,* gladly subordinating my plans to Your infinitely wise Master Plan.

In Your wondrous Name, amen.

*When You said, "Seek My face," my heart said to You,
"Your face, LORD, I will seek." —PSALM 27:8 NKJV*

*"For as the heavens are higher than the earth, so are My ways higher than
your ways, and My thoughts than your thoughts." —ISAIAH 55:9 NKJV*

*"As for God, his way is perfect; the word of the LORD is flawless. He
is a shield for all who take refuge in him." —2 SAMUEL 22:31*

But I trust in your unfailing love; my heart rejoices in your salvation. —PSALM 13:5

My great God,

Teach me how to approach problems with a light touch. When my mind moves toward a problem area, I tend to focus on that situation so intensely that I lose sight of You. I pit myself against the difficulty as if I must conquer it immediately. My mind gears up for battle, and my body becomes tense and anxious. Unless I achieve total victory, I feel defeated.

I know there is a better way! When a problem starts to overshadow my thoughts, please prompt me to bring the matter to You—talking it over with You and examining it *in the Light of Your Presence*. This puts some much-needed space between me and my concern, enabling me to see it more from Your perspective. Sometimes I even end up laughing at myself for being so serious about something that's insignificant.

I realize *I will always face trouble in this world*. But more importantly, I will always have *You* with me—equipping me to handle whatever I encounter. Help me approach problems with a light touch by viewing them in Your revealing Light.

In Your brilliant Name, Jesus, amen.

"Who of you by worrying can add a single hour to his life? Since you cannot do this very little thing, why do you worry about the rest?" —LUKE 12:25–26

Blessed are those who have learned to acclaim you, who walk in the light of your presence, O LORD. —PSALM 89:15

" I have told you these things so that in me you may have peace. In the world you have trouble and suffering, but take courage —I have conquered the world." —JOHN 16:33 NET

Promise-keeping Lord,

It's awesome that You have an eternal grip on me—Your Love will never let me go! I live in a world that is unpredictable and unsafe in so many ways. As I look around me, I see broken promises littering the landscape.

Thankfully, Your Love is a promise that will *never* be broken. *Though the mountains be shaken and the hills be removed, Your unfailing Love for me will not be shaken.* This verse paints a picture of dire circumstances: quaking mountains and disappearing hills. Yet no matter *what* is happening, Your Love remains unshakable. I can build my life on it!

I admit that it's difficult for me to receive Your Love in full measure. Please *strengthen me with power through Your Spirit*—helping me to really *grasp how wide and long and high and deep is Your Love* for me. Lord, I yearn to *know this Love that surpasses knowledge*!

I ask You to set me free from faulty self-images so I can view myself as You see me—radiant in Your *robe of righteousness*, wrapped in luminous Love.

In Your righteous Name, Jesus, amen.

*"Though the mountains be shaken and the hills be removed,
yet my unfailing love for you will not be shaken . . . ," says the
Lord, who has compassion on you.* —Isaiah 54:10

*I pray that . . . he may strengthen you with power through his Spirit. . . . And I
pray that you, being rooted and established in love, may have power, together
with all the saints, to grasp how wide and long and high and deep is the love
of Christ, and to know this love that surpasses knowledge —that you may
be filled to the measure of all the fullness of God.* —Ephesians 3:16–19

*I greatly rejoice in the Lord, I exult in my God; for He has clothed me with the
garments of salvation and wrapped me in a robe of righteousness, as a groom wears
a turban and as a bride adorns herself with her jewels.* —Isaiah 61:10 HCSB

Worthy Jesus,

Help me to stay mindful of You as I go step by step through this day. Your Presence with me is a precious promise—and a comforting protection. After Your resurrection, You reassured Your followers, *"Surely I am with you always, to the very end of the age."* That promise was for *all* Your followers—including me!

While journeying with You, I've seen that Your Presence is a powerful, essential protection. As I walk along my life-path, there are numerous pitfalls nearby. Just a few steps away from my true path are pits of self-pity and despair, plateaus of pride and self-will. Various voices compete for my attention—trying to entice me to go their way. If I take my eyes off of You and follow someone else's path, I am in real danger. I realize that even good friends can lead me astray if I let them usurp Your place in my life.

Thank You for showing me that the way to stay on *the path of Life* is to keep my focus on You. Awareness of Your loving Presence both protects me *and* delights me!

In Your comforting, protecting Name, amen.

"And teaching them to obey everything I have commanded you. And surely I am with you always, to the very end of the age." —MATTHEW 28:20

Therefore, since we are surrounded by such a great cloud of witnesses, let us throw off everything that hinders and the sin that so easily entangles, and let us run with perseverance the race marked out for us. —HEBREWS 12:1

You will show me the path of life; in Your presence is fullness of joy; at Your right hand are pleasures forevermore. —PSALM 16:11 NKJV

Compassionate Jesus,

You are the One who keeps me safe. My natural tendency is to rely heavily on my thinking and planning, as if that is where my security lies. When I start to feel anxious about something, my mind goes into overdrive—searching for solutions, seeking to feel secure. All the while *You are with me, holding me by my right hand.* Help me to remember and rely on Your continual Presence with me.

Instead of *trusting in myself,* which is foolish, I want to *walk in wisdom* and depend on You to keep me safe. You're teaching me that biblical wisdom involves trusting in You more than in myself or other people. You are always ready to *guide me with Your counsel,* so I can bring all my concerns to You. Sometimes writing out my prayers clarifies my thinking, especially when I'm feeling confused.

Please show me the way forward as I wait in Your Presence—asking You to guide my mind while I focus on You and Your Word. Whispering "Jesus" is one way I stay focused on You. *Your Name is a strong tower;* when *I run into it I am safe.*

In Your strong Name, amen.

Nevertheless I am continually with You; You hold me by my right hand. You will guide me with Your counsel, and afterward receive me to glory. —PSALM 73:23–24 NKJV

He who trusts in himself is a fool, but he who walks in wisdom is kept safe. —PROVERBS 28:26

The name of the LORD is a strong tower; the righteous man runs into it and is safe. —PROVERBS 18:10 ESV

Eternal God,

In Your Presence there is fullness of Joy, perfect Peace, and unfailing Love. I delight in walking with You along *the path of Life*, enjoying Your company each step of the way. Because You are continually by my side, the Joy of Your Presence is always available to me!

You have promised to *keep me in perfect Peace* as I *fix my thoughts on You.* Please help me stay in communication with You through my spoken words, thoughts, and songs. When I spend ample time absorbing Your Word—letting it soak into my mind—it changes the way I think and live. As I ponder who You really are, Your Light shines warmly into my heart and *blesses me with Peace.*

Lord, I want to flourish in Your Presence—*like an olive tree flourishing in the house of God.* As the sunlight of Your Presence shines upon me, it nourishes me so I can produce fruit in Your Kingdom. And the more *I trust in Your unfailing Love*, the more I realize how utterly secure I am in You!

In Your bright, loving Name, Jesus, amen.

You make known to me the path of life; in your presence there is fullness of joy; at your right hand are pleasures forevermore. —PSALM 16:11 ESV

You will keep in perfect peace all who trust in you, all whose thoughts are fixed on you! —ISAIAH 26:3 NLT

The LORD gives strength to his people; the LORD blesses his people with peace. —PSALM 29:11

But I am like an olive tree flourishing in the house of God; I trust in God's unfailing love for ever and ever. —PSALM 52:8

November

Let us come before His presence with thanksgiving; let us make a joyful noise to Him with songs of praise! —Psalm 95:2 ampc

Blessed Savior,

Thank You for the glorious gift of grace! Your Word teaches that *by grace I have been saved through faith. And this is not my own doing; it's not a result of my works.* Even the faith I needed to believe in You—to receive salvation—is a gift from You. Through Your finished work on the cross, I've been given the astonishing blessing of *eternal Life.* Help me respond to Your amazing generosity with a grateful heart. I can never thank You too fervently or too frequently for grace.

During this Thanksgiving season, I want to take time to ponder what it means to have all my sins forgiven. I am no longer on a pathway to hell; my ultimate destination is *a new heaven and a new earth.* This guaranteed heavenly inheritance gives me a great reason to rejoice every day of my life.

As I walk with You today, I'll try to thank You often for the matchless gift of grace. I pray that my gratitude for grace may increase my awareness of the many *other* blessings You provide—making me even *more* thankful.

In Your gracious Name, Jesus, amen.

For by grace you have been saved through faith. And this is not your own doing; it is the gift of God, not a result of works, so that no one may boast. —EPHESIANS 2:8–9 ESV

"For God so loved the world that he gave his one and only Son, that whoever believes in him shall not perish but have eternal life." —JOHN 3:16

"Do not be afraid of those who kill the body but cannot kill the soul. Rather, be afraid of the One who can destroy both soul and body in hell." —MATTHEW 10:28

Now I saw a new heaven and a new earth, for the first heaven and the first earth had passed away. Also there was no more sea. —REVELATION 21:1 NKJV

Precious Savior,

I rejoice and exult in hope! I have good reason to be joyful, because I'm on my way to heaven. Thank You, Lord, for paying the penalty for all my sins and for clothing me in Your own righteousness. *This* is the basis of my hope—a hope that is secure, regardless of my circumstances. *No one can snatch me out of Your hand.* In You I have absolute, eternal security!

Your Word instructs me to *be constant in prayer.* I need this communication with You at all times, but especially when I'm struggling. Yet during trials, my ability to focus on You can be hampered by stress and fatigue. So I'm grateful for the amazing source of strength I have within me: Your Holy Spirit. As I ask Your Spirit to *control my mind*, He strengthens me and enables me to pray. I'm glad that my prayers don't have to be eloquent or organized; I can just let them flow freely out of my circumstances.

Lord, please help me stay in communication with You, especially during times of adversity—so that I can *be steadfast and patient in suffering.*

In Your hopeful Name, Jesus, amen.

Rejoice and exult in hope; be steadfast and patient in suffering and tribulation; be constant in prayer. —ROMANS 12:12 AMPC

"I give them eternal life, and they will never perish —ever! No one will snatch them out of My hand." —JOHN 10:28 HCSB

The mind of sinful man is death, but the mind controlled by the Spirit is life and peace. —ROMANS 8:6

My great God,

Please train me in steadiness. I confess that too many things interrupt my awareness of You. I live in a world of sight and sound, but I don't want to be a slave to the stimuli that surround me. I know it's possible to be aware of Your Presence in all circumstances, no matter what is happening. This is the steadiness that I deeply desire to practice in my life.

Help me not to let unexpected events throw me off course. Instead of getting upset or anxious, I want to respond calmly and confidently—remembering that *You are with me.* As soon as something grabs my attention, I can talk with You about it. Thus I share both my joys and my sorrows with You—and You enable me to cope with whatever is before me.

Lord, I invite You to live in me more fully and to work Your ways both in me and through me. I want to be a channel for Your Peace to flow into this troubled world.

In Your soothing Name, Jesus, amen.

He will have no fear of bad news; his heart is steadfast,
trusting in the LORD. —PSALM 112:7

"Fear not, for I am with you; be not dismayed, for I am your
God. I will strengthen you, yes, I will help you, I will uphold you
*with My righteous right hand." —*ISAIAH 41:10 NKJV

God is our refuge and strength, an ever-present help in trouble.
Therefore we will not fear, though the earth give way and the
*mountains fall into the heart of the sea. —*PSALM 46:1–2

*Be joyful always; pray continually. —*1 THESSALONIANS 5:16–17

My strong Deliverer,

As I face the circumstances of this day, I need to *lean on You*. Everyone leans on *something*: physical strength, intelligence, beauty, wealth, achievements, family, friends. All of these are gifts from You, and I want to enjoy Your blessings gratefully. But I've learned that depending on any of these things is risky—every single one of them can let me down.

When I'm facing challenging circumstances and I'm feeling weak, I tend to obsess about how I'm going to make it through the day. This wastes a lot of time and energy; even worse, it distracts me from my relationship with You. Whenever this happens, please open my eyes so I can find You in the midst of my circumstances. Enable me to "see" You standing nearby, with Your strong arms extended to me— offering me Your help. Instead of pretending that I have it all together or that I'm stronger than I really am, I can lean hard on You. As I do, You *bear my burdens* and show me how to deal with my difficulties.

I rejoice in You, *my Strength*. And *I sing praises to You, my loving God*.

In Your splendid Name, Jesus, amen.

Lean on, trust in, and be confident in the Lord with all your heart and mind and do not rely on your own insight or understanding. —PROVERBS 3:5 AMPC

Praise be to the Lord, to God our Savior, who daily bears our burdens. —PSALM 68:19

O my Strength, I sing praise to you; you, O God, are my fortress, my loving God. —PSALM 59:17

Almighty God,

Help me *not to be overcome by evil but to overcome evil with good.* Sometimes I feel bombarded by all the bad things happening in the world. News reports are alarming, and people are *calling evil good and good evil.* All of this can be overwhelming unless I stay in communication with You. It's so comforting to know that You are not stunned by the horrors of this world that appall me. You have perfect understanding of the *deceitful, desperately wicked* condition of human hearts. Nothing takes You by surprise!

Instead of being disheartened by the condition of this world, I long to be a light shining in the darkness. When evil appears to be winning, I need to be more determined than ever to accomplish *something* good! Sometimes this involves working directly against the bad things that are troubling me. At other times, I just try to do whatever I can to promote true goodness—according to my abilities and opportunities. Either way, I want to focus less on bemoaning evil circumstances and more on *doing the good works that You prepared in advance for me to do.*

In Your sovereign Name, Jesus, amen.

Do not be overcome by evil, but overcome evil with good. —ROMANS 12:21

Woe to those who call evil good and good evil, who put darkness for light and light for darkness, who put bitter for sweet and sweet for bitter. —ISAIAH 5:20

"The heart is deceitful above all things, and desperately wicked; who can know it?" —JEREMIAH 17:9 NKJV

For we are God's workmanship, created in Christ Jesus to do good works, which God prepared in advance for us to do. —EPHESIANS 2:10

Dear Jesus,

Help me to lead a victorious life by living in deep dependence on You. I used to associate victory with success—not falling or stumbling, not making mistakes. But being successful in my own strength made me vulnerable to going my own way, forgetting about You. It is through problems and failure, weakness and need, that I'm learning to rely on You.

I realize that true dependence is not simply asking You to bless what I have decided to do. It involves coming to You with an open mind and heart—inviting You to plant Your desires within me.

Sometimes You instill a dream in me that seems far beyond my reach. I know that my own resources are inadequate for attaining such a goal. Thus begins my journey of profound dependence on You. It's a faith-walk, taken one step at a time, leaning on You for strength and guidance. This is not a path of continual success but a way of multiple failures. However, each failure is followed by a growth spurt—nourished by increasing reliance on You. I want to enjoy the blessedness of a victorious life by deepening my dependence on You.

In Your victorious Name, amen.

The righteous cry out, and the LORD hears them; he delivers them from all their troubles. The LORD is close to the brokenhearted and saves those who are crushed in spirit. —PSALM 34:17–18

For we walk by faith, not by sight. —2 CORINTHIANS 5:7 NKJV

I can do all things through Christ who strengthens me. —PHILIPPIANS 4:13 NKJV

Ever-present Jesus,

As I sit quietly with You, my fears and worries bubble up to the surface of my mind. Here, in the Light of Your Presence, the bubbles pop and disappear. However, some of my fears surface again and again, especially fear of the future. My thoughts tend to leap into the next day, week, month, year, or decade—and I imagine myself coping badly during the tough times I'm anticipating. But I realize that my worry-thoughts are meaningless because they don't include *You*. Those dreaded times of walking alone through adversity will *not* come to pass since Your Presence will be with me at *all* times. You have promised that *You will never leave me or forsake me*!

When a future-oriented worry attacks me, help me to capture it and bring it into Your Presence. As I remember that You will be with me then and always, I gain confidence that I *can* cope—even during my toughest times.

Lord, please keep calling me back to the present moment, where there is Peace in Your Presence.

In Your calming Name, amen.

*Then Jesus said to his disciples: "Therefore I tell you, do not worry about your life, what you will eat; or about your body, what you will wear. Life is more than food, and the body more than clothes." —*Luke 12:22–23

"Be strong and courageous. Do not be afraid or terrified because of them, for the Lord *your God goes with you; he will never leave you nor forsake you." —*Deuteronomy 31:6

*We demolish arguments and every pretension that sets itself up against the knowledge of God, and we take captive every thought to make it obedient to Christ. —*2 Corinthians 10:5

Trustworthy Lord,

My times are in Your hands. Your holy hands are absolutely capable of caring for me and meeting my needs. Please help me relax in Your sovereign watchcare—trusting You to do what is best. I know it's safe to commit both the "whats" and the "whens" of my life into Your hands because You are utterly trustworthy.

I realize I'll have to submit to the reality of time as long as I remain on this side of heaven. When I'm excitedly looking forward to a future event, I yearn to fast-forward to that delightful day. But my longing doesn't change the passage of time; I must wait. When I am suffering, I long for relief—and want it as soon as possible—but I must wait for that too.

Lord, You live above the tyranny of time. In fact, You are its Master. Whenever I'm struggling with having to wait for something, I need to turn to You in trusting acceptance—rather than fight against what I cannot change. I rejoice in knowing that You, the Master of time, understand my struggles perfectly and *love me with an everlasting Love.*

In Your merciful Name, Jesus, amen.

But I trust in you, O Lord; I say, "You are my God." My times are in your hands; deliver me from my enemies and from those who pursue me. —PSALM 31:14–15

Trust in Him at all times, you people; pour out your heart before Him; God is a refuge for us. Selah. —PSALM 62:8 NKJV

The Lord appeared to us in the past, saying: "I have loved you with an everlasting love; I have drawn you with loving-kindness." —JEREMIAH 31:3

Sovereign Lord,

Please help me trust You *here* and *now*. I feel as if I'm in rigorous training—following an adventurous trail that is arduous and challenging for me. The path I'm on is not of my choosing, but I accept it as Your way for me. I realize You are doing things that are far beyond my understanding. As I turn my attention more fully to You, I can hear You whisper in my mind, "Trust Me, beloved."

I feel as if I'm in a thick jungle, where I can't clearly see what is before me, behind me, or beside me. I cling to Your hand as I follow this trail through shadowy darkness. Even though it's hard for me to see where I'm going, I know that Your Presence with me is rock-solid reality. So I look hopefully to You, Jesus, trusting that You are in full control of this situation.

I need to focus on enjoying You and all that You are to me—even though my circumstances are clamoring for resolution. I refuse to obsess about my problems and how I'm going to fix them. Instead, I choose to affirm my trust in You and wait expectantly in Your Presence—*watching in hope* to see what You will do.

In Your all-sufficient Name, Jesus, amen.

Who among you fears the LORD and obeys the word of his servant?
Let him who walks in the dark, who has no light, trust in the
name of the LORD and rely on his God. —ISAIAH 50:10

We wait in hope for the LORD; he is our help and our shield. In him our
hearts rejoice, for we trust in his holy name. —PSALM 33:20–21

But as for me, I will watch expectantly for the LORD; I will wait for the
God of my salvation. My God will hear me. —MICAH 7:7 NASB 1995

My Savior-God,

You've been showing me that a thankful attitude opens windows of heaven—openings through which spiritual blessings fall freely. As I look up with a grateful heart, I gain glimpses of Your Glory. Even though I cannot yet live in heaven, I can experience foretastes of my ultimate home. These samples of heavenly fare revive my hope and fill me with Joy. Thankfulness opens me up to these experiences, giving me further reasons to be grateful. Thus my path becomes an upward spiral—ever increasing in gladness.

I realize that thankfulness is not some sort of magic formula; it's the language of Love, enabling me to communicate intimately with You. You've been training me to maintain a thankful mind-set—without denying reality with all its problems. Please help me to *be joyful in You, my Savior,* even in the midst of trials and troubles. I'm grateful that *You are my Refuge and Strength, a very present and well-proved help in trouble.*

In Your strong Name, Jesus, amen.

Praise be to the God and Father of our Lord Jesus Christ, who has blessed us in the heavenly realms with every spiritual blessing in Christ. —EPHESIANS 1:3

Though the fig tree does not bud and there are no grapes on the vines, though the olive crop fails and the fields produce no food, though there are no sheep in the pen and no cattle in the stalls, yet I will rejoice in the LORD, I will be joyful in God my Savior. —HABAKKUK 3:17–18

God is our Refuge and Strength [mighty and impenetrable to temptation], a very present and well-proved help in trouble. —PSALM 46:1 AMPC

Beloved Jesus,

Your Word tells me that *You call me by name and You lead me. You know me*—You know every detail about me! I am never a number or statistic to You. Your involvement in my life is wonderfully personal and intimate. I love to hear You whisper in my heart: "Beloved, *follow Me.*"

After Your resurrection, when Mary Magdalene mistook You for the gardener, You spoke just one word to her: *"Mary."* Hearing You say her name, she recognized You at once and *cried out in Aramaic, "Rabboni!" (Teacher).*

Because I am Your follower, You also speak *my* name—in the depths of my spirit. When I take time to hear You speaking to me personally in Scripture, reassuring me of Your Love, I am blessed. I delight in these beautiful words of blessing: *I called you out of darkness into My marvelous Light*, and *I have loved you with an everlasting Love.* The unshakable knowledge that You love me forever provides a firm foundation for my life. Help me to follow You faithfully and joyfully—*proclaiming Your praises* as I journey through my life.

In Your magnificent Name, amen.

*"He calls his own sheep by name and leads them out. . . . My sheep listen to my voice; I know them, and they follow me." —*John 10:3, 27

*Jesus said to her, "Mary." She turned toward him and cried out in Aramaic, "Rabboni!" (which means Teacher). —*John 20:16

*You are a . . . His own special people, that you may proclaim the praises of Him who called you out of darkness into His marvelous light. —*1 Peter 2:9 nkjv

The Lord *has appeared of old to me, saying: "Yes, I have loved you with an everlasting love; therefore with lovingkindness I have drawn you." —*Jeremiah 31:3 nkjv

Delightful God,

You've been showing me that I can find *Joy in Your Presence* no matter what my circumstances may be. On some days, Joy is generously strewn along my life-path, glistening in the sunshine. During these bright, cheerful days, being content is as easy for me as breathing the next breath. But other days are overcast and gloomy, and I feel the strain of the journey—which seems endless. Dull, gray rocks greet my gaze and cause my feet to ache. On gray days, I must search for Joy *as for hidden treasure.*

Help me remember that You have created this day; it is *not* a chance occurrence. Please remind me throughout my day that You are present with me—whether I sense Your Presence or not.

I'm thankful I can talk with You about whatever is on my mind. I rejoice in the truth that You understand me perfectly and You know exactly what I'm experiencing. I've found that if I stay in communication with You, my mood gradually lightens. Awareness of Your marvelous Companionship can infuse Joy into the grayest day!

In Your glad Name, Jesus, amen.

Surely you have granted him eternal blessings and made him glad with the joy of your presence. —Psalm 21:6

And if you look for it as for silver and search for it as for hidden treasure. —Proverbs 2:4

For by Him all things were created that are in heaven and that are on earth, visible and invisible, whether thrones or dominions or principalities or powers. All things were created through Him and for Him. —Colossians 1:16 NKJV

Jesus, my Redeemer,

I long to experience more fully the riches of my salvation—the Joy of being loved constantly and perfectly. Yet I confess that I tend to judge myself in superficial ways: based on how I look or behave or feel. If I look in the mirror and like what I see, I feel a bit more worthy of Your Love. When things in my life are going smoothly and I think my performance is adequate, I find it easier to believe that I'm Your beloved child. When I feel discouraged, I tend to look inward so I can figure out what is wrong and correct it.

Instead of trying to fix myself, help me *fix my thoughts on You*, the Lover of my soul. Rather than using my energy to judge myself, I need to redirect it to communicating with You—trusting and praising You. I'm so thankful that You view me wrapped in *Your righteousness*, radiant in Your perfect Love.

In Your holy Name, amen.

For it is by grace you have been saved, through faith —and this not from yourselves, it is the gift of God —not by works, so that no one can boast. —EPHESIANS 2:8–9

Therefore, holy brothers, who share in the heavenly calling, fix your thoughts on Jesus, the apostle and high priest whom we confess. —HEBREWS 3:1

They rejoice in Your name all day long, and they are exalted by Your righteousness. —PSALM 89:16 HCSB

Those who look to him are radiant, and their faces shall never be ashamed. —PSALM 34:5 ESV

Mighty Savior,

Your plan for my life is unfolding before me. Sometimes the road I'm traveling seems blocked, or it opens up so slowly that I must reduce my pace considerably. Then, when the time is right, the way before me suddenly opens—through no effort of my own. You present to me freely, as pure gift, what I have been longing for and working for. I'm astonished by the ease with which You operate in the world—and I glimpse *Your Power and Your Glory.*

As I stand in awe of Your majestic grandeur, I become vividly aware of how weak I am. But instead of being discouraged by my weakness, I want to view it as the stage on which Your Power and Glory perform most brilliantly!

While I persevere along the path You have prepared for me, I'll depend on Your strength to sustain me. Please help me to stay alert—and to be on the lookout for miracles. Though miracles are not always visible to the naked eye, those who *live by faith* are able to see more clearly. *Living by faith, not by sight*, keeps me close to You and open to Your awesome works.

In Your glorious Name, Jesus, amen.

*I have seen you in the sanctuary and beheld your
power and your glory.* —Psalm 63:2

*But he said to me, "My grace is sufficient for you, for my power is made
perfect in weakness." Therefore I will boast all the more gladly about my
weaknesses, so that Christ's power may rest on me.* —2 Corinthians 12:9

We live by faith, not by sight. —2 Corinthians 5:7

*Jesus said to her, "Didn't I tell you that if you believed you
would see the glory of God?"* —John 11:40 HCSB

Compassionate Jesus,

I delight in hearing You whisper these comforting words: *"Nothing can separate you from My Love."* As I relax in Your Presence, this divine declaration trickles through my mind and into my heart and soul. Whenever I start to feel fearful or anxious, please remind me to pray this promise back to You: "Nothing can separate me from Your Love, Jesus. Nothing!"

Much of mankind's misery—including mine—stems from feeling unloved. In the midst of adverse circumstances, it's easy to feel as if Your Love has been withdrawn and I have been forsaken. This feeling of abandonment can be worse than the adversity itself. So I'm grateful for Your reassurance that You will never abandon me—or any of Your children—even momentarily. I'm encouraged by these promises in Your Word: *I will not leave you or forsake you. I have engraved you on the palms of My hands.*

Lord, I rejoice in knowing that Your Presence *watches over me* continually.

In Your loving Name, amen.

For I am convinced that neither death nor life . . . nor anything else in all creation, will be able to separate us from the love of God that is in Christ Jesus our Lord. —ROMANS 8:38–39

"Be strong and courageous. Do not fear or be in dread of them, for it is the LORD your God who goes with you. He will not leave you or forsake you." —DEUTERONOMY 31:6 ESV

"See, I have engraved you on the palms of my hands; your walls are ever before me." —ISAIAH 49:15

He will not let your foot slip —he who watches over you will not slumber. —PSALM 121:3

My Shepherd-King,

Your Word tells me that *You are a Shield for all who take refuge in You*. So I draw near to You, Lord, and I find shelter under the umbrella of Your shielding Presence.

Sometimes I feel unprotected and exposed to danger. This happens when I crawl out from under Your protective Presence and try to face the world on my own. I do this unconsciously—forgetting the essential truth that I need You every moment. Please use the fear I feel at such times to alert me that I have wandered from You. Then point me to the remedy: taking refuge in You.

I'm so grateful that *You are my Shepherd*! You're always vigilant, and You know exactly what is on the path ahead of me. You anticipate perilous situations and prepare me for them. Because You're a masterful Shepherd, You can shield me from danger so skillfully that I remain blissfully unaware of it. Moreover, You are totally trustworthy—the only absolutely *Good Shepherd*. As I seek to follow You and Your ways, I thank You for protecting me from both danger *and* fear.

In Your sheltering Name, Jesus, amen.

"As for God, his way is perfect; the word of the Lord is flawless. He is a shield for all who take refuge in him." —2 Samuel 22:31

The Lord is my shepherd, I shall not be in want. . . . Even though I walk through the valley of the shadow of death, I will fear no evil, for you are with me; your rod and your staff, they comfort me. —Psalm 23:1, 4

"I am the Good Shepherd. The Good Shepherd gives His life for the sheep. . . . I am the Good Shepherd. I know My sheep and My sheep know Me." —John 10:11, 14 NLV

Jesus,

Please train me to trust You one day at a time. This practice will keep me close to You, responsive to Your will. I confess that trust does not come easily to me at all; I find it extremely challenging. But I know that You are absolutely trustworthy, regardless of my feelings. I'm so thankful for Your Spirit within me—my resident Tutor who helps me learn difficult lessons. I long to become increasingly sensitive to the Spirit's promptings and yield to His gentle touch.

Lord, teach me to trust You in *all* circumstances—without letting my desire to understand distract me from Your loving Presence. I want to get through this day victoriously by living in joyful dependence on You.

Tomorrow is busy worrying about itself. Instead of getting tangled up in tomorrow's worry-webs, I seek to trust You today—one moment at a time!

In Your strong, reliable Name, amen.

O LORD Almighty, blessed is the man who trusts in you. —PSALM 84:12

Do you not know that your body is a temple of the Holy Spirit, who is in you, whom you have received from God? You are not your own. —1 CORINTHIANS 6:19

"Blessed is the man who trusts in the LORD, and whose hope is the LORD." —JEREMIAH 17:7 NKJV

"Therefore do not worry about tomorrow, for tomorrow will worry about itself. Each day has enough trouble of its own." —MATTHEW 6:34

Exalted God,

Your paths are beyond tracing out! Help me to draw near You with a humble heart—relinquishing my demand to understand, accepting the fact that many things are simply beyond my comprehension. You are infinitely intelligent and I am finite. Because of my mind's limitations, much of what happens in my life and in the world doesn't make sense to me. So I need to make room for *mystery* in my ponderings.

I realize I'm privileged to know many things that were formerly mysteries—things that were *kept hidden for ages and generations.* The New Testament is full of revelation that came through Your incarnation, life, death, and resurrection. I'm immeasurably blessed to have this priceless knowledge!

Still, the ways You work in my world are often mysterious to me—frustrating my craving to comprehend. This presents me with a choice: to challenge Your ways or to bow before You in worshipful wonder. I choose to approach You with worship and wonder—marveling at *the depth of the riches of Your wisdom and knowledge.*

In Your marvelous Name, Jesus, amen.

Oh, the depth of the riches of the wisdom and knowledge of God! How unsearchable his judgments, and his paths beyond tracing out! —ROMANS 11:33

Trust in the LORD with all your heart; do not depend on your own understanding. —PROVERBS 3:5 NLT

The mystery that has been kept hidden for ages and generations, but is now disclosed to the saints. —COLOSSIANS 1:26

My living Lord,

I rejoice that *You are the living One who sees me.* You are far more fully, gloriously alive than I can begin to imagine. When I see You *face to Face* in all Your Glory, I know I will be awestruck! Now, though, *I see in a mirror dimly.* My view of You is obscured by my fallen condition.

It's wonderful—and rather daunting—that You see *me* with perfect clarity. You know everything about me, including my most secret thoughts and feelings. You understand how broken and weak I am: *You remember that I am dust.* But in spite of all my flaws and failures, You choose to love me with everlasting Love.

Help me to remember that the gift of Your Love was immeasurably costly. You endured unspeakable agony to save me from my sins. You *became sin for me so that I might become righteous in You.* I love to ponder this wondrous truth: Your perfect righteousness has been credited to me forever! This gift of infinite value has been mine ever since I trusted You as my Savior. I'm so thankful that the living One who sees me always is the same One who loves me eternally!

In Your saving Name, Jesus, amen.

Therefore the well was called Beer-lahai-roi [A well to the Living One Who sees me]; it is between Kadesh and Bered. —GENESIS 16:14 AMPC

For now we see in a mirror dimly, but then face to face. Now I know in part; then I shall know fully, even as I have been fully known. —1 CORINTHIANS 13:12 ESV

For He knows our frame; He remembers that we are dust. —PSALM 103:14 NKJV

God made him who had no sin to be sin for us, so that in him we might become the righteousness of God. —2 CORINTHIANS 5:21

Precious Jesus,

I've discovered that thanking You frequently not only awakens my heart to Your Presence but sharpens my mind. So when I'm feeling out of focus or out of touch with You, I need to make every effort to thank You for *something*. There is always an abundance of things to choose from: eternal gifts—such as salvation, grace, and faith—as well as ordinary, everyday blessings.

You've been training me to look back over the previous twenty-four hours and make note of all the good things You've provided—jotting down some of them in a journal. This discipline lifts my spirits and energizes me, enabling me to think more clearly.

The Bible teaches that *my enemy the devil prowls around like a roaring lion looking for someone to devour.* So it's very important for me to *be self-controlled and alert.* When I lose focus and let my thoughts drift, I'm much more vulnerable to the evil one's attacks. Please alert me whenever I'm in this vulnerable condition, and help me to drive away the enemy by thanking and praising You. This is warfare worship!

In Your praiseworthy Name, amen.

For by grace you have been saved through faith. And this is not your own doing; it is the gift of God, not a result of works, so that no one may boast. —Ephesians 2:8–9 ESV

Be self-controlled and alert. Your enemy the devil prowls around like a roaring lion looking for someone to devour. —1 Peter 5:8

Thanks be to God for His indescribable gift! —2 Corinthians 9:15 NKJV

Glorious God,

I offer You the sacrifice of thanksgiving. I don't want to take any of Your good gifts for granted—not even the rising of the sun. Thankfulness does not come naturally to me, but You've been training me to respond *super*naturally.

Your Word teaches me how important it is to have a grateful attitude. Before the serpent tempted Eve in the Garden of Eden, thankfulness was a natural response. But the evil one's temptation pointed her to the one thing that was forbidden. Though the garden was full of delicious fruits that were freely available, Eve focused on the one fruit that was off-limits. This negative focus darkened her mind, and she succumbed to temptation.

When *I* focus on things that I want but can't have, or on situations that displease me, my mind also becomes darkened. I take for granted life, salvation, sunshine, loved ones, and countless other gifts from You. I look for what is wrong and refuse to enjoy life until that situation is fixed. But when I approach You with thanksgiving, the Light of Your Presence pours into me, transforming me in the depths of my being. Help me to *walk in the Light* with You, Lord—*delighting in You* and practicing the discipline of thanksgiving.

In Jesus' wondrous Name, amen.

I will offer to You the sacrifice of thanksgiving. —PSALM 116:17 NKJV

The woman saw that the fruit of the tree was good for food and pleasing to the eye. —GENESIS 3:6

If we walk in the light as He is in the light, we have fellowship with one another, and the blood of Jesus Christ His Son cleanses us from all sin. —1 JOHN 1:7 NKJV

Delight yourself in the LORD. —PSALM 37:4

Faithful God,

I've learned that thankfulness and trust are like close friends who are always ready to help me. I need to rely on these faithful friends at all times, but especially when my day looks bleak or the world seems scary. Lord, You're teaching me to stop during these times and look around me—searching for beauty and blessings. When I thank You for what I find, I connect with You in a wonderful way. It blesses me to speak to You in glowing terms about the many good gifts You provide—making the effort to thank You enthusiastically, regardless of how I feel. If I persist in expressing my gratitude to You, my mood becomes brighter and lighter.

You are absolutely trustworthy! Voicing my trust in You reminds me that You are with me, taking care of me. I know there are areas of my life where I need to trust You more fully. When hard times come, help me view them as opportunities to expand the scope of my trust—*living by faith* in these challenging situations. Instead of wasting these opportunities, I want to use them to *come closer to You*. I rejoice that You welcome me warmly—with open arms!

> In Your compassionate Name, Jesus, amen.

It is good to give thanks to the LORD, and to sing praises to Your name, O Most High; to declare Your lovingkindness in the morning, and Your faithfulness every night. —PSALM 92:1 NKJV

You are my God, and I will give you thanks; you are my God, and I will exalt you. —PSALM 118:28

We live by faith, not by sight. —2 CORINTHIANS 5:7

Come close to God, and God will come close to you. Wash your hands, you sinners; purify your hearts. —JAMES 4:8 NLT

Gracious God,

Thank You for showering so many blessings on me! Everything I have is a gift from You, including each breath I breathe. I rarely think about the wonder of inhaling Your Life continually. Yet it was only when You breathed *the breath of Life* into Adam that he *became a living being*.

Sometimes I like to sit quietly in Your Presence, thanking You silently each time I inhale and affirming my trust in You as I exhale. I've found that the longer I do this, the more relaxed I become.

Lord, please help me to appreciate and thank You for blessings I often overlook—birds and trees, light and colors, loved ones and daily comforts. The list is endless! The more I look for good things in my life, the clearer my vision becomes.

Of course, my greatest gratitude is for *eternal Life*, which is mine because I *believe in You*. This priceless forever-gift fills me with ever-increasing *Joy in Your Presence*!

In Your generous Name, Jesus, amen.

The LORD God formed the man from the dust of the ground and breathed into his nostrils the breath of life, and the man became a living being. —GENESIS 2:7

"For God so loved the world that he gave his one and only Son, that whoever believes in him shall not perish but have eternal life." —JOHN 3:16

You have made known to me the path of life; you will fill me with joy in your presence, with eternal pleasures at your right hand. —PSALM 16:11

My loving Lord,

I ask You to increase my thankfulness. I've learned that being thankful not only brightens my day but opens my heart more fully to You. I long to encounter *You* in the midst of my circumstances. So I'll look for signs of Your Presence as I walk along *the path of Life*. A grateful attitude opens both my heart and my eyes—enabling me to see You in myriad tiny details as well as in the big picture of my life. I need to slow down and take time to notice all Your blessings—thanking You for them and enjoying Your many gifts.

I ask You also to train me in trusting You more consistently. Well-developed, sturdy trust enables me to walk across treacherous terrain without stumbling. The more challenging my journey, the more frequently I need to voice my confidence in You: "Lord, *I trust in Your unfailing Love*." This short prayer reminds me that You are with me, You are taking care of me, and You love me forever!

I have good reason to *be joyful* because You are absolutely worthy of my thankfulness and trust!

In Your great Name, Jesus, amen.

Be joyful always; pray continually; give thanks in all circumstances, for this is God's will for you in Christ Jesus. —1 THESSALONIANS 5:16–18

Devote yourselves to prayer, being watchful and thankful. —COLOSSIANS 4:2

You will show me the path of life; in Your presence is fullness of joy; at Your right hand are pleasures forevermore. —PSALM 16:11 NKJV

But I am like an olive tree flourishing in the house of God; I trust in God's unfailing love for ever and ever. —PSALM 52:8

Merciful God,

Please help me to linger in gratitude. This is a most delightful place—where the Joy of Your Presence shines warmly upon me.

Often I pray fervently for something and wait hopefully for the answer. If You grant my request, I respond joyfully and thankfully. But my tendency is to move on rather quickly to seeking the next thing. Instead of experiencing only a short-lived burst of gratitude, I want to remain in an attitude of thankful Joy—letting my gratefulness flow freely into the future. I need to train myself to remember Your gracious response to my request. One way is to tell others about the blessing I've received from You. Another way is to write down the prayer-answer someplace where I'll see it again and again.

Lord, teach me to *remember Your marvelous works* with thankfulness. You've been showing me that gratefulness blesses me doubly—with happy memories of answered prayer and with the delight of sharing Joy with You!

In Your joyful Name, Jesus, amen.

Let us come before His presence with thanksgiving; let us shout joyfully to Him with psalms. —PSALM 95:2 NKJV

But thanks be to God! He gives us the victory through our Lord Jesus Christ. —1 CORINTHIANS 15:57

Remember His marvelous works which He has done, His wonders, and the judgments of His mouth. —1 CHRONICLES 16:12 NKJV

Caring Jesus,

I want to live close to You and open to You—aware of, attentive to, trusting, and thanking You. I know You are always near me. So I open myself fully—heart, mind, and spirit—to Your living Presence.

Please help me stay aware of You as I follow my path through this day. I'm comforted by knowing there is never a moment when You are not fully aware of me. I want to be attentive—alert and listening carefully—not only to You but to the people You bring into my life. I've found that listening to others with full, prayerful attention blesses both them and me.

The Bible is full of instruction to trust You and thank You. Because You're supremely trustworthy, believing in You and Your promises provides a firm foundation for my life. Moreover, You understand my weakness and You *help me overcome my unbelief.*

You've been teaching me the importance of thanking You throughout the day. This delightful discipline blesses me greatly—keeping me close to You and increasing my joy!

In Your trustworthy Name, amen.

"I am the Living One; I was dead, and behold I am alive for ever and ever! And I hold the keys of death and Hades." —REVELATION 1:18

My dear brothers, take note of this: Everyone should be quick to listen, slow to speak and slow to become angry. —JAMES 1:19

Immediately the boy's father exclaimed, "I do believe; help me overcome my unbelief!" —MARK 9:24

The LORD is my strength and my shield; my heart trusts in him, and I am helped. My heart leaps for joy and I will give thanks to him in song. —PSALM 28:7

Bountiful Jesus,

I *give thanks to You, for You are good; Your Love endures forever.* I want to take time to think about the many blessings You provide. Thank You, Lord, for the gift of life—for every breath You give me. I'm grateful also for everyday provisions: food and water, shelter, clothing, family and friends. But the greatest gift I've received from You, my Savior, is everlasting Life!

As I consider all that You have done for me, I delight in who You are—the great *I Am*! You are one hundred percent good. There is not even a speck of darkness in You, *the Light of the world*! Moreover, Your Love is unending; it goes on and on throughout eternity.

Because I belong to You, I am never separated from Your loving Presence. I know that You are always near, so I don't need to worry about whether or not I sense Your Presence. Instead of focusing on my feelings, help me to simply trust that You are with me—and to *thank You for Your unfailing Love.*

In Your blessed Name, amen.

Give thanks to the LORD, *for he is good; his love endures forever.* —PSALM 107:1

Jesus said to them, "Most assuredly, I say to you, before Abraham was, I AM." —JOHN 8:58 NKJV

Again Jesus spoke to them, saying, "I am the light of the world. Whoever follows me will not walk in darkness, but will have the light of life." —JOHN 8:12 ESV

Let them give thanks to the LORD *for his unfailing love and his wonderful deeds for men.* —PSALM 107:8

Dear Jesus,

You've been showing me that thankfulness takes the sting out of adversity. Moreover, the Bible instructs me to *give thanks for every-thing.* I see an element of mystery in this transaction: I give You thanks, regardless of my feelings, and You give me Joy, regardless of my circumstances. This is a spiritual act of obedience—at times, blind obedience. Thanking You for heartrending hardships can seem irrational or even impossible. But I've learned that when I obey You in this way, I am blessed, even though difficulties remain.

Thankfulness opens my heart to Your Presence and my mind to Your thoughts. I may still be in the same place—facing the same set of circumstances—but it's as if a light has been switched on, enabling me to see from Your perspective more clearly. It is this *Light of Your Presence* that removes the sting from adversity. Help me, Lord, to *walk in the Light* with You more and more!

In Your luminous Name, amen.

And give thanks for everything to God the Father in the name of our Lord Jesus Christ. —EPHESIANS 5:20 NLT

O give thanks to the Lord, for He is good; for His mercy and loving-kindness endure forever! —PSALM 118:1 AMPC

Blessed are those who have learned to acclaim you, who walk in the light of your presence, O LORD. They rejoice in your name all day long; they exult in your righteousness. —PSALM 89:15–16

Everlasting God,

Help me to worship You only—making You first and foremost in my life. The Bible teaches that You are *a jealous God* and that idolatry has always been the downfall of Your people. Current idols are more subtle than ancient ones because today's false gods are often secular. People, possessions, status, and wealth are some of the most popular idols these days. To avoid the pitfall of bowing down before these things, I must *be self-controlled and alert*.

You've been showing me that false gods never satisfy; instead, they stir up lust for more and more. When I seek *You* instead of the world's idols, I experience Your *Joy and Peace*. These priceless intangibles quench the thirst of my soul, providing deep satisfaction. The glitter of the world is tinny and temporal. The Light of Your Presence is brilliant and everlasting. I want to *walk in the Light* with You—becoming a beacon through whom others are drawn to You.

In Your priceless Name, Jesus, amen.

*"Do not worship any other god, for the LORD, whose name is Jealous, is a jealous God." —*EXODUS 34:14

*Be self-controlled and alert. Your enemy the devil prowls around like a roaring lion looking for someone to devour. —*1 PETER 5:8

*May the God of hope fill you with all joy and peace as you trust in him, so that you may overflow with hope by the power of the Holy Spirit. —*ROMANS 15:13

*But if we walk in the light as He is in the light, we have fellowship with one another, and the blood of Jesus Christ His Son cleanses us from all sin. —*1 JOHN 1:7 NKJV

Glorious Lord,

I receive this day of life as a precious gift from You. I want to treat it as the treasure it is by *seeking Your Face* and prayerfully prioritizing. As I look at the day that stretches out before me, please help me discern what is most important. Show me how to set priorities according to Your will—using them to guide me as I go along my way. This will enable me to make good choices about the use of my time and energy. Then, when I reach the end of the day, I can feel at peace about the things I have done—and also about the things I have *not* done.

You've been teaching me to include You in everything I do. I've seen that even the briefest prayer is sufficient to invite You into my activities. By praying about everything, I acknowledge my continual need of You. I'm even learning to rejoice in my neediness—viewing it as a strong link to *Your glorious Presence*.

Although living in a dependent manner is countercultural, I've found that it's a blessed way to live—exulting in Your boundless sufficiency and *Your unfailing Love*.

In Your delightful Name, Jesus, amen.

This is the day the LORD has made; we will rejoice and be glad in it. —PSALM 118:24 NKJV

Glory in His holy name; let the heart of those who seek the LORD be glad. Seek the LORD and His strength; seek His face continually. —1 CHRONICLES 16:10–11 NASB 1995

To him who is able to keep you from falling and to present you before his glorious presence without fault and with great joy. —JUDE 24

May your unfailing love rest upon us, O LORD, even as we put our hope in you. —PSALM 33:22

December

The angel said to them, "Do not be afraid.
I bring you good news of great joy that
will be for all the people." —LUKE 2:10

Merciful Lord Jesus,

I come to You, asking You to prepare my heart for the celebration of Your birth. Christmas is the time to exult in Your miraculous incarnation, when You—*the Word—became flesh and made Your dwelling among us.* You identified with mankind to the ultimate extent: becoming a Man and taking up residence in our world. I don't want to let the familiarity of this astonishing miracle diminish its effect on me. You are the Gift above all gifts, and I *rejoice in You!*

A delightful way of opening up my heart to You is to spend time pondering the wonders of Your entrance into human history. I want to view these events from the perspective of *shepherds living out in the fields* near Bethlehem, *keeping watch over their flocks at night.* They witnessed first one angel and then *a great company of the heavenly host* lighting up the sky, proclaiming: *"Glory to God in the highest, and on earth Peace to those on whom His favor rests."*

Help me to gaze at the Glory of your birth, just as the shepherds did, and respond with childlike wonder.

In Your marvelous, wondrous Name, amen.

The voice of one crying in the wilderness: "Prepare the way of the LORD; make His paths straight." —MARK 1:3 NKJV

The Word became flesh and made his dwelling among us. —JOHN 1:14

Rejoice in the Lord always. —PHILIPPIANS 4:4 NKJV

There were shepherds living out in the fields nearby, keeping watch over their flocks at night. . . . Suddenly a great company of the heavenly host appeared with the angel, praising God and saying, "Glory to God in the highest, and on earth peace to men on whom his favor rests." —LUKE 2:8, 13–14

Vigilant Savior,

I'm trying desperately to keep my eyes on You! Waves of adversity are washing over me, and I feel tempted to give up. As my circumstances consume more and more of my attention, I'm afraid I will lose sight of You. But Your Word assures me that *You are continually with me, holding me by my right hand.* Moreover, I know that You're fully aware of my situation, and *You will not let me be tempted beyond what I can bear.*

You've been showing me that worrying about tomorrow not only displeases You but also drains my energy. I admit that I've been trying to carry tomorrow's burdens today, and I'm staggering under the heavy load. I realize that if I keep this up, I'll eventually fall flat on my face. I'm grateful that You are *God my Savior, who daily bears my burdens.*

Help me live within the boundaries of *today*—keeping my focus on Your Presence in the present. Please keep reminding me that *the present* is where I can walk close to You—leaning on You for strength and guidance.

In Your strong, guiding Name, Jesus, amen.

Nevertheless I am continually with You; You hold me by my right hand. —PSALM 73:23 NKJV

No temptation has seized you except what is common to man. And God is faithful; he will not let you be tempted beyond what you can bear. But when you are tempted, he will also provide a way out so that you can stand up under it. —1 CORINTHIANS 10:13

But encourage one another daily, as long as it is called Today, so that none of you may be hardened by sin's deceitfulness. —HEBREWS 3:13

Praise be to the LORD, to God our Savior, who daily bears our burdens. —PSALM 68:19

Supreme Savior,

I don't want to be weighed down by the clutter in my life—lots of little chores waiting to be done *sometime*, in no particular order. When I focus too much on these petty tasks, trying to get all of them out of the way, I discover that they are endless. They can eat up as much time as I devote to them!

Thank You for showing me that the remedy is to stop trying to do all my chores at once—and just focus on the ones I need to do today. Please help me choose the tasks You want me to accomplish this day, letting the rest of them slip into the background of my mind. This makes it possible for me to keep *You* in the forefront of my awareness.

My ultimate goal is living close to You—ready to respond to Your initiatives. I can communicate with You most freely when my mind is uncluttered and turned toward You. As I *seek Your Face* throughout this day, I ask for Your Presence to bring order to my thoughts and Peace into my entire being.

In Your redeeming Name, Jesus, amen.

Commit to the LORD whatever you do, and your plans will succeed. —PROVERBS 16:3

Lead me in Your truth and teach me, for You are the God of my salvation; for You I wait all the day. —PSALM 25:5 NASB 1995

When You said, "Seek My face," my heart said to You, "Your face, LORD, I will seek." —PSALM 27:8 NKJV

You will keep him in perfect peace, whose mind is stayed on You, because he trusts in You. —ISAIAH 26:3 NKJV

My loving Lord,

I delight in hearing You say to me, *"I have loved you with an ever-lasting Love."* I confess that I cannot comprehend Your constancy because My mind is ever so human. My emotions flicker and falter in the face of varying circumstances, and it's easy for me to project my fickle feelings onto You. This keeps me from benefiting fully from *Your unfailing Love.*

Please teach me how to look beyond the flux of circumstances and find You gazing lovingly back at me. Such awareness of Your Presence strengthens me—helping me become more receptive and responsive to Your Love. I'm so grateful that *You are the same yesterday, today, and forever*! I want to open up to You more fully—letting Your Love flow into me continually. My need for You is as constant as the endless outflow of Your Love to me.

In Your steadfast Name, Jesus, amen.

The LORD *appeared to us in the past, saying: "I have loved you with an everlasting love; I have drawn you with loving-kindness."* —JEREMIAH 31:3

"In your unfailing love you will lead the people you have redeemed. In your strength you will guide them to your holy dwelling." —EXODUS 15:13

Jesus Christ is the same yesterday, today, and forever. —HEBREWS 13:8 NKJV

Cherished Jesus,

You are *the Joy that no one can take away from me*. As I rest in Your Presence, I savor the wonders of this glorious gift. I rejoice that this blessing is mine forever—*You* are mine for all eternity!

Many things in this world can bring me pleasure for a while, but they are all passing away due to death and decay. In *You* I have a matchless Treasure—Joy in the One who *is the same yesterday and today and forever*. No one can rob me of this pleasure because You are faithful and unchanging.

I realize that whenever I'm feeling joyless, the problem is not in the source of Joy (You) but in the receiver (me). Sometimes I get so focused on other things—difficulties and distractions in my life—that I neglect my relationship with You. Help me remember to put You first in my life, relating to You continually as my *First Love*. And please increase my moment-by-moment receptivity to Your Presence. As I spend time *delighting myself in You*, I receive Joy in full measure!

In Your joyous Name, amen.

"So with you: Now is your time of grief, but I will see you again and you will rejoice, and no one will take away your joy." —JOHN 16:22

Jesus Christ is the same yesterday and today and forever. —HEBREWS 13:8 ESV

"Nevertheless I have this against you, that you have left your first love." —REVELATION 2:4 NKJV

Delight yourself in the LORD and he will give you the desires of your heart. —PSALM 37:4

Exalted Jesus,

You are *the Light from on high that dawns upon us—to give Light to those who sit in darkness.* Sometimes my circumstances are so difficult and confusing that I feel as if I'm surrounded by darkness. My mind offers up various solutions to my problems, but I've already tried them—without success. So I fret and wonder what to do next, feeling powerless and frustrated. At times like this, I need to look up and see Your Light shining upon me. As I gaze at You in childlike trust, I find hope and rest in Your Presence.

Your Word teaches me to *cease striving and know that You are God.* Please help me to set aside my problem-solving efforts and relax with You—remembering that You are the *Prince of Peace.* I find it soothing to breathe in Your peaceful Presence with each breath I take. The more of You I absorb, the calmer I become. After resting with You for a while, I'm ready to *pour out my heart* about my troubles—trusting You to show me the way I should go.

Lord, please *guide my feet into the way of Peace.*

In Your worthy Name, amen.

"A Light from on high will dawn upon us and visit [us] to shine upon and give light to those who sit in darkness . . . to direct and guide our feet in a straight line into the way of peace." —LUKE 1:78–79 AMPC

"Cease striving and know that I am God; I will be exalted among the nations, I will be exalted in the earth." —PSALM 46:10 NASB 1995

For to us a Child is born . . . and His name shall be called . . . Prince of Peace. —ISAIAH 9:6 AMPC

Trust in him at all times, O people; pour out your hearts to him, for God is our refuge. —PSALM 62:8

Beloved Jesus,

When my mind and heart are quiet, I can hear You inviting me to *draw near.* I delight in Your glorious invitation, proclaimed in holy whispers: *"Come to Me. Come to Me. Come to Me."* Drawing near to You requires no great effort on my part; it's more like surrendering to You and ceasing to resist the magnetic pull of Your Love.

Help me, *through Your Spirit,* to open myself more fully to Your loving Presence *so that I may be filled to the measure of all Your fullness.* I yearn to *have power to grasp how wide and long and high and deep is Your Love for me—and to know this Love that surpasses knowledge.* This vast ocean of Love cannot be measured or explained, but it can be experienced.

In Your amazing Name, amen.

Draw near to God and He will draw near to you. Cleanse your hands, you sinners; and purify your hearts, you double-minded. —JAMES 4:8 NASB 1995

"Come to Me, all who are weary and heavy-laden, and I will give you rest." —MATTHEW 11:28 NASB 1995

"Everyone the Father gives Me will come to Me, and the one who comes to Me I will never cast out." —JOHN 6:37 HCSB

I pray that out of his glorious riches he may strengthen you with power through his Spirit in your inner being, so that Christ may dwell in your hearts through faith. And I pray that you, being rooted and established in love, may have power, together with all the saints, to grasp how wide and long and high and deep is the love of Christ, and to know this love that surpasses knowledge —that you may be filled to the measure of all the fullness of God. —EPHESIANS 3:16–19

Brilliant Jesus,

You are the Light of the world! One way I like to celebrate Advent is by illuminating my home with candles and a lit-up tree. This is a way of symbolizing Your coming into our world—eternal Light breaking through the darkness and opening up the way to heaven. I'm grateful that nothing can reverse Your glorious plan of salvation. You've promised that all who trust You as Savior are adopted into Your royal family, to live with You forever!

Your Light shines on in the darkness, for the darkness has never overpowered it. No matter how much evil and unbelief I see in this dark world, You continue to shine brightly. So it's crucial for me to look toward the Light as much as possible—*fixing my eyes on You.* By making good thought-choices, I can see You as I journey through my days. Please help me to persevere in this delightful discipline of keeping my eyes on You. I find hope in these wonderful words that You spoke: *"Whoever follows Me will never walk in darkness, but will have the Light of Life."*

In Your bright, radiant Name, amen.

*When Jesus spoke again to the people, he said, "I am the light of the world. Whoever follows me will never walk in darkness, but will have the light of life." —*JOHN 8:12

*He did this by predestining us to adoption as his legal heirs through Jesus Christ, according to the pleasure of his will. —*EPHESIANS 1:5 NET

*The Light shines on in the darkness, and the darkness did not understand it or overpower it or appropriate it or absorb it [and is unreceptive to it]. —*JOHN 1:5 AMP

*Let us fix our eyes on Jesus, the author and perfecter of our faith, who for the joy set before him endured the cross, scorning its shame, and sat down at the right hand of the throne of God. —*HEBREWS 12:2

Jesus, my Creator,

Your Word tells me that *I am fearfully and wonderfully made.* You have built into my brain the amazing capacity to observe my own thoughts. So it's possible for me to monitor my thoughts and make choices about them. I've discovered that worry is often a result of thinking about things at the wrong time. If I think about things that trouble me while I'm lying in bed, it's all too easy for me to start worrying. But when I monitor my thinking, I can interrupt those anxious thoughts quickly—before I find myself deep in worry.

Teach me how to discipline my mind so I can minimize worry and maximize worship. Please alert me through Your Spirit when I'm thinking about something at the wrong time—a worrisome thought at a time when I can do nothing about it. Help me to direct my thinking *away* from that hurtful thought and *toward* You, Jesus. I delight in praying verses from the Psalms back to You—drawing near to You in worship by expressing my love for You and my trust in You. *I love You, O Lord, my Strength. I trust in You, O Lord; I say, "You are my God."*

In Your powerful Name, amen.

I praise you, for I am fearfully and wonderfully made. Wonderful are your works; my soul knows it very well. —Psalm 139:14 esv

Then Jesus said to his disciples: "Therefore I tell you, do not worry about your life, what you will eat; or about your body, what you will wear. . . . Who of you by worrying can add a single hour to his life? Since you cannot do this very little thing, why do you worry about the rest?" —Luke 12:22, 25–26

I love you, O Lord, my strength. —Psalm 18:1

But I trust in you, O Lord; I say, "You are my God." —Psalm 31:14

Precious Jesus,

You are my Treasure! You're immeasurably more valuable than anything I can see, hear, or touch. *Knowing You* is *the Prize* above every other prize.

Earthly treasures are often hoarded, worried over, or hidden for safekeeping. But the riches I have in You can never be lost or stolen or damaged. In fact, I've found that as I share You freely with others, I gain even *more* of You. Since You are infinite, there will always be more of You for me to discover—and to love.

My world often feels fragmented, with countless things—both small and large—vying for my attention. So much "stuff" keeps getting in the way of my desire to spend time enjoying Your Presence. I admit that being *worried and bothered about many things* comes naturally to me. But Your Word assures me that *only one thing is necessary.* When I make You that *one thing,* I choose *what will not be taken away from me.*

Help me to rejoice in Your continual nearness—and to let my awareness of Your Presence put everything else in perspective. You are the Treasure that can brighten all my moments!

In Your priceless Name, amen.

I press on toward the goal to win the prize for which God has called me heavenward in Christ Jesus. —PHILIPPIANS 3:14

"Do not store up for yourselves treasures on earth, where moth and rust destroy, and where thieves break in and steal." —MATTHEW 6:19

But the Lord answered and said to her, "Martha, Martha, you are worried and bothered about so many things; but only one thing is necessary, for Mary has chosen the good part, which shall not be taken away from her." —LUKE 10:41–42 NASB 1995

Mighty God,

You empower me—*infusing inner strength into me* so that I'm *ready for anything and equal to anything*. Please help me remember that this inner strength comes *through You*, Jesus, through my connection with You. It comes to me as I need it—as I take trusting steps of dependence, keeping my eyes on You. This promise is a powerful antidote to fear— especially my fear of being overwhelmed by the circumstances I see looming ahead. No matter how daunting they may look, I can trust that I am indeed ready for anything You bring into my life.

I'm thankful that You carefully control everything that happens to me. Moreover, You are constantly protecting me from both known and unknown dangers. And You provide strength, just when I need it, for coping with challenging circumstances.

You've been teaching me that many of the future things I anxiously anticipate will not actually reach me. Your promise is for the things I face in the present—and it is sufficient. So when I'm feeling the strain of an uphill journey, I need to stop and tell myself the truth: *"I have strength for all things in Christ who empowers me!"*

In Your strong Name, Jesus, amen.

I have strength for all things in Christ Who empowers me [I am ready for anything and equal to anything through Him Who infuses inner strength into me; I am self-sufficient in Christ's sufficiency]. —PHILIPPIANS 4:13 AMPC

"Abide in Me, and I in you. As the branch cannot bear fruit of itself, unless it abides in the vine, neither can you, unless you abide in Me." —JOHN 15:4 NKJV

"Therefore do not worry about tomorrow, for tomorrow will worry about itself. Each day has enough trouble of its own." —MATTHEW 6:34

My Jesus,

You designed me to live in union with You. I'm thankful that this union does not negate who I am. On the contrary, it makes me more fully myself. I've discovered that when I try to live independently of You—even for short periods of time—I experience emptiness and dissatisfaction. But when I *walk in the Light of Your Presence*, You bless me with deep, satisfying Joy. I delight in praising You—*exulting in Your righteousness.*

Help me to find fulfillment in living close to You, yielding to Your purposes for me. Sometimes You lead me along paths that feel alien to me. At such times I need to cling to You—trusting that You know what You're doing. When I follow You wholeheartedly, I can discover facets of myself that were previously hidden.

You know me intimately—far better than I know myself. In union with You, I am complete. In closeness to You, I am transformed more and more into the one You created me to be.

In Your beautiful, righteous Name, amen.

Blessed are those who have learned to acclaim you, who walk in the light of your presence, O Lord. They rejoice in your name all day long; they exult in your righteousness. —Psalm 89:15–16

My frame was not hidden from you when I was made in the secret place. When I was woven together in the depths of the earth, your eyes saw my unformed body. All the days ordained for me were written in your book before one of them came to be. —Psalm 139:15–16

And we all, with unveiled face, beholding the glory of the Lord, are being transformed into the same image from one degree of glory to another. For this comes from the Lord who is the Spirit. —2 Corinthians 3:18 esv

Ever-present Jesus,

I love to hear You whispering to me, *"I am with you. I am with you. I am with you."* It's as if heaven's bells are continually pealing with that promise of Your Presence. Sadly, some people never hear those glorious bells because their minds are earthbound and their hearts are closed to You. Others may hear the wondrous proclamations of Your Presence only once or twice in their lifetimes—in rare moments of seeking You above all else. You are my ever-present Shepherd, and I want to be a sheep who stays attentive to You—*listening to Your voice.*

Quietness is the classroom where You are teaching me to hear Your voice. I need a quiet place in order to calm my mind. I seem to be a slow learner, so please help me advance in this delightful discipline. Eventually, I hope to be able to carry the calmness with me wherever I go. Though I'm still a novice, sometimes I can hear those melodious bells when I step back into the bustle of life: *"I am with you. I am with you. I am with you."*

In Your delightful, calming Name, amen.

"Fear not, for I am with you; be not dismayed, for I am your God. I will strengthen you, yes, I will help you, I will uphold you with My righteous right hand." —ISAIAH 41:10 NKJV

"Then you will call upon me and come and pray to me, and I will listen to you. You will seek me and find me when you seek me with all your heart." —JEREMIAH 29:12–13

"I am the good shepherd; I know my sheep and my sheep know me. . . . My sheep listen to my voice; I know them, and they follow me. I give them eternal life, and they shall never perish; no one can snatch them out of my hand." —JOHN 10:14, 27–28

O Most High,

It is good to proclaim Your Love in the morning and Your faithfulness at night.

As I declare the wonders of Your loving Presence, I find strength and encouragement in You. This glorious blessing flows into me even more fully when I speak the words out loud. As I'm proclaiming Your Love, help me to *rejoice with Joy that's inexpressible and filled with Glory!*

Your amazing Love is sacrificial, unfailing, priceless, and boundless—*reaching to the heavens.* It shines so brightly that it can carry me through all my days, even the darkest ones.

When I get to the end of each day, it's time to declare Your faithfulness that *reaches to the skies.* As I look back over the day, I can see how skillfully You guided me and opened up the way before me. The more difficulties I encountered, the more You enabled, empowered, and equipped me to overcome the obstacles.

It is good to give voice to Your great faithfulness, especially at night, so that I can *lie down and sleep in peace.*

In Your peaceful Name, Jesus, amen.

It is good to praise the LORD and make music to your name, O Most High, to proclaim your love in the morning and your faithfulness at night. —PSALM 92:1–2

Though you have not seen him, you love him. Though you do not now see him, you believe in him and rejoice with joy that is inexpressible and filled with glory. —1 PETER 1:8 ESV

Your love, O LORD, reaches to the heavens, your faithfulness to the skies. —PSALM 36:5

I will lie down and sleep in peace, for you alone, O LORD, make me dwell in safety. —PSALM 4:8

Eternal God,

In the beginning was the Word, and the Word was with God, and the Word was God. You are *the Word that became flesh*—You have always been, and You will always be. Help me not to lose sight of Your divinity as I celebrate Your birth.

I'm so thankful that You grew up to become the Man-Savior who is God Almighty! If You were not God, Your sacrificial life and death would have been insufficient to provide salvation. I rejoice that You, who entered the world as a helpless infant, are the very same One who brought the world into existence.

Though You were rich, for my sake You became poor, so that through Your poverty I might become rich. No Christmas present could ever compare with the infinite treasure I have in You! Because of You, my sins have been removed *as far as the east is from the west*—freeing me from all condemnation. You have gifted me with unimaginably glorious Life that will never end! Thank You, Lord, for this breathtaking Gift; I embrace it joyously and gratefully.

In Your supreme Name, Jesus, amen.

In the beginning was the Word, and the Word was with God, and the Word was God. . . . The Word became flesh and made his dwelling among us. —JOHN 1:1, 14

In these last days, He has spoken to us by His Son. God has appointed Him heir of all things and made the universe through Him. —HEBREWS 1:2 HCSB

Though He was rich, yet for your sake He became poor, so that you through His poverty might become rich. —2 CORINTHIANS 8:9 NASB 1995

As far as the east is from the west, so far has He removed our transgressions from us. —PSALM 103:12 NKJV

Dear Jesus,

I come to You with my gaping neediness—asking You to fill me with the Light of Your Love. I realize that a heart yielded to You doesn't whine or rebel when the going gets tough. Instead, it musters up the courage to thank You during hard times. Subordinating my will to Yours is ultimately an act of trust.

I long to walk peacefully with You through this day, yet I'm distracted by wondering if I can cope with all that's expected of me. My natural tendency is to mentally rehearse how I will do this or that. Help me instead to keep my mind on Your Presence and on taking the next step. The more demanding my day, the more I need to depend on Your strength. Teach me to view my neediness as a blessing—believing that You designed me for deep dependence on You. Challenging times wake me up and amplify my awareness of my inadequacy.

When I don't know what to do next, I will wait for You to open the way before me. I want to be ready to follow Your lead—trusting that You know what You are doing. I rejoice in Your promise to *give me strength and bless me with Peace.*

In Your empowering Name, amen.

And give thanks for everything to God the Father in the name of our Lord Jesus Christ. —EPHESIANS 5:20 NLT

Wait for the LORD; be strong and take heart and wait for the LORD. —PSALM 27:14

"The bolts of your gates will be iron and bronze, and your strength will equal your days." —DEUTERONOMY 33:25

The LORD will give strength to His people; the LORD will bless His people with peace. —PSALM 29:11 NKJV

Faithful God,

Help me *hold unswervingly to the hope I profess*, trusting that *You are faithful*. Sometimes—especially when many things are going wrong—all I can do is hold on to You. I would love to be able to sort things out in my mind and find the way forward, but often this is impossible. At such times, what I really need to do is *seek Your Face* and *profess my hope*.

To profess hope is to affirm it openly. My words matter—not only to other people but also to me. Speaking negatively discourages me as well as the people around me. But when my words affirm my hope and trust in You, I gain confidence that You will show me the way to proceed.

The basis of my confidence is that *You are faithful*. Moreover, You have promised *You will not let me be tempted beyond my ability to endure*. Sometimes *the way of escape* You provide comes through my own words, such as: "I trust You, Jesus; You are my hope." This affirmation keeps me holding on to You as my hope—unswervingly and trustingly.

In Your hope-filled Name, Jesus, amen.

Let us hold unswervingly to the hope we profess, for he who promised is faithful. —HEBREWS 10:23

Hear, O LORD, when I cry with my voice! Have mercy also upon me, and answer me. When You said, "Seek My face," my heart said to You, "Your face, LORD, I will seek." —PSALM 27:7–8 NKJV

No temptation has overtaken you that is not common to man. God is faithful, and he will not let you be tempted beyond your ability, but with the temptation he will also provide the way of escape, that you may be able to endure it. —1 CORINTHIANS 10:13 ESV

All-wise God,

You have been teaching me that understanding will never bring me Peace. Your Word instructs me to *trust in You with all my heart instead of relying on my own understanding.* This verse challenges me every day of my life.

I confess that I have a voracious appetite for trying to figure things out—attempting to gain a sense of mastery over my life. But the world presents me with an endless series of problems. As soon as I master one set of difficulties, another set rises up and unsettles me. Soon my mind is gearing up again—striving for understanding and mastery instead of seeking *You*, my Master. Please forgive me, Lord, and help me to *seek You* above all else.

I'm thankful that Your Peace is not an elusive goal, hidden at the center of a complicated maze. Because I belong to You, I'm already enveloped in the Peace that is inherent in Your Presence. The more I look to You, Jesus, the more of Your precious Peace You give me.

In Your trustworthy Name, Jesus, amen.

Trust in the LORD *with all your heart, and do not rely on your own understanding.* —PROVERBS 3:5 HCSB

"You will seek me and find me when you seek me with all your heart." —JEREMIAH 29:13

Therefore, since we have been justified through faith, we have peace with God through our Lord Jesus Christ. —ROMANS 5:1

Now may the Lord of peace himself give you peace at all times and in every way. The Lord be with all of you. —2 THESSALONIANS 3:16

Beloved Jesus,

I love walking with You along the high road! I've noticed, though, that the path we're following has descents as well as ascents. In the distance I can see spectacular snow-covered peaks glistening in the sunlight. My longing to reach those peaks tempts me to take shortcuts, but I know my assignment is to *follow You*—trusting You to direct my steps. I'll let the heights beckon me onward; however, staying close to You must be my top priority.

One of the hardest times for me to trust You is when things go wrong. Disruptions to my routine tend to make me anxious, but You've shown me that difficulties are actually good for me. When I trustingly accept trials, they bring blessings that *far outweigh my troubles*. As I walk hand in hand with You along my path, I cling to the truth that You have lovingly planned every step of the way.

I pray that my faith will not falter when the path becomes rocky and steep. I'll hold tightly to Your hand and breathe deep draughts of Your Presence—listening for Your reassuring words: "Beloved, with M*y* help you can make it!"

In Your encouraging Name, amen.

Jesus said to him, "If I want him to remain until I come, what is that to you? You follow Me!" —JOHN 21:22 NASB 1995

For our light and momentary troubles are achieving for us an eternal glory that far outweighs them all. —2 CORINTHIANS 4:17

The Sovereign LORD is my strength; he makes my feet like the feet of a deer, he enables me to go on the heights. —HABAKKUK 3:19

Gracious God,

The Bible promises that *those who wait for You will gain new strength*. I love to spend time waiting in Your Presence, even though multitasking and staying busy have become the norm. During the Advent season, there are *more* things to do than usual. Please help me break free for a while from all the activity and demands. As I *seek Your Face* and enjoy Your Presence, I ponder the essential truth that Christmas is all about *You*.

Waiting with You is an act of faith—trusting that prayer really does make a difference. So I *come to You with my weariness and burdens*, being candidly real with You. While I rest in Your Presence and tell You about my concerns, You lift heavy burdens from my aching shoulders. I'm grateful that *You are able to do immeasurably more than all I ask or imagine*!

As I arise from these quiet moments with You, I delight in hearing You whisper, "I am with you." And I rejoice in the *new strength* gained through spending time with You.

In Your energizing Name, Jesus, amen.

*Yet those who wait for the L*ORD *will gain new strength; they will mount up with wings like eagles, they will run and not get tired, they will walk and not become weary.* —ISAIAH 40:31 NASB 1995

*Seek the L*ORD *and His strength; seek His face continually.* —PSALM 105:4 NASB 1995

"Come to me, all you who are weary and burdened, and I will give you rest." —MATTHEW 11:28

Now to him who is able to do immeasurably more than all we ask or imagine, according to his power that is at work within us. —EPHESIANS 3:20

Glorious Jesus,

As I wait attentively in Your Presence, *the Light of the knowledge of Your Glory* shines upon me. This radiant knowledge utterly transcends my understanding. Moreover, it transforms my entire being—renewing my mind, cleansing my heart, invigorating my body. Help me to open myself fully to Your glorious Presence!

I cannot imagine what You gave up when You came into our world as a baby. You set aside Your Glory so that You could identify with mankind—with me. You accepted the limitations of infancy under appalling conditions: born in a stable, with a feeding trough for Your crib. There was nothing glorious about the setting of Your birth, even though angels lit up the sky proclaiming "Glory!" to awestruck shepherds.

Sitting quietly with You, I experience the reverse of what You went through. *You became poor so that I might become rich.* As I draw nearer to You, heaven's vistas open up before me—granting me glimpses of Your Glory. O Lord, I sing hallelujahs to Your holy Name!

In Your sacred Name, amen.

God . . . made his light shine in our hearts to give us the light of the knowledge of the glory of God in the face of Christ. —2 CORINTHIANS 4:6

[Jesus] being in very nature God, did not consider equality with God something to be grasped, but made himself nothing, . . . being made in human likeness. —PHILIPPIANS 2:6–7

A great company of the heavenly host appeared with the angel, praising God and saying, "Glory to God in the highest, and on earth peace to men on whom his favor rests." —LUKE 2:13–14

For you know the grace of our Lord Jesus Christ, that though He was rich, yet for your sakes He became poor, that you through His poverty might become rich. —2 CORINTHIANS 8:9 NKJV

Compassionate Jesus,

You came into the world as a Light so that no one who believes in You would stay in darkness. You didn't just *bring* Light into the world; You are *the Light that shines on in the darkness, for the darkness has never overpowered it.* Nothing can extinguish this illumination because You are infinite and all-powerful!

When I believed in You, I became a *child of Light.* Your brightness entered into my inner being, enabling me to see from Your perspective—things in the world *and* things in my heart. When Your Spirit illumines the contents of my heart and shows me things that are displeasing to You, help me to repent and walk in Your ways. This is the road to freedom.

Lord, I rejoice in my brightened perspective. *The god of this age has blinded the minds of unbelievers so that they cannot see the Light of the gospel of Your Glory.* But because I belong to You, I have *the Light of the knowledge of Your Glory* shining in my heart! Thank You, Jesus!

In Your bright, illuminating Name, amen.

"I have come into the world as a light, so that no one who believes in me should stay in darkness." —JOHN 12:46

And the Light shines on in the darkness, for the darkness has never overpowered it [put it out or absorbed it or appropriated it, and is unreceptive to it]. —JOHN 1:5 AMPC

For you are all children of light, children of the day. We are not of the night or of the darkness. —1 THESSALONIANS 5:5 ESV

The god of this age has blinded the minds of unbelievers, so that they cannot see the light of the gospel of the glory of Christ, who is the image of God. . . . For God, who said, "Let light shine out of darkness," made his light shine in our hearts to give us the light of the knowledge of the glory of God in the face of Christ. —2 CORINTHIANS 4:4, 6

Immanuel,

You are *God with us*—at all times. This promise from Your Word provides a solid foundation for my Joy. Sometimes I try to pin my pleasure to temporary things, but Your Presence with me is an eternal blessing. I rejoice that You, my Savior, have promised *You will never leave me.*

The nature of time can make it difficult for me to fully enjoy my life. On those days when everything is going well, my awareness that the ideal conditions are fleeting can dampen my enjoyment. Even the most delightful vacation must eventually come to an end. Seasons of life also come and go, despite my longing at times to stop the clock and keep things as they are.

I don't want to look down on the temporary pleasures You provide, but I *do* need to accept their limitations—their inability to quench the thirst of my soul. Please help me remember that my search for lasting Joy will fail unless I make *You* the ultimate goal of my quest. *In Your Presence there is fullness of Joy.*

In Your joyful Name, Jesus, amen.

"Behold, the virgin shall be with child, and bear a Son, and they shall call His name Immanuel," which is translated, "God with us." —MATTHEW 1:23 NKJV

Your life should be free from the love of money. Be satisfied with what you have, for He Himself has said, I will never leave you or forsake you. —HEBREWS 13:5 HCSB

You will show me the path of life; in Your presence is fullness of joy; at Your right hand are pleasures forevermore. —PSALM 16:11 NKJV

King Jesus,

You are *King of kings and Lord of lords; You dwell in unapproachable Light!* I'm grateful that You are also my Shepherd, Companion, and Friend—the One who never lets go of my hand. I worship You in Your holy Majesty. And I draw near You to rest in Your loving Presence. I need You both as God and as Man. Only Your birth on that first, long-ago Christmas could meet all my needs.

Instead of trying to comprehend Your incarnation intellectually, I want to learn from the example of the wise men. They followed the leading of a spectacular star, then fell down in humble worship in Your Presence. Inspired by the magi, I long to respond to the wonder of Your holy birth with ardent adoration.

Please help me grow in my capacity to worship You as my Savior, Lord, and King. You held back nothing in Your amazing provision for me, and I rejoice in all that You are—all You have done!

You are *the Light from on high that dawns upon us, to direct and guide our feet into the way of Peace.*

In Your majestic Name, amen.

Which God will bring about in his own time —God, the blessed and only Ruler, the King of kings and Lord of lords, who alone is immortal and who lives in unapproachable light, whom no one has seen or can see. To him be honor and might forever. Amen. —1 TIMOTHY 6:15–16

When they saw the star, they rejoiced with exceedingly great joy. And when they had come into the house, they saw the young Child with Mary His mother, and fell down and worshiped Him. —MATTHEW 2:10–11 NKJV

"A Light from on high will dawn upon us and visit [us] to shine upon and give light to those who sit in darkness and in the shadow of death, to direct and guide our feet in a straight line into the way of peace." —LUKE 1:78–79 AMPC

Precious Lord Jesus,

When an angel announced Your birth to *shepherds living out in the fields* near Bethlehem, he told them: *"Do not be afraid. I bring you good tidings of great Joy."* This command to not be afraid is repeated frequently throughout the Bible. Thank You for providing this tender, merciful directive. You know how prone to fear I am, yet You do not condemn me for it. However, I do want to break free from my inclination to be fearful.

I've discovered that Joy is a powerful antidote to fear. And the greater the Joy, the more effective an antidote it is. The angel's announcement to the shepherds was one of *great* Joy! Help me never to lose sight of what amazingly good news the gospel is!

The moment I trusted You as my Savior, You forgave *all* my sins—past, present, and future. This glorious gift of grace ensures that my ultimate destination is heaven. Moreover, You gave me *Yourself*—the greatest treasure of all! You lavished Your Love on me and promised me Your Presence forever. As I ponder the angel's wondrous proclamation to the shepherds, I *rejoice in You*, my beloved Savior.

In Your magnificent Name, amen.

Now there were in the same country shepherds living out in the fields, keeping watch over their flock by night. And behold, an angel of the Lord stood before them, and the glory of the Lord shone around them, and they were greatly afraid. Then the angel said to them, "Do not be afraid, for behold, I bring you good tidings of great joy which will be to all people." —LUKE 2:8–10 NKJV

For by grace you have been saved through faith. And this is not your own doing; it is the gift of God. —EPHESIANS 2:8 ESV

Rejoice in the Lord always. I will say it again: Rejoice! —PHILIPPIANS 4:4

Wonderful Jesus,

Your Word teaches that *I am in You, and You are in me.* This is such a profound mystery! You are the infinite Creator and Sustainer of the universe, and I am a finite, fallen human being. Yet You and I live not only *with* each other but *in* each other. I am *filled with Your fullness—flooded with You Yourself!* This is a deeper, richer union than I can find in any human relationship. You know everything about me, from my deepest thoughts and feelings to the events I will encounter throughout my life. Because I belong to You, feelings of aloneness are really just an illusion. The whole earth is full of Your glorious Presence!

In You I live and move and have my being. Every step I take, every word I speak, every breath I breathe—all is done in Your watchful, embracing Presence. I'm immersed in Your invisible yet ever-so-real Being! The more aware of You I am, the more alive and complete I feel. Please strengthen my awareness of Your loving Presence as I go step by step through this day.

In Your watchful, loving Name, amen.

"On that day you will realize that I am in my Father, and you are in me, and I am in you." —JOHN 14:20

To them God has chosen to make known among the Gentiles the glorious riches of this mystery, which is Christ in you, the hope of glory. —COLOSSIANS 1:27

[That you may really come] to know [practically, through experience for yourselves] the love of Christ, which far surpasses mere knowledge [without experience]; that you may be filled [through all your being] unto all the fullness of God [may have the richest measure of the divine Presence, and become a body wholly filled and flooded with God Himself]! —EPHESIANS 3:19 AMPC

"For in him we live and move and have our being." As some of your own poets have said, "We are his offspring." —ACTS 17:28

Steadfast Savior,

Help me find Joy in the midst of brokenness. One of the hardest times for me to be joyful is when I'm dealing with multiple problems—seeking solutions but finding none—and then suddenly I'm faced with a new problem. I've found that if I focus too much on searching for solutions, I start to sink under the weight of all my difficulties. Please remind me at such times that You are present with me in the midst of my *various trials*. I need to trust that You're at work in my situation and that You're able to bring good out of evil. Your matchless wisdom and sovereign strength enable You to outsmart evil with good!

I want to encounter *You* in my difficult circumstances—believing that You are near me in my troubles. I need to unplug my emotions from all the problems and plug them into Your Presence. By connecting with You, my dark mood grows steadily lighter and brighter. Also, as I *remain in You*—plugged in to Your radiant Presence—You enable me to see things from Your perspective.

I can be joyful even during adversity by staying connected to You. *There is abundant Joy in Your Presence!*

In Your joyous Name, Jesus, amen.

Consider it nothing but joy . . . whenever you fall into various trials. Be assured that the testing of your faith [through experience] produces endurance. —JAMES 1:2–3 AMP

Oh, the depth of the riches of the wisdom and knowledge of God! How unsearchable his judgments. —ROMANS 11:33

"Remain in me, and I will remain in you. No branch can bear fruit by itself; it must remain in the vine. Neither can you bear fruit unless you remain in me." —JOHN 15:4

You reveal the path of life to me; in Your presence is abundant joy; in Your right hand are eternal pleasures. —PSALM 16:11 HCSB

Delightful Lord,

I love listening to the song that You continually sing to me: "*I take great delight in you; I renew you by My Love; I shout for Joy over you.*" The voices of this world are a cacophony of chaos, pulling me this way and that. Help me not to listen to those voices but to challenge them with Your Word. Show me how to take breaks from the noise of the world—finding a place to be still in Your Presence so I can hear Your voice.

I believe there is immense hidden treasure to be found through listening to You. You are always pouring out blessings upon me, but some of Your richest blessings have to be actively sought. I rejoice when You reveal Yourself to me—through Your Word, Your people, and the wonders of creation.

Having a seeking heart opens me up to receive more of You. The Bible gives me clear instructions: *Keep on asking and it will be given to you; keep on seeking and you will find; keep on knocking and the door will be opened to you.*

In Your generous Name, Jesus, amen.

*"The Lord your God is in your midst; he is a warrior who can deliver. He takes great delight in you; he renews you by his love; he shouts for joy over you." —*Zephaniah 3:17 net

*While he was still speaking, a bright cloud overshadowed them, and behold, a voice out of the cloud said, "This is My beloved Son, with whom I am well-pleased; listen to Him!" —*Matthew 17:5 nasb 1995

*"Ask and keep on asking and it will be given to you; seek and keep on seeking and you will find; knock and keep on knocking and the door will be opened to you." —*Matthew 7:7 amp

Restful Lord Jesus,

I come to You, seeking to find rest in Your Presence. *How precious it is, Lord, to realize that You are thinking about me constantly!* I long to be increasingly mindful of You. You've been teaching me that awareness of Your Presence can *give me rest* even when I'm very busy. An inner peacefulness flows out of remembering that *You are with me always.* This remembrance permeates my heart, mind, and spirit—filling me with Joy.

I confess that sometimes I get so focused on the problems I see and the predictions I hear that my joy gets buried under layers of worry and fear. When this happens, I need to bring my concerns to You—talking with You about each one, seeking Your help and guidance, asking You to remove those worry-layers. As I entrust My concerns into Your care and keeping, Joy begins to emerge again. I've learned that the most effective way for me to nurture this gladness is speaking and singing praises to You—*the King of Glory*!

In Your praiseworthy Name, amen.

"Come to me, all you who are weary and burdened,
*and I will give you rest." —*MATTHEW 11:28

How precious it is, Lord, to realize that you are thinking about
me constantly! I can't even count how many times a day your
*thoughts turn toward me. —*PSALM 139:17 TLB

"And teaching them to obey everything I have commanded you. And surely
*I am with you always, to the very end of the age." —*MATTHEW 28:20

Lift up your heads, O you gates! And be lifted up, you everlasting
*doors! And the King of glory shall come in. —*PSALM 24:7 NKJV

My loving Savior,

I want to become increasingly preoccupied with You. Yet I confess that my default state of mind is to be preoccupied with myself: my needs, my desires, my goals, my appearance, and so on. I hate this sinful tendency, and I know that it's displeasing to You. I long to break free from this bondage!

People who are deeply in love tend to focus on each other. So learning to love *You* more fully—*with all my heart and soul and mind*—is the best way to become more focused on You. The Bible refers to this teaching as *the greatest commandment*, and it is a most worthy goal! I realize I cannot do it perfectly in this life. But the more I'm able to comprehend Your boundless, *unfailing Love* for me—and take delight in it—the more lovingly I can respond to You. This is a glorious quest!

Help me learn to receive Your Love in greater height, depth, breadth, and constancy—and to respond with ever-increasing love for You. This will *set me free* from the bondage of self-absorption and empower me to grow increasingly preoccupied with You, my Savior-King. Then *I will be free indeed*!

In Your liberating Name, Jesus, amen.

Jesus replied: "'Love the Lord your God with all your heart and with all your soul and with all your mind.' This is the first and greatest commandment." —MATTHEW 22:37–38

But I am like an olive tree flourishing in the house of God; I trust in God's unfailing love for ever and ever. —PSALM 52:8

We love Him because He first loved us. —1 JOHN 4:19 NKJV

"So if the Son sets you free, you will be free indeed." —JOHN 8:36

My guiding God,

As I come to the end of this year, I need to take some time to look back—and also to look ahead. Please guide me as I review the highlights of this year: hard times as well as good times. Help me to see *You* in these memories, for I know You have been close beside me every step of the way.

When I was clinging to You for help in the midst of tough times, You comforted me with Your loving Presence. You were also richly present in circumstances that filled me with great Joy. You were with me on the mountain peaks, in the valleys, and everywhere in between!

My future stretches out before me, all the way into eternity, and You are the Companion who will never leave me—the Guide who knows every step of the way ahead. The Joy that awaits me in heaven is *inexpressible and full of Glory*! As I prepare to step into a new year, I ask for Your glorious Light to shine upon me and brighten the path before me.

In Your triumphant Name, Jesus, amen.

"For I am the LORD, your God, who takes hold of your right hand and says to you, Do not fear; I will help you." —ISAIAH 41:13

For this God is our God for ever and ever; he will be our guide even to the end. —PSALM 48:14

And though you have not seen Him, you love Him, and though you do not see Him now, but believe in Him, you greatly rejoice with joy inexpressible and full of glory, obtaining as the outcome of your faith the salvation of your souls. —1 PETER 1:8–9 NASB 1995

Then Jesus spoke to them again, saying, "I am the light of the world. He who follows Me shall not walk in darkness, but have the light of life." —JOHN 8:12 NKJV

About the Author

Sarah Young, author of the bestselling 365-day devotionals *Jesus Calling*® and *Jesus Listens*, was a missionary alongside her husband, Stephen, for forty-five years. In her writing and in her mission work, Sarah was committed to helping people connect with Jesus and the Bible. Her books have sold more than 45 million copies worldwide. *Jesus Calling*® has appeared on all major bestseller lists. Sarah's writings include *Jesus Calling*®, *Jesus Listens*, *Jesus Always*, *Jesus Today*®, *Jesus Lives*™, *Dear Jesus*, *Jesus Calling*® *for Little Ones*, *Jesus Calling*® *Bible Storybook*, *Jesus Calling*®: 365 *Devotions for Kids*, and more, each encouraging readers in their journeys toward intimacy with Christ. Sarah believed praying for her readers was a privilege and God-given responsibility and did so daily even amidst her own health challenges.

Connect with Jesus Calling at:

Facebook.com/JesusCalling

Instagram.com/JesusCalling

YouTube.com/JesusCallingBook

Pinterest.com/JesusCalling

Experience a Deeper Relationship with Jesus Through the *Jesus Calling®* App

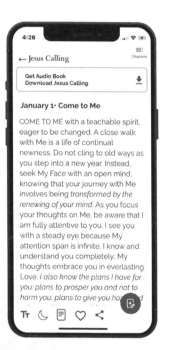

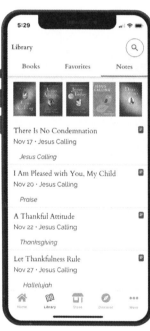

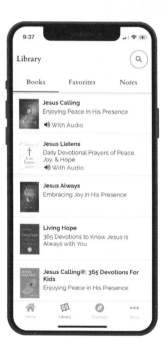

Get inspiring content for every day of the year! App users can read the *Jesus Calling® Magazine*, listen to the *Jesus Calling®* podcast, access other Sarah Young devotionals, browse readings by topic, take notes as you read, and more!

Get started today for free.